C000260396

Also available at all good book stores

9781785315985

9781785315541

9781785315633

9781785315442

9781785315312

9781785315411

9781785314995

9781785314902

9781785314384

A TOURNAMENT
FROZEN
IN TIME

A TOURNAMENT

FROZEN IN TIME

The Wonderful Randomness of the
European Cup Winners' Cup

STEVEN SCRAGG

First published by Pitch Publishing, 2019

Pitch Publishing
A2 Yeoman Gate
Yeoman Way
Worthing
Sussex
BN13 3QZ
www.pitchpublishing.co.uk
info@pitchpublishing.co.uk

© 2019, Steven Scragg

Every effort has been made to trace the copyright.
Any oversight will be rectified in future editions at the
earliest opportunity by the publisher.

All rights reserved. No part of this book may be reproduced,
sold or utilised in any form or transmitted in any form or by
any means, electronic or mechanical, including photocopying,
recording or by any information storage and retrieval system,
without prior permission in writing from the Publisher.

A CIP catalogue record is available for this book
from the British Library.

ISBN 978 1 78531 538 1

Typesetting and origination by Pitch Publishing
Printed and bound in India by Replika Press Pvt. Ltd.

Contents

Dedication

For my lovely mum, whom we lost on 5 October 2018. Had it not been for you allowing me to misspend so much of my youth on football, I'd never have become the unashamed football hipster I am today. Also, for my dad, who gifted me my team of choice, for Alison and David who had to put up with the constantly obstructive Subbuteo pitch throughout childhood, and for Bev, Sam, Elsie and Florence who are my world.

Acknowledgements

THIS BOOK was born from a podcast. Around a year ago, for *These Football Times*, we put together a series of podcasts on the glory days of the European Cup, the UEFA Cup and the European Cup Winners' Cup.

The Cup Winners' Cup podcast particularly hit the spot for listeners and as a throwaway remark my *These Football Times* comrade, Will Sharp, implored me to put a Cup Winners' Cup book on my to-do list. Well Will, here it is. You really do have a lot to answer for.

These Football Times has been an unmitigated joy to be a part of. A collection of like-minded souls who embrace the history of the game, finding untold stories or offering a different angle on well-known topics. This book wouldn't have been possible without me being a part of this wonderful environment, provided to us by its creator, the brilliant Omar Saleem.

Being encouraged and cheered on by the likes of Stuart Horsfield, Gary Thacker, Dan Williamson, Chris Weir, Jon Townsend, Andrew Flint and Matt Evans has been invaluable in seeing me get this book over the finish line. Another motivation was to fulfil a prophesy of one of our collective that we sadly lost in 2018: the legendary Jim Hart. Jim believed in his team of writers and offered nothing but positivity. All he ever wanted to do was absorb your passion for football. He remains much missed.

In putting this book together, I have been overwhelmed by the support and help of Hyder Jawád. Those endless evenings of talking the football of the past has stirred the mind and the soul, while nobody has shouted the concept of this book as long and loudly as the fantastic Graham Denton and Jeff Goulding.

I have also been supported in every single word I've ever written by Hayley Coleman, my most spectacular of friends, plus Andy and Carrie Knott. Each of these are people I am a better person for knowing.

Mostly, however, I must thank my wife, Bev, for insisting I start writing again in late 2013, after what was an almost decade-long hiatus, and our children, Sam, Elsie and Florence for accepting they couldn't play on the laptop, because I was on a roll with Dinamo Tbilisi.

I could not have done this without the presence of each one of you. Many thanks.

Introduction

FOR ANYBODY aged above 40 (although it could as easily be a sensory experience that belongs to me alone, I suppose), the European Cup Winners' Cup can't fail to evoke, from the misty ether of your mind, the theme tune to *Sportsnight* – the BBC's long-running, but generation-since defunct, midweek sports televisual digest.

If that has struck a nerve, then I dare imagine that very theme tune will be circulating in your head right now?

Glorious, isn't it?

Even ITV's rival version of *Sportsnight*, *Midweek Sports Special*, could boast an infectious opening musical salvo. Along with its BBC counterpart, it retrospectively speaks of a plate of cheese on toast in front of the TV as well as the bonus of being allowed to stay up late on a school night to watch Ray Clemence fumble a speculative effort from the Barcelona defender Antonio Olmo into his own goal when on duty for Tottenham Hotspur in the first leg of the 1982 semi-final. Of course, the Cup Winners' Cup wasn't always as glamorous as Spurs vs Barcelona and, even when it was that glamorous, it was often tinged with a dark edge. That game at White Hart Lane in April 1982 was one which most neutrals had expected to be infused with skill and beauty. However, it turned out to be one enveloped in spite, violence and rancour, as Barcelona opted to kick their opponents almost as much as the football, panicked as they were by the prospect of not reaching a final that was to be hosted at the Camp Nou five weeks later.

No, the Cup Winners' Cup was at its very best when it was being oblique. A beautiful randomness that meant Castilla, the Real Madrid reserve side, qualified for the 1980/81 contesting of the tournament having reached and lost the 1980 Copa del Rey Final, in which they had faced the recently crowned La Liga champions, Real Madrid.

The 1980/81 Cup Winners' Cup offered peak randomness. Upon the front cover of this book is a photo from the 1981 final. The photo shows everything you could possibly want, visually. A huge electronic scoreboard, which was magnificently of its era, set with the scoreline at 1-0 a mere four minutes beyond Carl Zeiss Jena having opened the scoring. The game stands at 1-1, however, and Vladimir Gutsaev is wheeling away, arms raised in celebration at having plundered the equalising goal for Dinamo Tbilisi. Two of his team-mates are angling their bodies towards the direction of Gutsaev's running trajectory, intending to ambush their hero of the moment.

Add into this evocative landscape the resting ball itself, an iconic Adidas Tango, two beautifully simplistic kits, the players in those Carl Zeiss Jena colours with hands on hips in resignation at the unfolding events. And then there is the fact that it is all being played out in a sparsely populated stadium, in West Germany, where only a reputed 4,750 spectators have assembled, making it one of the smallest attendances ever for a major European final.

It all speaks to me of a beautifully desolate utopia, a million miles away from the obscene amounts of money being paid for television rights, of brand recognition, of players who are detached from the mundanities of everyday life as they disembark from a space-age coach while cocooned from the outside world by their oversized headphones that aren't even plugged in to anything. The photo on the front of this book is a million miles away from 'Zadok the Priest' and being implored to favour Continental over all other tyre manufacturers.

The 1980/81 tournament encompasses the first chapter of this book. There is no better or more eccentric season to start with. Yet it isn't alone in its random nature and eccentricities: just as, by the traditional way in, there is no rhyme or reason behind a domestic cup success, sometimes neither was there anything particularly consistent about the Cup Winners' Cup. There were no 'usual suspects' thanks to that random-generator system of qualification.

With all of that in mind, this book is designed to be a homage to the awkward sibling of the European Cup and the UEFA Cup. This book is designed to honour a simpler time, when the playing field of European football was far more level and, in the case of the Cup Winners' Cup, was sometimes a playing field which was tilted in favour of the minnows rather than the elite.

All three major European club competitions had very distinct personalities, almost like three markedly different children. While the European Cup was for the high achievers and the UEFA Cup was where the cool kids often hung out, the Cup Winners' Cup threw out its own uniquely random and out-of-proportion shapes. If it were a reveller on the dance floor on a Friday night, it would have been that one you stand back from and inwardly admire, as others leave an unspoken exclusion zone around them, out of concern for getting hit by a stray arm or a saccadic kick from the oblivious dancer in question.

The Cup Winners' Cup was different from the very start. Only ten teams took part in the inaugural tournament during the 1960/61 season and, despite owning the name 'European Cup Winners' Cup', only 60 per cent of the field had won their domestic cup competition in 1960.

In the case of Ferencváros, there hadn't even been a domestic cup competition in Hungary in 1960. They were present in that first playing of the Cup Winners' Cup partially due to winning the startlingly elongated 1955–58 version of the Magyar Kupa – a tournament that would remain in stasis until it resumed once more in 1964 – and in part due to finishing runner-up to Vasas SC in the 1960/61 Nemzeti Bajnokság I, the top division of Hungarian club football.

Even when it came to the very first game to be played in the Cup Winners' Cup, a preliminary-round tie between Vorwärts Berlin of East Germany and Rudá Hvezda Brno of Czechoslovakia, neither side were the holders of their respective nation's domestic cup competition. Vorwärts had been given preference by their national footballing body to take part as the runner-up of the 1959 DDR-Oberliga. Missing out were SC Dynamo Berlin, the winners of that season's FDGB-Pokal, the East German domestic cup competition.

As for Vorwärts's opponents that day (1 August 1960) – Rudá Hvezda Brno – there wasn't an official Czechoslovak Cup until the 1960/61 season. Prior to this, there had only been intermittent unofficial versions, and Czechoslovakia's representatives in the first playing of the Cup Winners' Cup hadn't even won that in 1960. By the 1961/62 season, Rudá Hvezda Brno no longer existed, as they were absorbed into city rivals Spartak ZJŠ Brno.

It all adds to the peculiarities of the inaugural Cup Winners' Cup campaign: the only season when a two-legged final took place; the only season when the original handle-free trophy was awarded.

As UEFA didn't take on full responsibilities for the running of the tournament until the 1961/62 season, it wasn't until 1963 that European football's governing body bestowed the 1960/61 version with official historical status.

What that first erratic season of the tournament did though, was concentrate the minds of Europe's individual national footballing rulers on delivering a structured, annual, domestic knockout cup competition of purpose. While many of these domestic cup competitions remained largely unloved in their own nations, the carrot that dangled beyond them became something of value. The enduring legacy of the Cup Winners' Cup is that it energised, revived and even saved many domestic cup competitions across Europe.

From a small band of ten teams in 1960/61, by the middle of the decade the Cup Winners' Cup had a full complement of 32 competitors, and sometimes more. By the final playing of the tournament, in 1998/99, it boasted 49 entrants, thanks to the proliferation of the former communist collectives into their myriad of fragmented independent states.

The random nature of domestic cup success was what traditionally gained a club entry to the tournament and upon occasion being a losing finalist was enough. Even a beaten semi-finalist qualified during the tournament's autumn years, bringing a richer diversity of entrants than the competition's more celebrated counterparts.

Yes, some clubs would reappear intermittently, but others would be cast in a cameo role and rarely, if ever, be seen again. Barcelona, for instance, had 13 seasons playing in the Cup Winners' Cup, while Real Madrid set sail in the tournament on only four occasions. Ajax appeared five times but had a pronounced absence from it between contesting the 1961/62 and 1981/82 campaigns. AC Milan, Liverpool and Bayern Munich could also all count the amount of times they qualified for the Cup Winners' Cup on one hand. It was certainly rare if two megalithic giants of the game landed in the tournament together, let alone crossed paths with one another within it.

The great thing about the Cup Winners' Cup was that the spotlight rested wherever it wanted to. It wasn't dictated to by the elite. It danced to its own tune. You still had to be a very good team to win it, but there weren't many multiple winners as such. Football teams don't tend to win successions of domestic cups in the way they can league titles, so not many football teams come back to the Cup Winners' Cup year, after year, after year.

It was the exception to be a 'regular' in the Cup Winners' Cup, rather than the rule. Mechelen are a case in point. When they won in 1988 they were competing in the tournament for the very first time; and they would do so again in 1988/89 as holders, yet they never played in it ever again after their semi-final exit in 1989.

The Cup Winners' Cup was also a trophy which eluded the clutches of European royalty such as Real Madrid, Liverpool and Inter Milan. It remains, however, the only European honour for both Paris Saint-Germain and Manchester City, despite their current financial advantages. It is the tournament which immortalised the likes of Magdeburg, Slovan Bratislava and Dinamo Tbilisi, while it gave English football its first ever European glory.

Call it abstract, call it eccentric if you like, but the European footballing currency of old finally went out of circulation when the Cup Winners' Cup came to an end at Villa Park on 19 May 1999, where an expensively assembled Lazio side won the final final.

These are the eccentric fables of the European Cup Winners' Cup.

Chapter One

1980/81

THE 1980/81 edition of the European Cup Winners' Cup was just about as abstract as the tournament got. In a competition which offered the type of theatre that married football's A-list actors to jobbing extras when it came to the clubs involved, this was a season in which anything was possible. And yet the winners melted into the background as far as the wider history of the game was concerned, as did the runner-up.

Dinamo Tbilisi will mean nothing to an entire generation of football watchers, yet to my generation they will elicit an enigmatic smile and maybe even a moistening of the eye. It might sound strange to the uninitiated, but you'd be amazed just how many British football supporters go misty-eyed with joy at the memory of seeing their team of choice being knocked out of European competition by what would colloquially be referred to as a 'crack eastern European outfit'.

Of those great unknown sides to emerge from behind the Iron Curtain, Dinamo Tbilisi were one of the most clinical and unremitting. Fast and precise, they hit you on the break and they hit you hard. For those who saw them, they were unforgettable.

In the quarter-finals, at the beginning of March 1981, West Ham United were systematically dismantled by Dinamo Tbilisi at Upton Park.

Slicing straight through the West Ham midfield and defence time and time again, they enabled Aleksandre Chivadze, Vladimir Gutsaev and Ramaz Shengelia to score goals that were as beautiful as they were devastating. Ray Stewart, the West Ham right-back and penalty-taker extraordinaire was particularly tormented by the Dinamo Tbilisi offensive. He was caught in precarious possession of the ball for the second goal, when ludicrously left to man the West Ham defence all on his own.

What made the situation so ludicrous was that Stewart's team-mates had piled forward, as if chasing a last-minute equaliser, when instead, the first leg of the game was only 31 minutes old. Everything was still to play for. West Ham had fallen a goal behind a mere seven minutes earlier and even by the standards of March 1981 this was an admirably gung-ho approach from John Lyall and his players.

One botched corner, a lofted Dinamo Tbilisi clearance, an ill-advised header from Stewart and a flash of the white-shirted Gutsaev later, and the ball was once again in the back of Phil Parkes's net. It was as shocking as it was swift.

It wasn't as though Dinamo Tbilisi hadn't already sent advance word of their bewitching and ruthless blend of football. They had taken the mighty Liverpool apart during the early exchanges of the previous season's European Cup; they had surgically unpicked the Liverpool of Ray Clemence, Alan Hansen, Graeme Souness and Kenny Dalglish with a performance which left you feeling the Georgians should have been wearing operating gowns, face masks and sterilised gloves.

They had even put five goals, without reply, past Waterford FC in the round prior to taking on West Ham. When it came to Dinamo Tbilisi, there shouldn't have been any shortage of easily accessible victim statements to draw research from.

West Ham's 1980/81 season might have been spent in the Second Division, a third successive campaign in which they had been playing second-tier football, but it was a far from insignificant West Ham vintage. Without a defeat at Upton Park for almost seven months, West Ham were running away with the Second Division title in style. They were ten days away from facing Liverpool at Wembley, in the League Cup Final. And while they had been knocked out of the FA Cup in the third round after a trilogy of games against Wrexham, they were still technically the holders of the FA Cup.

Along with Stewart and Parkes, the latter at one stage the most expensive goalkeeper in the world, West Ham could boast the services of talents such as Trevor Brooking, Billy Bonds, Alan Devonshire, Frank Lampard senior and Alvin Martin. They had a team which was the envy of many First Division clubs.

Dinamo Tbilisi dispensed with the 1980/81 West Ham with almost obscene ease. There was a wonderful sense of spectacular misadventure to the east London side's Cup Winners' Cup run that season.

Before their hypnotic bemusement at Dinamo Tbilisi, West Ham had faced Castilla, Real Madrid's reserve side, in the first round. Their Spanish opponents had defied the odds to reach the 1980 Copa del Rey Final, where they were thrashed 6-1 by their older sibling. Castilla had defeated Athletic Bilbao, Real Sociedad and Sporting Gijón on the way to that Copa del Rey Final. Sociedad had only narrowly missed out on the La Liga title in 1979/80, making amends by taking the title for the following two seasons, while Gijón ended the campaign in third place. Bilbao rolled over the finish line in seventh.

During that remarkable cup run, Castilla had benefitted from the services of the likes of Ricardo Gallego, Javier Castañeda and Francisco Pineda, all of whom had moved forward to bigger things: with the Real Madrid senior side in the cases of Gallego and Pineda, and with Osasuna for Castañeda.

Despite the diaspora of talent during the summer of 1980, Castilla still beat West Ham's star-studded line-up in the first leg in Madrid. West Ham dominated the first half at the Santiago Bernabéu, David Cross putting the visitors ahead after only 15 minutes. From this solid foundation, however, they missed a succession of chances to put the game out of reach of Castilla, prior to the half-time whistle. There was a heavy price to pay for West Ham as Castilla threw together a stunning 12-minute spell during the second half, scoring three times to accumulate a hard-earned yet somehow fortuitous 3-1 lead to take to London for the second leg.

To double the woe for Lyall and his players, crowd disturbances led to approximately 50 West Ham supporters being chased across the terraces and ejected from the stadium after violence was ignited by one travelling fan urinating from an upper tier of the Bernabéu on to Castilla followers below. Outside the ground after the game, a West Ham supporter was killed when struck by a bus, completing their misery.

Within the slipstream of events in Madrid, West Ham were threatened with being banned from the tournament. It had been the club's first European venture since they had competed in the 1976 Cup Winners' Cup Final. However, the prospect of an outright ban was eventually averted. Instead, UEFA mirrored a similar sanction placed on Manchester United during the 1977/78 season which led to them playing at Plymouth Argyle's Home Park after altercations away to St Etienne. This consisted of a £7,750 fine and an insistence that West Ham's next two home European ties take place at least 300 kilometres (187 miles) away from Upton Park.

Having been offered the use of Sunderland's Roker Park, Lyall piloted West Ham through a Zürich appeal process which downgraded their punishment to no fine and one home tie to be played at Upton Park behind closed doors.

Thus, the second leg against Castilla was lent an almost eerie, and certainly echoey, atmosphere, accentuated by the added amplification of the referee's whistle, the increased 'doof' sound as foot met ball, and the audio of on-pitch shouts, which seemed to bounce back from the empty terraces. It was a sensation that was as close as you could get to a fusion of European club competition and a local five-a-side night.

Yet none of this was enough to stop West Ham from running up a 5-1 victory that saw them through to the second round, all witnessed by 200 invited and UEFA-approved guests, 16 ball boys and the ITV production team, inclusive of their match commentator, Martin Tyler.

The first-round eccentricities didn't end with West Ham and Castilla either. AS Roma, Serie A's representatives in the tournament, stormed to a 3-0 first-leg win over Carl Zeiss Jena at the Stadio Olimpico, courtesy of goals from Roberto Pruzzo, Falcão and a young Carlo Ancelotti. They were then steamrollered 4-0 in the second leg at the Ernst-Abbe-Sportfeld in Jena.

Added to this heady concoction, Celtic fumbled their way out of the tournament at the first hurdle when they succumbed to the Romanians, FC Politehnica Timişoara, who were taking part in only their second ever European campaign. West Ham would deal with them comfortably in the next round, in what maybe should have been a 'Battle of Britain' encounter instead. Although UEFA, the FA, the SFA and the police forces of the east ends of both London and Glasgow might have breathed a long sigh of relief that Britain had swerved that battleground being drawn out on their respective doorsteps.

While an all-British spat was avoided, there was still a United Kingdom derby played out in that intriguing opening round of the 1980/81 Cup Winners' Cup. Newport County, Welsh of blood and geographical positioning, but of the English Third Division, found themselves in European combat as winners of the 1980 Welsh Cup Final, where they had defeated Shrewsbury Town, a club hailing from the English county of Shropshire.

I know. You might have to re-read that paragraph a couple more times for the cross-border complexities to sink in.

Newport breezed past Crusaders, winning the first leg 4-0 at Somerton Park, before drifting along to a goalless draw having crossed the Irish Sea for the return game.

In the second round there was a similar outcome, except in reverse. Newport, armed with the goals of John Aldridge, cruised past the Norwegians of SK Hauger 6-0 in the second leg to propel themselves into an unlikely quarter-final towards the spring, having played out another goalless draw in the first leg, when once again on their travels.

For Carl Zeiss Jena, after their incredible comeback against Roma, they were dubiously rewarded by being paired with the tournament holders, Valencia. A 3-1 victory in the first leg in Jena proved to be marginally enough for the East Germans, when a 1-0 scoreline to Valencia at the Mestalla in the second leg brought the holders to within one more strike of an away-goal superiority.

Given the voracity of Carl Zeiss Jena's opponents during the first two rounds of the 1980/81 Cup Winners' Cup, it made the quarter-final prospect of Newport a welcoming mirage. This was also a Newport side who were denied the goal-getting services of the injured Aldridge.

At the Ernst-Abbe-Sportfeld however, Newport managed something which had proved to be beyond the capabilities of both Roma and Valencia. Len Ashurst's men returned to South Wales with a positive result following an impressive 2-2 draw, thanks to a brace of equalisers from the prolific lower-league marksman Tommy Tynan. The second of those two levellers came with almost the last kick of the game.

In a game which was played out on the same evening as Dinamo Tbilisi were taking West Ham apart at Upton Park, the performances of the two remaining British clubs in the 1980/81 Cup Winners' Cup were the complete opposite in outcome to what had been expected.

Back at Somerton Park, Newport had a once-in-a-lifetime opportunity to become the first Third Division team to reach the semi-finals of a major European competition. However, they couldn't take advantage of either their hard work from the first leg or the fact that Carl Zeiss Jena were nursing both injuries and suspensions. The only goal of the game fell the way of the East Germans shortly before the half-hour mark, when Lothar Kurbjuweit struck a low free kick that swept past the defensive wall and caught the Newport goalkeeper, Gary Plumley, wrong-footed.

Plumley later gained national notoriety once again when he made a one-off appearance for Watford in the 1987 FA Cup semi-final, coming to the aid of Graham Taylor's side during a goalkeeping injury crisis. Plumley's father, Eddie, being the chief executive of the Vicarage Road club, had sent out the emergency call.

Newport's exit from the Cup Winners' Cup wasn't an insipid one, however, as they largely dominated the game and were denied progression to the semi-finals by a succession of reaction saves from the Carl Zeiss Jena goalkeeper, Hans-Ulrich Grapenthin. The goalposts and an outrageous number of goal-line clearances also thwarted Newport on the occasions that Grapenthin was unable to stop the multitude of goal-bound Newport efforts.

Within the eccentric spirit of the Cup Winners' Cup, Newport, having pushed Carl Zeiss Jena harder than both Roma and Valencia, went on to a mid-table Third Division finish, via a very real flirtation with relegation to the Fourth Division.

After being on the brink of bankruptcy just three years earlier, Newport would slip out of the Football League in 1988 and then go out of business less than a year later. The club swiftly reformed and started their climb back to the Football League from the Hellenic League, effectively four divisions below the promised land of the professional game. It was a stark eight-year step from the brink of the Cup Winners' Cup semi-final to the oblivion of February 1989.

Along with Dinamo Tbilisi and Carl Zeiss Jena, it was Benfica and Feyenoord who also made the semi-finals. Two former European Cup winners and members of an incredible list of 14 teams who won European football's biggest prize during the lifespan of the Cup Winners' Cup, yet never managed to win the latter tournament.

For Feyenoord, it was, remarkably, their first ever Cup Winners' Cup campaign. Neither they nor Benfica would ever make it beyond the semi-finals. While Feyenoord's path to the semi-finals hadn't been overly taxing, Benfica's had been an arduous one. Beginning with the preliminary round, they faced down the stubborn Dinamo Zagreb, the beaten 1979 European Cup finalists Malmö, and then Fortuna Düsseldorf, just two years on from them having faced Barcelona in perhaps the greatest Cup Winners' Cup Final of the lot.

Being made host to the 1981 final was possibly a nod of appreciation to Düsseldorf from UEFA for the part Fortuna played in that indelible 1979 final. Indeed, Barcelona, for their part, hosted the 1982 final.

Both Feyenoord and Benfica were disadvantaged after the first legs of their respective semi-finals. Feyenoord were defeated 3-0 in Tbilisi, while Benfica lost 2-0 in Jena. In the return fixtures, both Feyenoord and Benfica drew to within one goal of levelling their ties, with over half an hour still to play. However, the energy they expended in chasing their Eastern Bloc opponents, especially ones who were known for their pace and endurance levels, was quickly spent.

The prospect of a historically pleasing and almost reassuring Benfica vs Feyenoord 1981 Cup Winners' Cup Final was instead exchanged for the hipster's utopia of a Carl Zeiss Jena vs Dinamo Tbilisi final.

Carl Zeiss Jena had been semi-finalists in 1962, under the name of SC Motor Jena. Comfortably beaten by Atlético Madrid, they had even embraced another trip to South Wales long before their visit to Somerton Park to take on Newport in 1981. They had faced Swansea Town in the 1961/62 preliminary round.

A peculiar link was provided by the Austrian referee, Friedrich Seipelt. Kept busy by the players of Swansea Town and SC Motor Jena in the late summer of 1961, he was a referee of purpose. He had officiated in Sweden at the 1958 World Cup where he took charge of the group game between Czechoslovakia and Northern Ireland, plus the Brazil vs Wales quarter-final. After handing in his whistle in 1966, Seipelt was employed by FIFA as a referee instructor, eventually becoming the president of UEFA's Arbitration Commission in 1972. It was a position he held until his unexpected death while waiting for a flight at

Vienna International Airport, just short of one week prior to the 1981 Cup Winners' Cup Final.

On a day of strange events, just two hours before kick-off, Pope John Paul II was shot four times in St Peter's Square by the gunman Mehmet Ali Ağca.

It turned out that 13 May 1981 was a fittingly eccentric day for Carl Zeiss Jena and Dinamo Tbilisi to be contesting the Cup Winners' Cup Final, in front of such a small gathering of spectators. Around 1,000 made the journey from East Germany, while there were arguably as many members of the Dinamo Tbilisi official party as there were supporters making the trip from Georgia. In their desperation to pad out the crowd at the 68,000-capacity Rheinstadion, UEFA gave away 2,000 free tickets to local schools. While it may have been a commercial disaster for UEFA, the game itself was one which deserved a full house.

With Carl Zeiss Jena's well-organised man-to-man marking system and Dinamo Tbilisi looking to exploit their own propensity for speed, it made for an intriguing and absorbing game of football.

During the early exchanges of the first half in Düsseldorf, the game was brought to a halt as the ball harmlessly rolled out of play for a Carl Zeiss Jena throw-in. A period of silence was then observed for Seipelt before the game resumed. Gerhard Hoppe opened the scoring for Carl Zeiss Jena in the 63rd minute, finishing off a timeless pass-and-move passage of play during which they played Dinamo Tbilisi at their own counter-attacking game. Hoppe scored with the outside of his right foot at the end of a nine-pass move which swept from one end of the pitch to the other.

It was a lead which lasted for only four minutes, as a succession of rash Carl Zeiss Jena attempts to halt the Dinamo Tbilisi tide simply gifted Gutsaev the opportunity to drive the equaliser home. With Carl Zeiss Jena's play becoming more ragged, and Dinamo Tbilisi pondering whether to stick or twist as extra time loomed on the horizon, the winning goal came with only four minutes left to play.

Vitaly Daraselia scored that winning goal.

The following night, at Wembley Stadium, Tottenham Hotspur won the 1981 FA Cup Final replay, gaining with it a place in the 1981/82 Cup Winners' Cup. Ricardo Villa's winning goal against Manchester City has been shown so many times, as a homage to the FA Cup, it is almost as if a watching world became desensitised to it. This is nothing other than insane, of course. Villa's goal remains one of the greatest of all time.

Unbeknown to many football watchers, Daraselia's winning goal for Dinamo Tbilisi, not much more than 24 hours earlier, bore striking similarities to the goal Villa would score to win the FA Cup. While the two goals weren't identical, they share that unmistakable twist and turn within the penalty area that totally sells the respective defences. They were even both scored at the same end of the pitch from the perspectives of where the television cameras were situated in Düsseldorf and London.

And with that, the 1981 Cup Winners' Cup was won. A team of immense speed, skill and beauty, it would have been a travesty had Dinamo Tbilisi not had their moment of European glory. They would reach the semi-final as holders and supply four members of the Soviet Union's

1982 World Cup squad, yet they were also a team shaded by darkness.

In December 1982, Daraselia was tragically killed when his car fell from a mountain road and was swept away by a raging river. He was just 25. Kipiani, the talented attacking midfielder, also died as a result of injuries he received in a car crash, in 2001, at the age of 49, while Shengelia died at 55 of a brain haemorrhage, in 2012. Their legendary moments flicker on to the observant but fall under the radar of those who never knew the simple pleasures of seeing their team of choice dismantled by opponents from behind the Iron Curtain.

The 1980/81 Cup Winners' Cup remains a mystery to many; the 1980/81 Cup Winners' Cup remains one of football's best kept secrets.

Chapter Two

Bloc Party

IT WASN'T just about Dinamo Tbilisi and Carl Zeiss Jena when it came to the European Cup Winners' Cup adventures of teams from behind the Iron Curtain. The first finalist in a major European tournament to emerge from behind the Iron Curtain was MTK Hungaria when they reached the 1964 Cup Winners' Cup Final.

MTK were by no means the first team from a subjugated nation to reach a major European final. Some 11 months earlier, Dinamo Zagreb made their way to the Inter-Cities Fairs Cup Final and, while Yugoslavia wasn't classed as being behind the Iron Curtain, it had been a member of the Eastern Bloc and it lived under undemocratic rule. To the untrained eye, Yugoslavia were an associate member of the 'Iron Curtain Club' in the same way that the cities of Kiev and Tbilisi were often considered to be in Russia.

To muddy the game of dictatorship further, when the fans of Real Madrid, Benfica, Barcelona and Valencia had watched their respective teams contest major European finals during the second half of the 1950s and the early 1960s, prior to MTK's run to the 1964 Cup Winners' Cup Final, they had done so while living under the imposed rules of General Franco and the unelected Portuguese Prime Minister Antonio de Oliveira Salazar.

Despite the highly questionable political regimes from which the great and the good of Spanish, Portuguese and Yugoslavian football had had to operate and strike forth to challenge for European glory, it was MTK who were the first team to peer from behind the Iron Curtain itself.

With the Magyar Kupa not being brought back to life until 1964, MTK took up Hungary's berth in the 1963/64 Cup Winners' Cup via being distant runner-up to Ferencváros in the 1962/63 Nemzeti Bajnokság I. As far as western Europe was concerned, the stealth with which MTK moved through their 1963/64 Cup Winners' Cup run was massively impressive as they largely slipped under the radar until the second leg of the semi-final.

MTK's progress in the tournament had all occurred against clubs from the east. They overcame Slavia Sofia and Motor Zwickau in the opening two rounds before a quarter-final play-off success in front of just 700 spectators over Fenerbahçe in Rome's cavernous Stadio Olimpico.

When MTK rolled into Glasgow to face Jock Stein's Celtic in the first leg of the semi-final, they were ruthlessly dismissed 3-0. Celtic were fast and powerful, bludgeoning even. Against the perceived delicate wallflowers of MTK, a team of great intelligence and artistry, Stein's side were simply too forceful in their play for MTK to repel the onslaught. The sensitive artisans of Budapest were stopped in their tracks by a punch to the face in the east end of Glasgow. Having finally ventured into northern Europe, their performance once they got there was such that they remained firmly beneath the radar, returning to Budapest a well-beaten side.

However, at Celtic Park there had been enough signs to suggest there was more to MTK than met the eye initially. They had made the semi-finals of the 1962 Inter-Cities Fairs Cup, where they had been beaten 10-3 on aggregate by Valencia and, although MTK were universally viewed as being aesthetically pleasing to watch, another semi-final defeat by a large margin was still expected. Yet in Glasgow, MTK had been shorn of three injured players of international standing; the biggest of those losses being that of Károly Sándor, their free-scoring and devilishly skilful right-winger. While everything pointed to Celtic reaching their first major European final, there at least should have been a vague sense of foreboding. Manchester United's recent blowing of a 4-1 first-leg advantage in the very same competition, in the quarter-finals against Sporting CP, was still fresh in the mind.

During the closing stages of the game in Glasgow, Thomas Chambers, having scored two of Celtic's three goals, squandered the opportunity of claiming a hat-trick and what would have been a vital fourth goal for Stein's men. Celtic were left to regret that miss as, at the Nep Stadion two weeks later, MTK stormed to a 4-0 victory that surprised even their own supporters and saw them march on to the final in Brussels against Manchester United's Portuguese conquerors.

Given that MTK had only managed to score eight goals throughout the entirety of the tournament up until that point, meaning that they were left with the task of scoring half of their own season's tally in the match without conceding any further in order to reach the final, the general Budapest public wasn't overly sold on MTK's chances of prevailing against their Scottish opponents.

Having countenanced a shift of venue from MTK's Hungária körúti stadion to the Nep Stadion because it would generate larger and more vociferous backing for MTK's hopes of reaching the final, and with one eye upon swelling gate receipts as a most agreeable side effect, the move backfired in two ways.

Firstly, due to the heavy deficit MTK had to overturn, many supporters stayed away from the Nep Stadion where, for the second leg of the semi-final, the attendance was lower than it had been at the Hungária körúti stadion for the first leg of their quarter-final against Fenerbahçe.

Secondly, the shift to the Nep Stadion also meant a wonderful sensory image was lost to football history, as the legacy of the game was denied the evocative images of Celtic facing MTK against the backdrop used for the film *Escape to Victory* in which Bobby Moore, Michael Caine, Sylvester Stallone, Pelé et al defeated their German oppressors.

Ultimately, however, none of this mattered a jot to MTK and they swept to the 4-0 victory they had needed to progress to the final, thanks to their relentless speed of action which the Hungarians balanced perfectly with the subtleties of their artisan footballing crafts. Sándor was quick to make up for the lost time of the first leg, setting up MTK's first goal for István Kuti and then scoring the goal that levelled the tie himself, before Kuti struck the winner.

It was a stunning turnaround in the fortunes of MTK and one which has left a lasting question mark over whether it was a referee-assisted result or not. While Celtic did indeed have two goals disallowed before the half-time break, Stein's side were guilty of their own profligacy in front of goal and in the generosity of their defensive gifts.

MTK's second goal came via the penalty spot after the Celtic left-back Tommy Gemmell contrived to punch the ball over the bar. The pressure and skill that MTK applied was unremitting and the first 20 minutes of the game were spent almost exclusively in the Celtic half of the pitch, the ball being predominantly within MTK's possession.

There was a naïvety to how Celtic played during the second leg, which was defiantly of its time. Still on a learning curve, Stein's players didn't know whether they should stick or twist after the second MTK goal was scored shortly after the beginning of the second half. They opted to push forward and they paid a hefty cost for their bravado. Kuti's winning goal came eight minutes from time.

The teachings of the great Jimmy Hogan had come home to roost. Widely credited as the man who taught the Hungarians how to play football, this son of the town of Nelson in Lancashire had had a spell in the early 1950s as a coach at Celtic Park. Yet, as was the case during many of his coaching roles in British football, he was viewed with suspicion because of his preaching for greater ball control. Hogan was revered on the continent and only appreciated in his homeland in more recent times, many years beyond his death at the age of 91, in January 1974.

Thanks to the need for a play-off match to settle the outcome of the other semi-final, MTK only found out the identity of their opponents for the 1964 Cup Winners' Cup Final eight days prior to the game. Sporting CP narrowly edged out Olympique Lyonnais, at the Estadio Metropolitano de Madrid, the former home of Atlético Madrid.

Just 3,208 spectators made the pilgrimage to the Heysel Stadium for the final, the lowest ever attendance for a major European final. Those who did make the effort were, however, richly rewarded for their presence and a classic was played out which drifted one way and then the other, and back again. Sándor scored MTK's first two goals in a swaying and dramatic 3-3 draw, where they led 1-0, trailed 2-1, then led again at 3-2, before succumbing to one last equaliser. In a game which remained finely balanced throughout, Mascarenhas missed a golden opportunity to win it for Sporting CP in extra time.

Two days later, at the Bosuilstadion in Antwerp, on an evening that attracted over 10,000 more spectators than had been present in Brussels, MTK lost a tighter contest 1-0, in marvellously eccentric circumstances of course, when João Morais's decisive goal flew in directly from a corner. A massive chance had come MTK's way, but it had passed them by.

It would take a further five years for the Cup Winners' Cup to finally be taken behind the Iron Curtain and even then it was during a season when there was a large-scale boycott of the tournament by teams from eastern Europe. A boycott which was repeated in the European Cup. When UEFA made the decision to split eastern and western clubs in the draw for their two major tournaments, the old Inter-Cities Fairs Cup not being within UEFA's jurisdiction, it resulted in a swathe of teams withdrawing.

The reason for UEFA opting for an East–West divide for the 1968/69 season was the 21 August 1968 Warsaw Pact invasion of Czechoslovakia, led by the Soviet Union and supported by Poland, Hungary, Bulgaria and to a lesser extent by East Germany. It was an invasion in the name of supressing a campaign for political liberalisation and reform, the brainchild of the new first secretary of the Communist Party of Czechoslovakia, Alexander Dubček. Around 20 years ahead of his time, Dubček was apprehended in Prague and flown to Moscow where a quiet word was had.

In the Cup Winners' Cup, Dynamo Moscow, Górnik Zabrze, Raba Vasos ETO, FC Spartak and Union Berlin's combined withdrawal meant that the Soviet Union, Poland, Hungary, Bulgaria and East Germany would not be represented in UEFA's secondary tournament for the 1968/69 season, essentially because they were nations which were represented politically, uninvited, in Czechoslovakia. Czechoslovakia played on, though, and it was Slovan Bratislava who took to the Cup Winners' Cup field having been narrow winners of the 1968 Czechoslovak Cup Final against the team of choice for fans of the irreverent band Half Man Half Biscuit, Dukla Prague.

Some occurrences in football seem to have their scripts set in stone. If there had to be one and one season only in which a major European trophy headed to Czechoslovakia, I doubt there could have been any other campaign in which it would have happened.

Overcoming FK Bor of Yugoslavia in the first round, a team from one of the few eastern European nations that defied the Soviet Union's point of view to instead openly sympathise with Czechoslovakia's plight, Slovan won the first leg 3-0. Yet they were left to cling on desperately at 2-0 down in the second leg to edge through to a stunning second-round tie against FC Porto.

Having lost the opening game in Bratislava 1-0, Slovan headed to Oporto for the return, where they destroyed their hosts 4-0. They followed that, in the new year, with home and away victories against a physical and awkward Torino.

This was a win which set Slovan up with an intriguing semi-final against Dunfermline Athletic, a semi-final which, from half a century's worth of introspection, appears to have been one of the most implausible major European semi-finals of all time.

Led by Blackpool's 1953 FA Cup-winning goalkeeper, George Farm, this was the final flourish of a Dunfermline golden period that had been initially instigated by the great Jock Stein when he took the Pars to Scottish Cup glory in 1961, something that Farm emulated in 1968. Between those two successes, Willie Cunningham had taken the club close to a league and cup double, missing out on the title by just one point and losing a closely contested Scottish Cup Final to Stein's Celtic, during the 1964/65 season.

Slovan, meanwhile, were a team of substance too. Seven of their Cup Winners' Cup-winning side travelled to the 1970 World Cup in Mexico, at the end of a domestic season in which they had won the Czechoslovak First League for the first time in 15 years.

Jozef Čapkovič, one of a minority of the Slovan players on duty in the 1969 Cup Winners' Cup Final not to go to Mexico, would go on to be an integral part of the Czechoslovakia side that won the 1976 European Championship. Alexander Vencel would also pick up a winner's medal as back-up goalkeeper to his Dukla Prague rival, Ivo Viktor.

The scorer of the crucial away goal, seven minutes from the end of the first leg at East End Park, was Jozef's twin brother, Ján Čapkovič. Coming against the run of play and obtaining a 1-1 draw, the goal took the wind out of Dunfermline's sails and a 1-0 win for Slovan in the second leg was enough to see them through to the final in Basel, against Barcelona.

On an evening when great bravery was needed to be able to compete with Barcelona, Slovan took the game to their illustrious opponents, taking the lead after just two minutes thanks to a smart finish from Ľudovít Cvetler. Even when José Antonio Zaldúa levelled the score with the game still within its formative stage, Slovan didn't blink, and it was with great persistence that Vladimír Hrivnák reclaimed the lead for his side on the half-hour mark when he powered through on the Barcelona goalkeeper, Salvador Sadurní, finishing with a calm intelligence that belied the fact that he was a centre-back. If Barcelona thought that they would find Slovan in a benevolent enough mood to allow a second equaliser before the half-time break, they were rudely awoken by the Ján of the Čapkovičs when he seized upon some Barcelona defensive indecision to strike a third goal for Slovan in the 42nd minute. Despite Carles Rexach trimming the deficit for the Catalans early in the second half, Slovan repelled wave upon wave of Barcelona attacks to hang on for wonderfully improbable glory.

A year later, it was Poland's turn. Górnik Zabrze went all the way to the final, mostly thanks to the bewitching skills of future England tormentor Włodzimierz Lubański. He was particularly pivotal in the semi-final against a Fabio Capello-inspired AS Roma, in a trilogy of games because the tie rolled on to a play-off match after a 3-3 draw on aggregate.

It was a game which shifted the sands of European football. While the away-goals rule had been introduced to the Cup Winners' Cup in the 1965/66 season, it was only in operation for the early rounds of the tournament, not at the business end. Thus, when Górnik faced Roma in the 1970 semi-finals, the away-goals rule wasn't implemented. Had it been so, then Roma would have advanced to play Manchester City in Vienna in the final, rather than the Polish side.

There was a spectacular shape to the progression of the Górnik vs Roma saga, which was magnetically drawn to a majestically manic climax. Having drawn the first leg at the Stadio Olimpico in Rome 1-1, the second leg at the Silesian Stadium in Chorzów was drifting Roma's way at 1-0. With Capello set to be the hero of the piece, up stepped Lubański with an injury-time penalty to take the game into extra time. Within three minutes of the start of extra time, Lubański had scored again and the tie was on its head, only for Francesco Scaratti to drive in the equaliser for Roma from distance, with almost the last kick of the game. Both sides had come to within seconds of reaching the final, and for Roma the relief of a last-gasp reprieve was tempered by the fact that under the away-goals rule they would have done enough to reach the final.

In the Strasbourg play-off Lubański put Górnik ahead in the first half, while Capello equalised for Roma in the second half. Joined at the hip throughout 330 minutes of football, the only sensible thing UEFA could come up with to decide the outcome was to toss a coin. Górnik won the duel of heads vs tails and advanced to the final.

Persuaded of the unsatisfactory nature of how this game was settled, for the 1970/71 season, the away-goals rule was extended by UEFA to be applicable all the way to the semi-finals, while the concept of the penalty shoot-out was adopted as a replacement for the toss of a coin. Presumably, penalties pushed rock, paper, scissors and consulting a Ouija board into second and third place.

Eastern Europe absorbed another final defeat in 1972, this time for Dynamo Moscow, who would remain the only team from the Russian capital to reach a major European final until CSKA Moscow lifted the UEFA Cup in 2005.

A new Cup Winners' Cup success was on the horizon in the east, however. Magdeburg, the only East German team to win a major European trophy, began and ended their run to 1973/74 glory at Feyenoord's De Kuip. A goalless draw against NAC Breda in the first leg of the first round, and a seemingly incomprehensible victory over Giovanni Trapattoni's AC Milan in the final itself, bookended a stirring run which was the perfect warm-up act to the East German national team competing in their one-and-only major international tournament at the 1974 World Cup finals, over the heavily militarised border in West Germany.

Jürgen Sparwasser wrote his name in football history when he scored the only goal on the day West and East Germany met one another at the Volksparkstadion in Hamburg, during the opening group stages of the 1974 World Cup. He was by no means a one-hit wonder of a player but Sparwasser without question had the season of his life in 1973/74. Not only would he score his nation's most iconic international goal, not only would he be the driving force of Magdeburg's greatest moment, but his goals also propelled his team to DDR-Oberliga success.

The only thing which is incomprehensible about Magdeburg's success is that it should be classed a shock.

Time tends to warp perceptions of the circumstances surrounding the overall contemporary landscape upon which games from the past were played out. As far as the broader history of the game is concerned, AC Milan are AC Milan after all. Only Real Madrid have won the European Cup/Champions League more times. In contrast, Magdeburg have struggled to find their feet since East and West German club football was reunited in the summer of 1991.

Magdeburg were asset-stripped of their best and brightest playing and coaching talents in 1990, a cataclysmic diaspora which meant they had to wait until 2018 to reach the 2. Bundesliga as a result of their frail attempts to fight back from the regional outer reaches of the unified German league pyramid, only to go straight back down once they got there. To put this into context, beyond winning the Cup Winners' Cup in 1974, Magdeburg finished outside the top six places in the DDR-Oberliga only twice; the second of those occurrences was the very last season, when the tournament went by the name of the NOFV-Oberliga.

During that last season of the East German league system, the top two teams were allotted places in the 1. Bundesliga, the teams finishing third to sixth were guaranteed places in the 2. Bundesliga, while those in seventh to 12th were given the chance to play off for a place in the 2. Bundesliga. Everybody else was automatically marooned in the NOFV-Oberliga which, for the 1991/92 season, became one of the three regionalised third-tier divisions.

In 1990/91 Magdeburg finished tenth, failing to win any of their six play-off games; thus, they found themselves cut adrift in the NOFV-Oberliga. A broken club, they have never truly recovered. Their recent high of a belated rise to the second tier of German football had been slow in coming, and their existence there was ultimately a short-lived one.

Persuading somebody today, whether they remember or know nothing of the proud past of those teams to have starred in the DDR-Oberliga, of the once-significant standing of an entity such as Magdeburg would probably leave you feeling like you were speaking a very different language to them. But to this very day, Magdeburg have still won as many European trophies as the moneyed current-day behemoths Manchester City and Paris Saint-Germain have. You can also repeat this with regards to Dinamo Tbilisi and Slovan Bratislava of course. While that fact lasts, and it is a peculiar fact that is surely on borrowed time, there is wonderful comfort to be found within the concept that, in terms of

European honours won, Magdeburg stand in the queue next to the two most affluent teams in contemporary world football.

In 1973/74, after dispensing with the stubborn NAC Breda in that first round, Magdeburg overturned a 2-0 first-leg deficit in the second round against Banik Ostrava. During a spectacular second-leg fightback at the Ernst Grube Stadium the home side came within six minutes of exiting the tournament, until Martin Hoffmann saved the day. Sparwasser produced the winning goal to be the extra-time hero.

Remaining east for the quarter-finals, Magdeburg faced the Bulgarian side PFC Beroe Stara Zagora, winning the first leg 2-0. The 1-1 scoreline of the second leg doesn't tell the whole story of the nervous evening Magdeburg spent in the city of Stara Zagora. Clinging on desperately as Beroe relentlessly attacked, in search of the goal that would send the game into extra time, Magdeburg sprang. Hans-Jürgen Hermann snatched the crucial away goal that killed off the tie and put his team into the semi-finals.

In the last four Magdeburg were up against Sporting CP, the 1964 winners. When Sparwasser opened the scoring in Lisbon during the first leg, it provoked an avalanche of attacks from Sporting, one of which found the back of the net, one of which struck the post. The game ended 1-1.

Despite laying the foundations for a comfortable second leg back in Magdeburg and running into a 2-0 lead thanks once again to Sparwasser, who got the second goal after Jürgen Pommerenke had netted the first, a goal back for Sporting from Marinho set up another frenetic finish as the Portuguese side drew to within one more goal of an away-goal victory. It was a relieved Magdeburg side that embraced the final whistle.

A watching world fully expected an AC Milan victory in the final, back at De Kuip.

Retrospectively, it is an *I Rossoneri* defeat that jars somewhat. The Italian side was led by Giovanni Trapattoni; but this was a young Trapattoni who was at the helm on a caretaker basis only, after the club had sacked Cesare Maldini after a run of poor results in early April. What might appear a shocking event from a distance of 45 years was arguably no shock at all.

Going into the final, Magdeburg hadn't lost a game since December. They had won their domestic league and four members of their line-up would go to the World Cup. Conversely, AC Milan had won only one of their last nine Serie A fixtures, yet had shocked Borussia Mönchengladbach in the semi-finals. The 2-0 victory in the first leg at the San Siro had been Trapattoni's first game in charge.

While Magdeburg were the form side, that's not to say it was a feeble and disorganised AC Milan that they beat. In just a short space of time, Trapattoni had instilled a renewed solidity to his defence. The 1974 Cup Winners' Cup Final was his seventh game in temporary control of the team and, despite having won only two of those previous six games, they had kept four clean sheets and conceded only two goals. Their last game before the final was a win at Genoa.

Captained by the legendary Gianni Rivera and infused with the first sprinklings of Trapattoni's coaching magic, it all combined to level the playing field of the final. Magdeburg had played only Cup Winners' Cup football during the month prior to the game as their domestic season had ended in early April, on the very same day when a 2-1 loss at Verona had been the last straw for Maldini and AC Milan. As Magdeburg were being crowned DDR-Oberliga champions, Trapattoni was still waiting in the San Siro wings. Over the space of a month, this celestial coach-to-be transformed AC Milan, yet his pupils fell flat on their collective face in Rotterdam, and the hierarchy of the club sent Trapattoni back to their coaching ranks for a further year before teaming him up with Nereo Rocco for the 1975/76 season.

By the summer of 1976 Trapattoni was employed by Juventus, and AC Milan had followed a similar path to Decca when they allowed The Beatles to slip from their grasp. So synonymous with AC Milan as a player, Trapattoni's coaching genius was instead embraced elsewhere.

Given what Trapattoni had done in such a short amount of time, the images of Enrico Lanzi lunging to cut out a Magdeburg cross into the AC Milan penalty area only to successfully divert it into his own goal are still shocking now. They are images that are totally at odds with the work Trapattoni had put in. Also shocking was the lethargic and futile attempt of the fantastically named AC Milan goalkeeper, Pierluigi Pizzaballa, in keeping the ball out of his net. Shortly before half-time, it was a demoralising moment for the Italians. Amidst the sounds of klaxons, echoey cheers and polite applause, Wolfgang Seguin plundered Magdeburg's second goal, much to the delight of the small band of travelling fans from East Germany who were amongst the 6,461 spectators that were rattling around the bare-looking stands of De Kuip.

East Germany's one and only European trophy – there is great joy to be found in the fact that it wasn't won by one of the DDR-Oberliga teams who operated beneath the wing of the Socialist Unity Party of Germany, the only fully fledged political party of the one-party state that was East Germany.

Heinz Krügel, the legendary yet rarely celebrated coach of Magdeburg, a man who led the club to three DDR-Oberliga titles, two FDGB-Pokal wins and, of course, to Cup Winners' Cup glory, was as impressive a personality as he was a coach.

After the red tape had been bound too tightly to allow the 1974 Super Cup games between Magdeburg and Bayern Munich to take place (and you can draw your own conclusions as to whether it was coincidence or not), the two teams were drawn together in the second round of the 1974/75 European Cup. When the second leg of the tie was played on the eastern side of the divide, legend has it that Krügel refused Stasi-harvested information on Bayern's plans, after the East German secret police had set up recording equipment in the visitors' dressing room. Whether or not this was true, Krügel was out of not only his job at Magdeburg, but out of East German football permanently by 1976. His card was rumoured to have been marked by the authorities as an East–West reconciliatory supporter after he turned down the chance to listen in to Udo Lattek's half-time team talk.

Charged with the vague and highly questionable crime of not sufficiently promoting the performance and development of the East German Olympic footballers within his squad, Krügel was banned by the authorities and, as he was not allowed to leave for the west, he saw his football career effectively ended when, at the age of 55, he still had much to give.

Magdeburg never again won the DDR-Oberliga after his departure, and Krügel, after reunification, was brought back symbolically as their executive director of football. Later, having been made an honorary member, he continued to watch games on a regular basis until his death in 2008.

Followed in reaching the final of the Cup Winners' Cup by Carl Zeiss Jena seven years later, and by Lokomotive Leipzig in 1987, Magdeburg are arguably the most 'frozen in time' element of all, when it comes to the Cup Winners' Cup.

When Lokomotive made the final in 1987 they were the last eastern European side to do so. The very first official German champions in 1903, under the alias of VfB Leipzig, they added two further national championships to their honours list in 1906 and 1913, narrowly missing out on two more occasions, in 1911 and 1914. Irrefutably their golden era, it was a time they've simply been unable to live up to for the majority of the last 100 or so years.

When East and West Germany were partitioned, Lokomotive, beyond a series of mergers, amalgamations and structural reorganisations of league systems, found themselves part of the DDR-Oberliga. Despite their origins as one of German football's first powerhouses and very first champions, the East German league title remained tantalisingly out of reach. The closest they came was an agonising loss in the 1987/88 season, when they were edged out on goal difference by the shadowy and state-approved force of Dynamo Berlin. What they lacked in league titles during those Cup Winners' Cup years, they made up for in FDGB-Pokal successes. Between 1976 and 1987 they lifted the East German domestic cup four times, becoming a regular sight in European competition between 1963 and 1988. Over the course of a 26-season span, Lokomotive ventured into European combat 18 times, also reaching the semi-finals of the UEFA Cup in 1974.

A balanced side without a standout hero, Lokomotive projected the perfect footballing visage of economic equality. Communism via the medium of football was, perhaps, never better displayed than it was by Lokomotive. While other teams from behind the Iron Curtain that prospered on the European stage showed a certain artistry, Lokomotive were a collective who toiled. It was almost a grey version of Total Football that they dealt in.

Their run to the 1987 Cup Winners' Cup Final was a dramatic one. Needing extra time to see off Rapid Vienna in the second round, Hans-Jörg Leitzke's goal came with only two minutes left to play, just as it seemed that a penalty shoot-out was unavoidable.

While spot kicks were narrowly avoided against the Austrian side, the semi-final did drift into a duel from 12 yards and, of course, as is customary in these circumstances, the Germanic team won the spoils against their stylish French victims, Girondins de Bordeaux, who were of massive standing at the time. Led by the future French World Cup-winning coach Aimé Jacquet, they were blessed with an eclectic array of talents – from the fantastically named goalkeeper, Dominique Dropsy, through to the free-scoring Philippe Fargeon, via the likes of fellow French internationals or internationals-to-be Patrick Battiston, Jean-Christophe Thouvenel, Alain Roche, René Girard, Jean Tigana, Philippe Vercruysse, José Touré, Jean-Marc Ferreri and the veteran Bernard Lacombe. It was a team accentuated further by the presence of the Yugoslav international twins Zoran and Zlatko Vujović, plus the German defender Gernot Rohr. As the coach of Bordeaux, Rohr would lead the club to the 1996 UEFA Cup Final.

Jacquet's team had battled for the crown of France's finest team since the sharp decline of Saint-Étienne in the early 1980s. Bordeaux's main rivals at that time were Nantes, Monaco and Paris Saint-Germain as they fought it out for most of the French domestic honours on offer until the late 1980s rise to power of Bernard Tapie's Olympique de Marseille. Bordeaux won the French First Division in 1983/84 and 1984/85, and won the Coupe de France in 1986 which gained them entry into the 1986/87 Cup Winners' Cup. They were well on the way to a domestic league and cup double as they faced Lokomotive, with eyes fixed on a possible treble.

There was a hint of unfinished European business for Bordeaux. They had come back from a 3-0 first-leg deficit to within one goal in the 1985 European Cup semi-final against Juventus, so very nearly altering the course of a tragic final in Brussels. It meant that the odds were heavily stacked against Lokomotive, a team that couldn't really compete with Bordeaux on a player-to-player basis. What did go in Lokomotive's favour, however, was the unity of their team. The collective was greater than the sum of the individual parts. They were defiantly a cup team and they swept in under the radar.

Uwe Bredow scored the only goal of the first leg in Bordeaux, at the wonderfully vibrant Stade Chaban-Delmas, heading home as the ball rebounded off the crossbar after the initial chance had been an outrageously sliced effort. In Leipzig a fortnight later, amidst a deafeningly hostile atmosphere, Zlatko Vujović claimed the goal that levelled the aggregate scoreline with just three minutes on the clock, although there was a sizeable hint that it was an own goal by Matthias Lindner instead. The following 117 minutes of football went without a goal, however, and it was the English referee George Courtney who presided over the inevitable outcome of the penalty shoot-out. Lindner made up for his part in Bordeaux's early goal when he rolled in Lokomotive's first penalty, in reply to Touré having successfully got the penalty shoot-out under way for the French team. After Vercruysse and the fabulously mulleted Matthias Liebers both contrived to see their respective teams' second penalties saved, Bordeaux and Lokomotive rediscovered their accuracy and the next six penalties were scored to take the shoot-out into sudden death. Lokomotive suffered a scare, however, when their fifth penalty, taken by Dieter Kühn, went in off the inside of the square goalposts of the cavernous Zentralstadion. The estimated 110,000 in attendance were much relieved.

Tigana for Bordeaux and Wolfgang Altmann for Lokomotive got sudden death off to a successful start, but it was a condemned-looking Zoran Vujović who stumbled forward to take the next one for Bordeaux. Almost spitting on himself as he dragged his body forward, his mind clearly not wanting to go, he looked down to the turf every step of the way; he seemed to know he was going to miss. Tapping the ball towards the penalty spot, then repositioning it for longer than is necessary, he was trying to delay the inevitable. Not casting an eye at the goalkeeper or his target, he turned away to retreat to his run-up position, looking down yet again, perhaps wondering if anybody would notice if he just kept on walking. He began his run, checked almost immediately, and restarted his run before checking again half a yard from the ball. René Müller, the Lokomotive goalkeeper, was virtually on the ground already when one of the worst penalties ever taken in a game of such magnitude rolled tamely into his body.

The roar of the Zentralstadion was awe-inspiring. It was a million miles away from the sparsely populated De Kuip and Rheinstadion where, reputedly, less than 12,000 combined watched the two Cup Winners' Cup finals contested by East German teams, in 1974 and 1981.

As if he hadn't done enough already, Müller got to his feet, placed the ball back on the penalty spot and lashed home the winning penalty for Lokomotive himself. The ultimate penalty shoot-out goalkeeping hero. Mobbed by team-mates, ball boys, photographers, reporters and even a brave few stray supporters, Müller was suddenly at the centre of the universe.

That night at the Zentralstadion was effectively Lokomotive conquering their mountain. The final, against Ajax, at a barely half-full Olympic Stadium in Athens, was a bridge too far.

Four years later, beyond reunification, Lokomotive won a play-off group to gain themselves a place in the 2. Bundesliga of the newly reconstituted system of the German football league pyramid. As with all clubs from the east, Lokomotive suffered a drain of their best talent, of which there wasn't that much to speak of given they were largely a collective of good, organised, yet workmanlike players. The striker, Olaf Marschall, who went on to win the Bundesliga with Kaiserslautern and made the Germany squad for the 1998 World Cup, was the pick of the litter.

Returning to the name VfB Leipzig, the club won promotion to the top flight in 1992/93, but it would only be a one-season stay. By 1998 they had slipped into the regionalised third tier. By 2001 it was the fourth, before they were declared bankrupt in 2004.

Reformed for the 2004/05 season through supporter power, and renamed Lokomotive once more, they began their rebirth in the 11th tier of the German game. Through a series of promotions and mergers, Lokomotive won promotion to the fourth tier at the end of the 2016/17 season.

Often accused of having a politically right-leaning supporter base, they are not out of place in a city which is the most divisive, in footballing terms, in Germany. The location was settled on by Red Bull for their latest product-placement venture within the game, when RB Leipzig were founded in 2009.

Twelve months prior to Lokomotive's run to the 1987 final, the last winners of the Cup Winners' Cup to emerge from behind the Iron Curtain and snatch the trophy were the wondrous Dynamo Kyiv. Winners in 1975, in the first all-eastern European major final, against the skilful and fearsome Ferencváros, Dynamo Kyiv are unique in being the only eastern European team to win two European trophies. That those two successes were 11 years apart, yet were won by the same coach, Valeriy Lobanovskyi, with the same number 11, Oleh Blokhin, in the respective line-ups, is still astounding now.

On top of that, Lobanovskyi led Dynamo Kyiv on three separate occasions, bridging almost three entire decades from first game to last, taking them to the 1977 European Cup semi-finals and to the semi-finals of the Champions League in 1999, being desperately unlucky not to reach both finals. In his 'spare time' he created one of the most bewitchingly beautiful international teams, the Soviet Union side of Igor Belanov et al, which went all the way to the final of the 1988 European Championship. Lobanovskyi has a case for being classed as the most metronomic of the lot when it comes to the great and the good of football coaching. Overseeing the renewed rise of a former Iron Curtain powerhouse a decade after the Soviet Union began to dissolve, as the cherry on the cake of all his other stunning achievements, arguably puts him at the very top of the tree.

The first of Dynamo Kyiv's two successes in the Cup Winners' Cup was a dominant one. Seeing their way past the growing force that was CSKA Sofia in the first round, Eintracht Frankfurt and PSV Eindhoven were also brushed aside as Lobanovskyi's team swept to the final in Basel.

Ferencváros, meanwhile, put both Liverpool and Red Star Belgrade out of the tournament, along with a Malmö side that would reach the European Cup Final just five years later. As a warm-up to defeating Liverpool on away goals in the second round, the Hungarians had breezed past Cardiff City. They were not short on complexity: a club which won the Inter-Cities Fairs Cup in 1965, two years after reaching the semi-finals, beating Manchester United in the last four, prior to heading to Turin for the final where they defeated Juventus in their own back yard. Ferencváros went on to reach the final again in 1968, only to be narrowly beaten over two legs by Don Revie's Leeds United. They also reached the semi-finals of the inaugural playing of the UEFA Cup in 1971/72, losing out to Wolverhampton Wanderers.

Yet, as much as they were an entity which could ruthlessly dissect their western European opponents, Ferencváros had an unerring habit of shooting themselves in the foot in the early rounds to fellow eastern European teams. For every Liverpool, Manchester United, Juventus, Roma, Bologna, Athletic Bilbao or Real Zaragoza that Ferencváros beat in European competition, in some instances on more than one occasion, there was a defeat against a Dinamo Zagreb, Sparta Prague, Gwardia Warsaw, Dynamo Dresden, Marek Dupnitsa, Magdeburg, Lokomotive Sofia or Banik Ostrava. In this respect, that they should have lost the 1975 Cup Winners' Cup Final to Dynamo Kyiv 3-0 couldn't have been much more Ferencváros if they had tried.

It was a masterclass of a performance from Dynamo Kyiv, with Blokhin and Volodymyr Onyshchenko incessant in attack, about both of whom Lobanovskyi had been happy to mislead journalists and his opponents alike, over their fitness for the game. When combined with Ferencváros being without their suspended defensive lynchpin, the 1975 Hungarian footballer of the year, László Balint, it made for a one-sided final. Dynamo Kyiv were simply too powerful for Ferencváros, with six members of their starting line-up having been in the Soviet Union squad which made the 1972 European Championship Final. Vladimir Muntyan had even played in Mexico at the 1970 World Cup, bookending a team in which Blokhin, as the opposite bookend, played in Mexico at the 1986 World Cup.

Just as during their run to glory in 1974/75, Dynamo Kyiv cruised to their second Cup Winners' Cup success in 1986, brushing aside Utrecht, Universitatea Craiova, Rapid Vienna and Dukla Prague along the way. A Kyiv side that included the winner of the 1986 Ballon d'Or, Belanov, scored a frightening 26 goals in their campaign to win a second Cup Winners' Cup.

Of the 16-man squad on duty for the 1986 Cup Winners' Cup Final for Dynamo Kyiv, Lobanovskyi took 12 of them to Mexico for the World Cup finals.

Standing in their way in the final, at Olympique Lyonnais' Stade de Gerland, was Luis Aragonés and his Atlético Madrid side. Winners of the Cup Winners' Cup in 1962 and beaten in the final the following year, Dynamo Kyiv made much lighter work of them than should have been the case. The 3-0 scoreline, matching the result of the 1975 final, did not flatter Lobanovskyi and his men. Unwittingly the last time an eastern European team would win the Cup Winners' Cup, it was a fitting way and a deserving collective to obtain that distinction.

The 1986 Cup Winners' Cup Final marked the beginning of the end of an era, a wonderful era of football when those mysterious nations from behind the Iron Curtain kept hold of their players, drawing a protective shield around them, ring-fencing their greatest talents, who would appear intermittently in European club competitions and biannually in major international tournaments.

It left the western European observer with a unique sensory experience, as if being allowed to briefly peer into a magic cauldron. The price of freedom for the shackled populations of many eastern European nations was a hammer blow to the souls of swathes of football hipsters to the west.

Football would never quite be the same ever again.

Chapter Three

Full of Eastern Promise

THERE WAS something about those goalposts and the netting at the Boleyn Ground. Well, at least until the Premier League era eventually brought a boring general uniformity to goalposts and netting, during the 1990s.

It was the way the gap between goal line and the back of the netting was so shallow. When a ball was hit at them, centrally and with power, it would often be propelled back out into the penalty area, rather than nestling for the beaten goalkeeper to retrieve.

Brimming with character, the old home of West Ham United was the perfect venue for European Cup Winners' Cup football. Compact in nature, the stands were close to the edge of the pitch, with terracing at each end, where the North and the South Banks resided. Unlike other grounds, its most iconic banking wasn't behind either of the goals, however. At West Ham, it was the Chicken Run that was both revered and feared, sometimes striking terror into their own players as much as it did the visiting ones. A stretch of terracing that ran the length of where the East Stand would later emerge, it was covered by a sloped roof and would live on in the terminology of the Boleyn Ground, with the name continuing to exist when tagged on as the name for the paddock enclosure at the front of the new East Stand, which was built in 1969.

When it came to West Ham and the Cup Winners' Cup there was always guaranteed entertainment, all the way up to those last games they ever played in the tournament, against Dinamo Tbilisi in the 1980/81 quarter-finals, via that game behind closed doors against Castilla.

West Ham undertook four Cup Winners' Cup campaigns. Winners of the FA Cup in 1964, 1975 and 1980, all three of their successes came within the Cup Winners' Cup era, while the highest First Division position West Ham finished in between their first and last Cup Winners' Cup games was sixth, during the 1972/73 season. It was the closest they came, up until that point, of qualifying for Europe via league positioning.

Even then, had they claimed just one extra point to have ended the season above Wolverhampton Wanderers, then West Ham would have still been denied a place in the 1973/74 UEFA Cup due to European football's governing body upholding the one city, one club criteria of the formative seasons of the UEFA Cup. A temporary leftover rule from the days of the Inter-Cities Fairs Cup, it was finally abandoned in the summer of 1975.

It could have been worse though for West Ham, had they found themselves in such circumstances. Arsenal, the

1972/73 First Division runners-up, were denied a shot at the 1973/74 UEFA Cup thanks to Tottenham Hotspur winning the 1973 League Cup. Wolves, who instead benefitted from the one city, one club rule, finished ten points behind Arsenal, during what was still the era of two points for a win.

Back in 1964 West Ham won their very first major trophy when they overcame Second Division Preston North End and a 17-year-old Howard Kendall in the FA Cup Final, some 41 years after the Hammers had fallen at the last hurdle against Bolton Wanderers.

Clawing their way back from a goal behind on two occasions, it was Ronnie Boyce who settled the game in the final minute, affording Preston very little room for a late manoeuvre.

There are some wonderful photos of West Ham manager Ron Greenwood, after the 1964 FA Cup Final, on his way home on the Tube. The trophy sits upon his knee, wrapped protectively in a blanket. Some of the photos were taken on board a train, some taken as he was sitting on the platform at Tottenham Court Road.

West Ham's subsequent and hard-earned European adventures began in Belgium, when drawn to face La Gantoise in the first round of the 1964/65 Cup Winners' Cup. La Gantoise, in 1971, would become the more recognisable K.A.A. Gent.

Expecting it to be a sedate task in a picturesque part of the Low Countries, it was that man again, Boyce, who scored West Ham's first ever goal in European competition. Lamented as a relatively uneventful 1-0 victory at the Jules Ottenstadion, in time it would be the type of performance that would be classed as being a textbook away European endeavour.

Despite doing much of the hard work in Belgium, West Ham contrived to make the second leg more difficult than necessary. Wasteful with a litany of early chances, Greenwood's side conceded an own goal through Martin Peters which levelled the tie on aggregate. But John Byrne snared the decisive strike which put West Ham through to a second-round encounter with Sparta Prague.

Here, they largely dominated the two games until the last 20 minutes when, at 3-0 down on aggregate, Sparta sprang to life, shrinking their deficit to 3-2, making West Ham sweat for their place in the quarter-finals.

At home in the first leg, West Ham had to cope with Sparta's dense defensive strategy. Unable to break through the massed ranks of the visiting defenders and retreating midfielders, it took an effort from distance by John Bond, the future Norwich City and Manchester City manager, to break the deadlock.

Bond's relationship with Greenwood seemed, from a distance, to be a bittersweet one. Given the nod ahead of younger right-back Joe Kirkup for the 1964 FA Cup Final, the decision went the opposite way for the 1965 Cup Winners' Cup Final. Bond played his last game for West Ham a month prior to them facing Max Merkel's TSV 1860 Munich at Wembley Stadium.

Bond was granted a testimonial game, played a year after his departure to Torquay United on a free transfer, but had to watch from the sidelines due to a groin injury. He pulled no punches a decade and a half later, however, when as Manchester City manager he was called upon by ITV as an analyst for their coverage of Greenwood's England and their erratic campaign to reach the 1982 World Cup.

Having survived Sparta's late fightback on a lovely warm Wednesday afternoon in Prague, inclusive of Jim Standen saving a penalty, West Ham went on to defeat Lausanne Sport both home and away in the quarter-finals, in two wonderfully open games.

This then set up an intriguing semi-final against Real Zaragoza, who had won the Inter-Cities Fairs Cup less than a year earlier, to go alongside their Copa Generalísimo success, the second of which had put them into the 1964/65 Cup Winners' Cup.

Three of Zaragoza's players had been part of the Spanish squad that won the 1964 European Championship, with Marcelino even scoring the winning goal in the final against the Soviet Union. In La Liga, *Los Maños* went on to finish third during the 1964/65 season, with only Real Madrid and Atlético Madrid ahead of them. They dropped just one point at La Romareda all season.

West Ham were up against one of the finest teams Zaragoza have ever produced.

Stretching into a 2-0 lead within the first 23 minutes of the first leg at the Boleyn Ground thanks to strikes from Brian Dear and John Byrne, West Ham were almost mocking their more accomplished and experienced Europe-exploring opponents.

At times during West Ham's 1964/65 Cup Winners' Cup run they had found themselves to be wanting, in terms of technical ability, against inferior opponents. They relied instead upon a more bludgeoning British power-based play that would prove too physical for their dainty and artisan mainland European opponents from Belgium, Czechoslovakia and Switzerland.

Being one of English football's great thinkers, Greenwood had absorbed all the lessons his team had attended, however. Against Zaragoza, it was West Ham who created the passing blizzard, playing the continent at its own game. At least in the first half. Impossible to keep the pace up for the full 90 minutes, West Ham ceded most of the ball to Zaragoza in the second half. Regaining their composure, the visitors got one goal back through the Brazilian international, Canario – who had been part of the Real Madrid side which had attained attacking perfection in the 1960 European Cup Final, at Hampden Park, against Eintracht Frankfurt – leaving the outcome of the second leg hugely unpredictable, yet with Zaragoza as the favourites to progress to the final.

Wave upon wave of Zaragoza attacks headed West Ham's way at La Romareda. With great style, speed and artistry, the home side incessantly threw themselves into the pursuit of goals. At times, Enrique Yarza, the Zaragoza captain and goalkeeper, was the only player to be found in their own half of the pitch. When Carlos Lapetra opened the scoring midway through the first half, nobody would have thought West Ham could have possibly had a chance of surviving the remainder of the game without conceding another. Through sheer stubbornness that is just what West Ham did, however, and when added to by John Sissons scoring against the run of play for Greenwood's side, it was a Bobby Moore-inspired rearguard effort that saw West Ham into the 1965 Cup Winners' Cup Final.

One of the great under-heralded European performances by a British football team – hidden behind an era of limited black-and-white television coverage and a lack of general understanding of just how good Real Zaragoza were in the mid-1960s – it was one of Moore's very finest moments and a masterclass in tactical preparation by Greenwood.

Made to wait a further week to see who their opponents would be at Wembley, thanks to 1860 Munich clawing back a two-goal first-leg deficit against Torino to force a play-off in Switzerland, Greenwood repaid his players' hard work in Aragon against Zaragoza by flying them out to take a look at their semi-final opponents in person at the deciding game.

Greenwood and West Ham were quick learners during their run to the 1965 Cup Winners' Cup Final. As they strode on to the Wembley turf, they were arguably purveyors of a more continental approach to football than their West German opponents were. In comparison, 1860 Munich were almost British in style, fast and direct; fair, yet bludgeoning.

Merkel, their head coach, was a master craftsman of the teams he led. Having taken Borussia Dortmund close to the German championship, he won the DFB-Pokal in 1964 with 1860 Munich, going on to lift the Bundesliga title in 1965/66. Their run to the 1965 Cup Winners' Cup Final slotted in between. Beyond Munich, Merkel won another Bundesliga title in 1967/68, at 1. FC Nürnberg, only to see them obtain the curious distinction of being relegated the following season, a month or so after he departed the club. He eventually resurfaced in Spain, firstly at Sevilla, before leading Atlético Madrid to La Liga glory, laying the foundations of the team which would reach the 1974 European Cup Final.

It all lent a certain magnitude to West Ham's success. At a near-capacity Wembley, 85 per cent of which was filled by West Ham supporters, Greenwood out-thought Merkel in a spectacularly open game in which both sides showed no fear in going for goals.

The only surprise was that it took until 20 minutes from the end for the first goal to arrive. When it did come, however, it was one of great beauty.

As the pressure mounted on the West Germans, Ron Boyce dispossessed 1860 Munich of the ball in midfield, striding forward until he drew a lunging challenge. He released the ball diagonally and to his right, playing in Alan Sealey who drove into the penalty area and lashed a rising shot into the top corner of Petar Radenković's net. Sealey performed a spontaneous somersault in celebration and the already electric atmosphere, generated by both sets of fans, spiralled ever upwards. Two minutes later Sealey scored again, powering the ball in from close range after a free kick had been clipped into the 1860 Munich penalty area.

Despite West Ham effectively killing off the game within a 120-second span, the Hammers still piled forward in search of more goals and Sissons was unfortunate not to add a third when he rattled the angle of post and crossbar from distance. It was a shot which left the Wembley goalposts reverberating and the crowd roaring their approval on what was one of the legendary old stadium's greatest nights. All the way up to the final whistle the pace of the game never dipped, with 1860 Munich working tirelessly to try to find a way back into the game and West Ham unwilling to sit back and invite more pressure. Virtually the last kick of the game was an uninhibited bicycle kick from Martin Peters, which was completely in keeping with the spirit of the game. It was left to Moore to lead his team up the famous Wembley steps to collect the trophy, which gleamed in the glare of the floodlights and the popping of the barrage of camera flashes.

A year later Moore would repeat the journey up those steps, to lift the World Cup. Romanticised daydreaming that actually came to pass, affording Moore his unique place in football history and iconography. He was not just the only man to lift the World Cup for England, but also the only man to walk up the Wembley steps three years in a row, to lift three different trophies.

West Ham's glory in the 1965 Cup Winners' Cup Final handed them the right to attempt to defend their title. Having finished ninth in the First Division, without beating 1860 Munich at Wembley, West Ham wouldn't have been able to enjoy another European adventure quite so swiftly. Saying that, however, West Ham's defence of the Cup Winners' Cup didn't begin until late November, after they received a first-round bye. Over six months separated them beating 1860 Munich in the 1965 final and taking to the pitch at the Boleyn Ground to face Olympiacos in the second round first leg of the 1965/66 campaign.

If European glory had been expected to usher in a new era for West Ham of rubbing shoulders with the biggest English clubs in a challenge for the league title, or at least regular qualification for Europe, then the first half of the 1965/66 season offered them a rude awakening. At the beginning of November, West Ham sank into the

First Division relegation zone and by the time they took on Olympiacos they had won only three league games. Locked within a run which would take them to the very last two-legged League Cup Final, along with their return to European football it was their cup exploits which rejuvenated Greenwood's fortunes.

Two goals from Geoff Hurst and one each from John Byrne and Peter Brabrook swept Olympiacos aside 4-0. In the return leg in Athens, Peters struck twice, either side of half-time, and West Ham looked capable of rolling onwards to another substantial victory. A careless own goal from Edward Bovington, and a bemusing penalty being given away when Ken Brown was penalised for nothing more than outjumping an opponent, instead allowed Olympiacos a second-leg draw.

Although the game was a near inconsequence given the margin of West Ham's first-leg lead, it still proved to be a valuable European lesson as Olympiacos took a heavy-handed approach to their challenges and the Azerbaijani referee, a certain Tofiq Bahramov, made a succession of bizarre and highly debatable decisions throughout the game.

Of course, just under eight months later, it was Bahramov who was the linesman in the 1966 World Cup Final who called England's controversial third goal a good one.

That West Ham's players didn't rise to the bait of wild tackles and erratic officiating was an act of impressive restraint. Added to the on-pitch tests they were given, off the pitch the crowd was hostile, with firecrackers and rockets being set off, while, with the game taking place during the hours of daylight, Greenwood's players had to contend with a glaring sun and strong winds which swept across the pitch.

By the time the quarter-finals arrived, West Ham's domestic form had improved. They were climbing steadily up the table and, while they had been knocked out of the FA Cup, they had reached the League Cup Final. Magdeburg, eight years prior to their moment of ultimate glory, were West Ham's opponents. The tie brought with it a second trip behind the Iron Curtain, following their trip to Prague the previous season.

Largely frustrated in the first leg at the Boleyn Ground, West Ham had to make do with a 1-0 lead to take to East Germany. Magdeburg were resolute in defence, defiant in midfield and unadventurous in attack. Their aim was to keep the first leg a low-scoring event, and they succeeded in their task.

A well-organised team, the defender Manfred Zapf and the midfielder Wolfgang Seguin would be survivors of the line-up that took on West Ham, who would go on to be part of the Magdeburg team that beat AC Milan in the 1974 Cup Winners' Cup Final.

It was with an outstanding degree of subterfuge that Magdeburg embraced the second leg at the Ernst Grube Stadium. Physical in their approach and getting their retaliation in first, it was Zapf who led by arguably malevolent example. This steel fist was classically covered by a velvet glove, however, as another Magdeburg hero of 1974 introduced himself to West Ham, having been shielded from the first leg. Magdeburg now unleashed a precocious 17-year-old by the name of Jürgen Sparwasser.

Sparwasser almost opened the scoring in the very first minute of the game when he instinctively attempted to divert the ball past Standen as it bounced back towards him, after it had thudded against the West Ham post via a venomous free kick by Günter Hirschmann.

Finding that the hostile atmosphere and the welcome they had experienced against Olympiacos in Athens to have been the ideal preparation, West Ham set out to play Magdeburg at their own defensive game. Disciplined and rigid in formation, they opted for a 'protect what we have' approach, inviting Magdeburg to be braver and bolder than they had been in east London.

That early near miss proved not to be a harbinger of doom for West Ham, as Magdeburg were easily repelled until the 76th minute, when Joachim Walter finally broke the resistance of Moore. The goal was set up by Sparwasser, with a hint of both handball and offside during the build-up.

Remaining calm, Sissons was on the end of a well-worked move just one minute later to kill the tie off. With UEFA experimenting with the away-goals rule, it meant Magdeburg needed to find two goals in not much more than ten minutes to progress to the semi-finals. Given how hard they had found it to score once, West Ham's goal left Magdeburg with a mountain to climb, although that didn't stop the hosts from throwing everything into their efforts to do so.

The following day in Cannes, West Ham avoided Liverpool and Celtic in the semi-final draw, finding themselves up against German opposition once again, this time from the west, in the shape of Borussia Dortmund. Finding themselves to be in a position which was simultaneously enviable and unenviable, when West Ham made the semi-finals of the 1965/66 Cup Winners' Cup, as holders, there was no obvious favourable draw to be found. While Celtic and Liverpool would pair off for a 'Battle of Britain' collision, Borussia Dortmund were by no means a prize to be celebrated, especially with the second leg to be played in Dortmund.

Both Celtic and Liverpool were on their way to their respective league titles in 1965/66, yet Borussia Dortmund were also sitting atop of the Bundesliga and looking strong favourites to lift the West German title. All the signs were foreboding ones.

That sense of peril was accentuated further due to West Ham's plight. Having improved vastly between defeating Olympiacos and Magdeburg, the wheels had fallen off since they had escaped East Germany with a place in the semi-finals. The League Cup Final had ended in a heavy loss to West Bromwich Albion, and they hadn't won for almost a month when they lined up for the first leg against Dortmund, amidst rumours of internal unrest at the club. Moore had even been replaced by Byrne as captain of the team. West Ham might have been the holders, but they were suddenly the weak link of the four teams to reach the semi-final. Dortmund, on the crest of a wave, could sense a vulnerability in their prey and they took full advantage of the situation.

At the Boleyn Ground, West Ham lifted what spirits they could, having already defied the odds several times along this wonderful European adventure of theirs. Riding their luck to a large extent, with five minutes remaining it looked like West Ham were going to head towards Germanic borders with another 1-0 advantage, thanks to a goal from Peters. Tormented down the right wing by Reinhard Libuda, West Ham couldn't hold firm, however, as two quick strikes from Lothar Emmerich changed the entire complexion of the tie within the blink of an eye.

At the Stadion Rote Erde, in the return game, Emmerich scored two more goals during the opening half hour, the first of which came within seconds of the kick-off. The game ended in a 3-1 defeat for West Ham, who exited the tournament 5-2 on aggregate. The incredible dream was over for West Ham, and they would have to wait almost nine and a half years until they could experience the European high life once again.

When they did, much had changed at the Boleyn Ground. While Greenwood was still at the club, he had taken on the role of general manager, yielding the managerial reigns to John Lyall, a former West Ham defender who had been forced to quit the game at the age of 23 due to a succession of knee problems. Lyall climbed through the ranks, from part-time youth coach to the manager's office, over the course of a decade. Greenwood was one of a collection of managerial icons of the English game to depart his job within a short span of time.

Between the final few exchanges of the 1972/73 season and the formative weeks of the 1974/75 campaign, Harry Catterick, Brian Clough, Bill Shankly, Don Revie and Bill Nicholson were joined by Greenwood in relinquishing their respective roles at Everton, Derby County, Liverpool, Leeds United and Tottenham Hotspur. Meanwhile, Matt

Busby had selected his last Manchester United line-up in 1971, as part of a round of musical chairs at Old Trafford which saw Wilf McGuinness, Frank O'Farrell and Tommy Docherty each appointed as manager of the club within just three and a half years of one another. Over on the blue side of the city, Joe Mercer had lost his job at Manchester City to his sidekick, Malcolm Allison, during a boardroom power struggle.

Allison himself was gone by March 1973 and the new Manchester City chairman, Peter Swales, had a revolving door fitted to the manager's office at Maine Road while, as a final flourish to the managerial upheaval, Clough departed Leeds after 44 days, having succeeded Revie.

Having fallen out with the Tottenham board and effectively been invited to leave the club after an advisory role was discussed for him, Nicholson was offered the same position by West Ham, joining up with Greenwood as Lyall's duo of invaluable and wise soothsayers.

The landscape of those in charge of the great and good of English football changed quickly and dramatically. There was an almost Bermuda Triangle effect and Lyall was part of the new wave of football managers. At the end of his first season, he had won West Ham their second FA Cup. Lyall would add more FA Cup glory in 1980, placing the club in to that almost bohemian 1980/81 playing of the Cup Winners' Cup. Over the course of an eventful 15 years at the helm of West Ham, Lyall not only delivered those two FA Cups, but there was also a League Cup Final, a third-place finish in the 1985/86 First Division and an epic run to the 1976 Cup Winners' Cup Final, all offset with two relegations and one runaway promotion.

It is fair to guess that life was never dull for the common or garden West Ham supporter of the Greenwood and Lyall eras.

There were no playing survivors in the West Ham squad of 1975/76 that had been part of the club's last European campaign. The heroes of the Moore, Peters and Hurst side had made way for new idols such as Frank Lampard senior, Billy Bonds and Trevor Brooking. Moore had even been in the Fulham side which faced West Ham in the 1975 FA Cup Final.

Bedecked in their wonderful 1970s Admiral kits, a sartorial twist which was perfect for the wider embracing of the colour television era, West Ham's run to the 1976 Cup Winners' Cup Final stood as an oasis amidst a barren spell for English clubs in the tournament.

There would not be another English finalist, beyond West Ham, until 1980, and no winner until 1985, a 14-year gap between English clubs succeeding in the Cup Winners' Cup. While all other English finalists reaching the showpiece event prior to them, in 1976, had played out their moments in the Cup Winners' Cup Final limelight within the ethereal flicker of black-and-white coverage – or in the case of Manchester City, not on British television at all – West Ham's run to the 1976 final feels like a peculiarity in comparison. A visual distortion that is of its era.

Relegation came to West Ham just three years later.

The 1975/76 West Ham were like a ship unwittingly sailing towards an iceberg. While a party was in full swing throughout the last long days of summer and the ever-darkening nights of autumn, there was danger ahead.

They made unnecessarily hard work of Reipas Lahti in the first round. The first leg, moved to Helsinki's Olympic Stadium, ended in a 2-2 draw in which West Ham twice had to come from behind, through the goals of Brooking and Bonds. With pretentions of rectifying their first-leg Helsinki meanderings, West Ham, while eventually running out 3-0 winners in the return game, had to wait until the hour mark to ease the shoulders of all those of a claret-and-blue persuasion. Keith Robson finally opened the scoring with a vicious volley; the second goal was added by Pat Holland before the substitute, Billy Jennings, made it 3-0. West Ham didn't go without their scares, however, and the frame of the goal was tested, as were the reflexes of their highly rated goalkeeper, Mervyn Day. It might have ended in a 5-2 aggregate win, but the scoreline didn't reflect the level of West Ham's overall complacency across the two games. At the time, Lyall's side were sitting in second position in the First Division and being spoken of as a credible challenger for the league title. They had topped the table in the early weeks of the season and would do so again in early November.

Bearing striking similarities to how Greenwood's 1964/65 side started their European odyssey, Lyall's 1975/76 vintage had no option but to learn on the job too. In the second round they were handed a trip into the Soviet Union, heading to Armenia via Moscow, to face the dangerous Ararat Yerevan.

Winners of the Soviet Top League as part of a domestic double just two years earlier and having reached the quarter-finals of the European Cup in 1974/75, where they only narrowly went out to Bayern Munich, Ararat were a true test of West Ham's abilities and an assignment that many other teams were delighted to have avoided.

At the vast Hrazdan Stadium in Yerevan it was a very different performance from West Ham, compared to the one they displayed in Helsinki. With the calibre of their opponents possibly focussing minds, West Ham were also unknowingly at the peak of their 1975/76 powers when they came up against Ararat. Weathering the Soviet storm, despite being depleted by injury and illness, Lyall and his players came away from Armenia with an impressive 1-1 draw.

Although they had been forced to operate with a predominantly defensive formation, the inspired goalkeeping of Day successfully kept Ararat frustrated. Alan Taylor, West Ham's FA Cup Final hero, was the beneficiary of the ball ricocheting towards him, when well placed to score. Completely against the run of play, the Hammers had the lead. West Ham were denied an unlikely but hard-earned win when Ararat equalised with a hugely contentious goal. Day, barged when collecting the ball in mid-air, seemed to have it kicked from his grasp on the ground. Samvel Petrosyan went both unpenalised and rewarded for his physical approach.

It was the other Petrosyan, Nazar, who scored for Ararat in the second leg, but to no avail as West Ham clicked through the higher gears to storm to a dominant 3-1 victory. Graham Paddon, Robson and Taylor scored with stylish efforts that were almost out of place on an evening when generally West Ham had opted for a succession of high balls into the Ararat penalty area, which the Armenians simply found impossible to deal with.

Between the two games against Ararat, West Ham beat Manchester United at home and demolished Birmingham City at St Andrew's. This was the white-hot zenith of their season and, in the very next game beyond dispatching Ararat, West Ham returned to the top of the First Division.

Anything seemed possible.

This bandwagon started to stutter, however. Over the course of their next six league games, West Ham won three and lost three. When they then travelled to Villa Park on Boxing Day, the wheels completely fell off and Lyall only managed to reattach them for European nights at the Boleyn Ground.

Contriving to win only one of their last 21 league games, West Ham defied football gravity when in Europe, in contrast to domestic capitulation. While they plummeted from the top of the First Division in mid-November all the way down to 18th position by mid-April, they still had eyes set firmly upon a trip to Brussels for the 1976 Cup Winners' Cup Final.

It was the random nature of the Cup Winners' Cup at its awkward best.

After brushing aside Ararat, West Ham would play five further games during their 1975/76 Cup Winners' Cup campaign. In the two games they played at home, they were imperious; in the three games they played in the Netherlands, West Germany and Belgium they lost and conceded a not insubstantial ten goals.

That isn't to say the travelling version of West Ham were entirely shambolic in Europe, but that they perhaps threw caution to the wind in the knowledge that they arguably had nothing to lose. Given their vulnerable domestic condition, maybe a more circumspect approach to the latter stages of the 1975/76 Cup Winners' Cup wouldn't have taken Lyall's team so close to glory. And they did come very close to incomprehensible glory in Brussels in May 1976.

In the quarter-finals West Ham were up against Den Haag, winners of the 1975 KNVB Cup Final, where they had beaten the 1975 UEFA Cup finalists, FC Twente. Whether Lyall was trying to convince his players as much as he was hoping to convince Den Haag, when it came to West Ham's defensive capabilities for the first leg, at the cacophonous Zuiderparkstadion, all bets were off within the first 45 minutes. At half-time, Den Haag went in 4-0 up. Even by West Ham's standards, it had been a wild first half. Aad Mansveld scored a hat-trick, two of his goals from the penalty spot: one of them harshly given, one of them guilty as charged.

Mansveld was a free-scoring sweeper, a former Netherlands international who had been denied a place in Rinus Michels's 1974 World Cup squad due to injury. He was so trusted and respected at Den Haag that he had been sent to England on a scouting mission, taking in West Ham's game against Leeds. That 1-1 draw had been one of West Ham's better recent performances. Had Mansveld instead viewed their following game, then he'd have witnessed Manchester United beating Lyall's team 4-0.

If the damage that Mansveld had administered to West Ham had been largely sublime, then the fourth goal, scored by Lex Schoenmaker, was purely absurd. After the referee was forced to pull up play near the halfway line, he resumed the game with a reassuringly old school drop-ball. As wonderful as this is to see, Rudi Glöckner – the

1970 World Cup Final referee no less – didn't adequately ensure that West Ham were as ready for it as Den Haag were. It was a bemused set of West Ham players who saw Den Haag accept the gift. As Paddon stood, with hands on hips, awaiting instruction from the referee, the man in black dropped the ball to the turf and Rob Ouwehand grasped the initiative and swept upfield where Schoenmaker coolly slotted the ball beneath Day.

The only solace for Lyall was that he wasn't in the Zuiderparkstadion to see his team's first-half capitulation in person. The latest victim of a West Ham influenza epidemic, he was back at the hotel. His star player, Brooking, was even further away, as he hadn't been well enough to make the journey at all.

Having reached the nadir, West Ham's depleted team relaxed in the second period, the half-time break halted Den Haag's momentum and Glöckner's refereeing became less erratic. Although that still didn't stop him bringing play to another halt to insist that all the West Ham players pull their socks up higher. This was a request that might have been taken figuratively along with the literal meaning of the East German referee's message. Inspired by the drive of Paddon down the left wing, Billy Jennings twice profited from his team-mate's hard work. While the first goal back was saluted with no more than a resigned sense of consolation, the second was embraced a little more enthusiastically. A vague inkling perhaps sneaking through the subconscious that what had seemed an inevitable exit at 4-0 down now felt redeemable with two away goals to go home with. If there was a supreme moment when doubt gripped Den Haag during the first leg, then it will have been when Tommy Taylor produced a bicycle-kick goal-line clearance, in the final few seconds of the game.

Clawing their way back to 4-2 gave West Ham a thin strand of hope, whereas conceding a fifth goal at the very end would have been soul-destroying for a team low on confidence, short on players, missing their manager and becoming ever more unfamiliar with the sensation and experience of winning games of football. Den Haag's serving of food for thought was bigger than they had been expecting to stomach.

After staying away from the first leg in the Netherlands, at the Boleyn Ground for the second leg Lyall finally came face-to-face with his Den Haag counterpart, Vujadin Boškov. The Serb would go on to lead Real Madrid to La Liga success and the 1981 European Cup Final, before winning Serie A with Sampdoria.

As Boškov's team rode out the initial wave of pressure, the home supporters began to get frustrated. It was an understandable response, given how West Ham had struggled since Christmas, yet it was ultimately a premature one. Just short of the half-hour mark West Ham made the breakthrough. A fine run and low shot from Brooking was fumbled by the Den Haag goalkeeper, Ton Thie, with the comedy of errors continuing during a goalmouth scramble which saw Taylor and Jennings get in each other's way, in their haste to force the ball over the goal line. With multiple Den Haag defenders getting in each other's way in their haste to clear the danger, the combined melée took on an Eton Wall Game theme, until Taylor was presented with the opportunity to prod the ball home.

The Boleyn Ground erupted.

Within five minutes the volume was even higher, as Lampard was cued up by Brooking to unleash an astonishing drive from 30 yards, which fizzed past Thie. After that catastrophic first half at the Zuiderstadion, it seemed ludicrous that West Ham now held a place in the semi-finals in the palm of their hand, thanks to their away-goal advantage. Tommy Taylor's late goal-line clearance at the end of the first leg now looked pivotal.

Incredulous onlookers, still recovering from the shock of the swiftness of the turnabout Boškov must have felt impossible, were soon left astounded when just three minutes later West Ham were awarded a penalty after Alan Taylor was clumsily brought down when charging through the Den Haag penalty area. Bonds was calmness personified as he sent Thie the wrong way. It was an almost identical re-enactment of the first leg, except in reverse.

This, of course, meant that for their part of the bargain Den Haag had to stage a second-half fightback, to mirror West Ham's first-leg second-half recovery. They very nearly did it too, with Schoenmaker scoring on the hour to level the aggregate score. With West Ham still in possession of the away-goal advantage, it made for an intense final half hour. Den Haag had a goal disallowed, as had West Ham not long after the restart. Den Haag even threw on the 19-year-old Martin Jol, as part of their chase for a winning goal. West Ham, going teenager for teenager in reply, introduced Alan Curbishley who had played from the start in the first leg in the absence of Brooking. With both teams going for another goal, while simultaneously harbouring nervous tendencies about the prospect of conceding again, it made for a white-knuckle ride for players, coaches and spectators alike, all the way up to the roar-inducing final whistle.

Despite their Cup Winners' Cup heroics, West Ham headed to Highbury three days later for a resumption of their laboured domestic endeavours and were thrashed 6-1, following that with a defeat at home to Norwich City.

It all left a huge question mark over which version of West Ham would show up for their semi-final against Eintracht Frankfurt.

At the Waldstadion, at the end of the first leg, West Ham were a beaten side for the 12th time since the turn of the year, yet there was something a little bit more assured about this loss. Away from domestic disharmony, the shackles were released from West Ham and they appeared to be enjoying themselves.

After another away goal procured when Paddon struck an early dipping effort from distance which provoked a wonderfully late dive from the Eintracht goalkeeper, Dr Peter Kunter – who went by the nickname 'The Flying Dentist' due the doctorate he gained in dentistry in 1969 – West Ham took the sting out of their opponent's technical superiority in one fell swoop. Although Eintracht would claim the lead early in the second half, that they had to start in arrears hadn't been part of the plan and it left them with a degree of indecision over how much risk they should put into extending their advantage for the second leg.

Push on, gambling with the potential for conceding a second away goal, in pursuit of more goals of their own, or settle for the lead they had obtained? Prompted by the World Cup winners Jürgen Grabowski and Bernd Hölzenbein, Eintracht were perhaps a little grateful for a win at all after Brooking spurned a couple of opportunities during the last 20 minutes of the game and West Ham again suffered with yet more disallowed goals.

Finely poised, it was all set up for one of the Boleyn Ground's greatest nights and the first half of the second leg was played at a frenetic pace. Eintracht were caught within a blur of West Ham attacking intent and mud, the turf having taken a series of saturations in the days and hours building up to the game. Goalless at half-time, Brooking, having not been at his best during the first leg, saw the tie turn on the flick of his head. A beautifully weighted ball from Lampard and a glancing header from Brooking put West Ham in provisional possession of a place in the final, alongside Anderlecht, who were running away with the other, very one-sided, semi-final, against the East Germans, BSG Sachsenring Zwickau.

Regaining composure, and with some of the pressure being released due to no longer holding the advantage, Eintracht began to grow into the game, Rüdiger Wenzel forcing Day into an impressive low save. It was Eintracht's first effort of substance, yet a shot had been delivered across West Ham's bows and it instigated a wave of attacks from the West Germans from which the Londoners were lucky to emerge unscathed. Within a short few seconds, from the resultant corner Day was forced into another smart save, his post was hit, and the ball was cleared off the line with a heavy hint of handball that left the Eintracht players appealing desperately for a penalty.

West Ham had again ridden their luck, yet if challenged would no doubt have pointed at the penalty they were denied in the opening minutes, karma perhaps being satisfied. It was knife-edge European second-leg football at its most dramatic.

With the game being split open wide, Eintracht ploughed forward in their attempt to obtain a place in the final, in the belief, or even hope, that their greater general cohesion and technique would be rewarded by success.

This, of course, left Eintracht vulnerable to the counter. A long cross-field pass from Brooking found Robson in generous amounts of space on the right-hand side. Perfectly played by Brooking, slightly misjudged by Robson, the recipient of the ball had to correct himself and his position, before looking up to assess just where Dr Kunter was. It is a testament to just how committed to attack Eintracht were at this point, that Robson had all the time in the world to circumnavigate his way around the ball to get it on to his favoured left foot, from where he unleashed a spectacular shot which flew into the top left-hand corner of Dr Kunter's net.

Bedlam ensued and, while the goal put West Ham 2-0 up, it didn't alter the fact that Eintracht still only needed one goal to save themselves. That hypothetical goal would now only be enough to force extra time rather than win the game outright, however.

The Boleyn Ground now measuring impressively on the Richter scale, emitting an atmosphere that it surely never eclipsed in any other game before or beyond, both teams continued to go for goal. Eintracht driving forward incessantly, West Ham hitting on the break with style: it made for irresistible footballing theatre. Robson's goal having come midway through the second half meant that there was still a lot of football to be played.

Brooking, scorer of their first, and having played a prominent role in West Ham's second goal, also then scored the third with just ten minutes remaining. Getting on to the end of a long pass played out of defence by Tommy Taylor, it was with what could almost have been a Stan Bowles-style drag back that Brooking cut across the Eintracht penalty area, sold his marker and rolled the ball under the advancing Dr Kunter.

At 3-0, leading 4-2 on aggregate, West Ham seemingly had their place in the 1976 Cup Winners' Cup Final assured. Eintracht refused to give up, however, and what unfolded next was a succession of saves, clearances, further penalty claims and near misses via wicked deflections, until Klaus Beverungen silenced the raucous West Ham congregation with a goal when there were still a few short minutes to spare for their pursuit of a clincher.

Despite the pressure Eintracht were applying, West Ham should have scored a fourth goal. It was a tired Jennings who failed to take a golden opportunity to ease West Ham's anxieties, with only a couple of minutes left to play, stumbling in the penalty area as he attempted to collect a descending ball. This simply invited Eintracht to make one final push and it was only a desperate, backs-to-the-wall rearguard effort that kept the West Germans out.

As the final whistle blew, the noise inside the Boleyn Ground was so deafening that the players of both sides continued to play for a good few seconds beyond the game ending. It was with a mixture of relief, disbelief, exhaustion and an almost numbed elation that the West Ham players embraced the fact that they had, against all odds, reached the final.

Three weeks away from the final, West Ham had three more league games to play, although they would be crammed into an eight-day span that afforded their physically shattered players an 11-day break before facing Anderlecht at the Heysel Stadium.

Still, Lyall's team couldn't buy a domestic victory, ending a peculiar league campaign with a draw at home to Aston Villa and defeats at Ipswich Town and Everton.

Over the course of their week and a half long sabbatical, West Ham took themselves off to Morecambe and faced Rochdale in a friendly, occasionally syphoning players off in small clusters to appear in testimonial games, as a way of keeping them sharp.

Given the nature of their season however, it would surely have felt odd to them if West Ham hadn't been thrown a pre-match curve ball. Their captain, Bonds, didn't fly out to Brussels with the rest of the squad, instead remaining at home due to helping look after his ill father-in-law, eventually catching up with the party the following day.

Lyall's selection options had increased. Injury problems having cleared for both Alan Taylor and Kevin Lock, the West Ham manager was left with the luxury of either bringing back two players who had been crucial components of the team prior to injury or sticking with the line-up which had defeated Eintracht in the semi-final. It would have been the very stereotypically English choice to stick rather than twist in these circumstances, and that is just what Lyall did. The West Ham players that walked out for the 1976 Cup Winners' Cup Final were the very same line-up that had got them past Eintracht.

There were also choices to be made by Hans Croon, the Anderlecht coach. Already aware that, regardless of the result, it was to be his last match in charge, Croon had made the difficult decision to leave out his captain, Erwin Vandendaele. Having been out for a prolonged spell, the skipper had returned to the team for the previous game in a bid to prove his fitness for the final. Vandendaele wasn't alone in providing a selection headache for Croon. Ludo Coeck did make the starting 11, but would last for just 32 minutes, before being replaced by the 20-year-old Franky Vercauteren.

Vercauteren would go on to greatness in the white of Anderlecht and the red of Belgium, but in his first season in the Anderlecht senior squad his development had been as painful as the injuries and operations he had had to endure.

Around 8,000 West Ham supporters made the trip to Brussels for the final but, given that Anderlecht are a product of the city, they were outnumbered by over 5-to-1, as part of what was effectively a home crowd. Home crowd or not, the travelling West Ham supporters could be heard loud and clear and it was their team who made the brighter start, a positivity that was rewarded in the 28th minute as Pat Holland guided the ball home after Bonds climbed the highest in the Anderlecht penalty area when challenging for a lofted cross from Paddon.

If West Ham embraced this most unexpected of opportunities enthusiastically, the 1976 Cup Winners' Cup Final hung around the neck of Anderlecht like an unwelcome weight until the 42nd minute. Gifted a way back into a game they hadn't yet aesthetically arrived at, the whole evening and the destination of the trophy itself pivoted in a Belgian direction when Lampard attempted to play a back pass to Day, from the left-hand side of his own penalty area. Partly scuffing the ball, partly kicking the turf, it was a costly error which was seized upon by Peter Ressel. He closed on the advancing West Ham goalkeeper before cutting the ball back to an eager Rob Rensenbrink, who rounded a prone Bonds and was then calm enough to pick his spot to place the equalising goal past Day and the covering West Ham defender on the goal line.

It was a massive blow to West Ham and it undid all the hard work they'd put in, which had looked set to see them go in for the half-time break with a 1-0 lead. Given Lampard's robust nature, it was perhaps unsurprising that not one of his team-mates remonstrated their frustration with him. Going from bad to worse for the West Ham left-back, within seconds of his mistake he suffered a groin strain and would not return for the second half. Compounding their unfortunate end to the first half, with Lampard's departure Lyall felt compelled to extensively rearrange his team, rather than go with as like-for-like a change as he possibly could. While defender Kevin Lock remained on the bench, Lyall instead opted to bring on striker Alan Taylor to play out of position on the right-hand side of midfield. Holland moved into a central midfield role and John McDowell was asked to drop to left-back to cover for Lampard. A versatile player, McDowell was generally a career full-back, but at right-back rather than left-back.

Three alterations had been made to cover the loss of one player, with two of them arguably makeshift choices. Within three minutes of the restart, West Ham were 2-1 down. Over the course of a six-minute swing, bridging each side of the half-time break, West Ham had conceded two goals and lost one of their most important players. The scorer of that second Anderlecht goal was the future West Ham player, François van der Elst. Stylistically beautiful, it wasn't to be his last goalscoring contribution to the game.

Rather than capitulate due to the cruelty of football, West Ham then had their most dominant period of the game. Having fought back from one setback after another to reach the final in the first place, it was entirely in keeping with them to fight on. Tommy Taylor was the unexpected proponent of a wonderful near miss when he caught an Anderlecht defensive clearance cleanly on the volley, sending the ball flying towards the top corner, where Jan Ruiter threw himself across goal to make a spectacular stop. Taylor's team-mates seemed as equally stunned that it didn't go in as they were about the identity of the player who had launched the effort.

For Anderlecht, it was only a temporary reprieve, however. Brooking, working his way down the left, sent in a low cross that Robson stooped to glance beyond Ruiter to make it 2-2. It was an equaliser that West Ham didn't get to use as a springboard for victory, however.

The direction of the pressure switched from one end to the other. As Anderlecht swarmed forward, West Ham didn't seem to know how to react to being back on level terms. Rensenbrink, Van der Elst and Ressel, along with Arie Haan, began to turn the screw on a West Ham defence that had kept just two clean sheets since the beginning of December. Day, with a series of fine saves, particularly from Vercauteren and Van der Elst, kept West Ham in the game for a while, but it was clear that Anderlecht were now in the ascendancy and Rensenbrink – heir of Cruyff – was leading the charge.

When Anderlecht's third goal came, it was in semi-contentious circumstances. Rensenbrink went to ground in the West Ham penalty area with 17 minutes to go. Holland had dived in to challenge him, when it was arguably wiser to stay on his feet, hooking his leg around Rensenbrink in a genuine attempt to get to the ball; it was Rensenbrink's momentum which took him over. Holland protested his innocence, while in Rensenbrink's defence, he was in such close proximity to the West Ham six-yard box that he was quickly back on his feet, sensing the chance to score. In contemporary terms, there would be eight different camera angles to clear the ambiguity up. Yet, even by 1976 standards, it looked more like it should have been a penalty than it shouldn't.

There was a strange combination of fine skill and unintended error in the build-up to Anderlecht being awarded their penalty. Haan sent Ressel away down the right-hand side, where he elicited an unfortunate slip from Tommy Taylor, gifting the attacker with a clear run, at an angle, at Day. Closed down by the advancing Day and the recovering Tommy Taylor, Ressel opted to cut the ball back across the West Ham penalty area, yet was a little heavy with his pass, leaving Rensenbrink half a second too late to take possession and Coleman swinging his foot at thin air, having possibly not expected the ball to drift across him. Vercauteren then picked the ball up, laying it off to Rensenbrink and making a run for a hoped-for return ball, only to find his team-mate was in the mood to hold on to it instead. Tormenting an increasingly ragged Coleman, Rensenbrink performed something which was akin to a reverse Cruyff turn, before accelerating towards his duel with Holland, which won him his penalty.

Grabbing the ball himself and powering it a little too centrally for comfort, Rensenbrink was blessed by Day diving the wrong way. Dave Sexton, the Queens Park Rangers manager acting as David Coleman's co-commentator for the game, added to the grey areas regarding the validity of the penalty being given. He declared that, while it was technically a penalty, Holland hadn't brought Rensenbrink down intentionally.

Despite reclaiming a slender lead, Anderlecht knowingly remained on the offensive, a common-sense approach given that West Ham's weaknesses were at the back and their strengths were further forward. Day continued to be regularly tested. As the West Ham threat diminished, Anderlecht sprang forward one more time in the 88th minute. Brooking was dispossessed of the ball by Jean Thissen and Gilbert Van Binst – the stand-in captain for Anderlecht in the absence of Vandendaele – close to the right-side corner flag, as he ran into a cul-de-sac in his attempt to conjure West Ham the goal which would have forced the game into extra time. Anderlecht swept from one end of the pitch to the other. From Thissen to Van Binst, the ball then moved on to Rensenbrink. Stretching his legs, Rensenbrink carried it towards the halfway line, waiting, waiting for the perfect moment to release it to Van der Elst. Tommy Taylor, arm raised, having stepped up to play the offside trap, was undone by McDowell who fell for the bait of trying to keep pace with Van der Elst.

It is here that the artistry escalated. Van der Elst, allowing McDowell to catch him up on the edge of the D, cut back in the opposite direction to goal, causing a bewildered McDowell to overshoot the ball by a considerable distance.

Turning the spinning McDowell inside out, when the West Ham defender returned to face him again, Van der Elst managed to leave the disorientated McDowell with his back to play and simultaneously sit Day on the floor, before rolling the ball into the West Ham net for 4-2, sinking to his knees in celebration.

It was one of the finest goals in the entire history of the Cup Winners' Cup and for West Ham, as disappointing as defeat was, there was no shame to be suffered in losing out to an Anderlecht side that would go on to reach the next two Cup Winners' Cup finals too.

West Ham's domestic troubles limped on into the following seasons. At the end of the 1977/78 campaign they were relegated to the Second Division. Their climb back to the big time in 1981 embraced the eccentricities of their encounters with Castilla and Dinamo Tbilisi in the 1980/81 Cup Winners' Cup.

They never appeared in the tournament again, the closest they drifted to it being when – with shades of winning the FA Cup in 1980 – they reached the semi-finals of the FA Cup in 1991, as a Second Division side. Their relationship with the Cup Winners' Cup stretched to four seasons, spanning 16 and a half years from first game to last, winning it once, losing another final, reaching a semi-final and a quarter-final. West Ham got a rich return from the tournament, as did the tournament from West Ham.

Despite there being other winners from their country, it's quite possible that no other English club embodied the wild randomness of the Cup Winners' Cup as much as West Ham did.

Chapter Four

A Catalan Love Affair and Other Iberian Adventures

BARCELONA ARE the most successful team in the history of the European Cup Winners' Cup. Four-time winners, twice-beaten finalists, they won every semi-final they reached and fell at the first hurdle only once. Competing in the tournament in 13 of its 39 seasons, they were present for over a third of its existence. Their four successes, won between 1979 and 1997, mean that Barcelona lifted the Cup Winners' Cup more times than all other Spanish teams put together.

Although Real Madrid took the European Cup by storm during its first five seasons, when Atlético Madrid won the 1960 Copa Generalísimo they did not take up the opportunity to compete in the first playing of the Cup Winners' Cup in 1960/61.

In 1961/62, however, they made up for lost time, after managing to retain their Copa Generalísimo when beating their city rivals from the Santiago Bernabéu, at the Santiago Bernabéu, in front of an estimated 120,000 spectators in the 1961 Spanish domestic cup final.

From over the border, Portugal also supplied its first entrant to the Cup Winners' Cup in 1961/62, when Leixões bravely dared to go where Belenenses didn't in 1960/61. Having passed up their 1960/61 opportunity, Belenenses would have to wait until the 1989/90 season before they got to compete for the Cup Winners' Cup, and by 'compete' I mean be bundled out of the tournament with ease by AS Monaco in the first round.

While Leixões made it to the quarter-finals in 1962, Atlético went all the way to the final at Hampden Park, where they faced the holders, the Ferruccio Valcareggi-led Fiorentina. Valcareggi was the man who would take Italy to glory in the 1968 European Championship and to the 1970 World Cup Final. Atlético eased their way to the final, breezing their way past Sedan, Leicester City, Werder Bremen and Motor Jena, scoring 19 goals along their route and not being truly tested until facing Fiorentina. The holders, meanwhile, were made to work in the quarter-finals against Dynamo Žilina, yet had little trouble with Rapid Vienna and Újpesti Dózsa either side of that.

The 1962 final was marked by the adjustment of it being a one-off final, as opposed to the inaugural final which was played over two legs. This, however, didn't stop the game needing two games to decide the outcome.

In Glasgow, on 10 May, the two sides played out a 1-1 draw, with Atlético drawing first blood through Joaquín

Peiró, before the legendary Swedish international, Kurt Hamrin, levelled the score for Fiorentina, all within the first half hour. With no further goals being added, and the era of the penalty shoot-out still almost a decade away, it meant that a replay would be required.

With no contingency plan for a rematch arranged and the 1962 World Cup finals beginning in Chile less than three weeks later, for which both Spain and Italy had qualified, the 1962 Cup Winners' Cup Final replay was put on hold until 5 September, almost a full four months after the playing of the original game at Hampden Park.

This time at the Neckarstadion, in Stuttgart, Atlético were comfortable 3-0 winners against a Fiorentina line-up with four changes to the team that played in Glasgow. One of those changes, Enrico Albertosi, in for the injured Giuliano Sarti, proved to be a devastating one, as rich a young talent as he was, having played in both legs of the 1961 final in the absence of Sarti. A man who would go on to play in the 1970 World Cup Final, a man who had travelled to the 1962 World Cup as one of Lorenzo Buffon's two back-ups, despite not even being first choice at Fiorentina, Albertosi was surprisingly at fault for at least two, if not all three, of Atlético's goals. Atlético finally had their Cup Winners' Cup glory, in a game which was played on the same day as the first leg of preliminary-round games for the 1962/63 Cup Winners' Cup campaign, inclusive of Bangor City defeating the Mighty Napoli 2-0 at Farrar Road.

Allowed just seven weeks to bask in their success, Atlético launched themselves into the defence of their trophy against Hibernians, of Malta. Brushing aside the limited threat of not only Hibernians, but also that of

Botev Plovdiv in the quarter-finals, it seemed – as they approached the semi-finals once more – like Atlético had no peers to speak of in the competition. It was all a little too easy for them.

If this had bred any air of superiority, or convinced Atlético that they were immortal as far as the Cup Winners' Cup was concerned, then a rude awakening was on the horizon. When Atlético travelled to West Germany, to face 1. FC Nürnberg in the first leg of the semi-final, they returned to the Spanish capital nursing their first ever Cup Winners' Cup defeat. Losing 2-1, however, left everything to fight for in the return game, which was switched from Atlético's Estadio Metropolitano de Madrid, to Real Madrid's Santiago Bernabéu.

With the Vicente Calderón under construction and still three years away from being habitable, as atmospheric and bijou as Atlético's Metropolitano was, the fact that over three times the number of spectators could attend the game if it were to be shifted to the home of their cross-city rivals won the debate over where to hold the game.

Approximately 86,000 spectators filed into the Bernabéu to watch a hard-fought battle between two clubs who were living in the vast shadows of rival clubs, in their respective nations. Emerging into the spotlight, they put on a display that would have been befitting of the final itself.

Atlético scored shortly before half-time and again before the hour mark, thanks to strikes from Chuzo and Mendonça. Combined with the crucial goal scored in West Germany, by Miguel Jones, a Bioko-born former economics student at the University of Bilbao, these were the goals that saw the holders reach the final once again.

Looking to achieve what was just beyond the capabilities of Fiorentina, in successfully defending the Cup Winners' Cup, Atlético's 5-1 margin of defeat in the 1963 Cup Winners' Cup Final is misleading. While Tottenham Hotspur were deservedly the victors, and they played well enough to warrant the result, Atlético were by no means out of the game until the last ten minutes. Trailing 2-0 at half-time, Atlético halved the deficit within two minutes of the restart, when their captain, Enrique Collar, confidently put a penalty away. This was a goal which encouraged Atlético's best spell of the final and they dominated the next 20 minutes, a spell in which another Atlético goal would have left Tottenham hugely vulnerable.

That second goal didn't come, however, and with Atlético on the early second-half offensive it left their Argentinian goalkeeper, Edgardo Madinabeytia, underemployed after he had been kept busy for most of the first half in repelling Tottenham attack after Tottenham attack. It was a fast and powerful wave of intent that Atlético simply hadn't foreseen. When Madinabeytia was brought back into action midway through the second half, it was in calamitous circumstances. He completely misjudged the flight of a miscued cross by Terry Dyson, which was lofted high into the Rotterdam night sky, only for it to come down just beneath Madinabeytia's crossbar, brushing the goalkeeper's fingers as it did and dropping into the Atlético net. It was a goal which came against the run of play and it automatically deflated the Atlético cause, the entire course of the game being altered in that one incredible moment.

Remarkable as it might seem, this would be the first of a hat-trick of speculatively similar moments in Cup Winners'

Cup finals involving English clubs. While Tottenham prospered in 1963, Liverpool in 1966 and Arsenal in 1995 were on the receiving end of such strokes of trophy-deciding misfortune.

As Atlético struggled to assimilate the events of Tottenham's third goal, the English side took full advantage and it was a drained Atlético who played out the final stretch of the game, up against a refreshed Tottenham side which now turned on all their best tricks to add a couple of extra goals.

With a result that doesn't tell the full story of the game, the 1963 Cup Winners' Cup Final has some similarities to Denmark's 1986 World Cup defeat to Spain by the same scoreline. Both sides had dominated spells of their respective games only to see their opponents run off into the distance, with a margin of victory that is virtually obscene when it comes to the wider context of the 90 minutes which has just unfolded.

Having been on the brink of back-to-back Cup Winners' Cup successes in 1963 and having, along with Fiorentina, forever set the rule that the holder shalt not retain the trophy, Atlético went from having had what appeared to be the perfect relationship with the Cup Winners' Cup to an almost uneasy and suspicious one.

It was as if the 1963 final had left an indelible and immovable curse upon Atlético when it came to the Cup Winners' Cup. They would never again win the tournament, as part of the peculiar wider fact that of the first seven winners of the Cup Winners' Cup, not one of them would go on to lift the trophy a second time. Tying in to the eccentric and random theme of the tournament, only five teams ever won the Cup Winners' Cup upon multiple occasions.

This isn't to say that Atlético never came close again. This they did; no more so than when they reached the 1986 final against Dynamo Kyiv. Yet, there were other flirtations towards the general direction of a reunion with the Cup Winners' Cup trophy, when they were beaten semi-finalists in 1977 and again in 1993.

In 1977 Atlético threw away a 3-1 semi-final first-leg lead, when they made the trip to West Germany for the return game against a pre-Kevin Keegan, Hamburger SV. La Liga champions-elect, they imploded during a nine-minute span towards the end of the first 30 minutes at the Volksparkstadion. It was a capitulation which was set in motion by a calamitous own goal from José Luis Capón when he cut across the vision of Miguel Reina – father of the future World Cup winner, Pepe – to deflect a free kick into the Atlético net. From there, there seemed to be only one likely winner. Yet even at 3-0 down, despite conceding three goals in such quick succession, the last 62 minutes of the game were played out on a knife edge. All Atlético needed to take the game into extra time was one goal.

That goal failed to materialise, and another chance of renewed Cup Winners' Cup glory had gone once again, just as it did against Dynamo Kyiv in 1986. On that occasion, in the final at the Stade de Gerland in Lyon, it was two late goals that cruelly increased the margin of defeat for Atlético. Although they had spent most of the match chasing Soviet shadows, nobody would have questioned the final score had it remained 1-0. The second of those near misses had been a largely arduous journey, which made the manner of Atlético's loss in the final more devastating.

After facing Celtic, evoking still only 11-year-old and extremely bitter memories of the two sides' brutal European Cup semi-final encounters of 1974, Atlético edged through to the second round where they faced an old nemesis of Napoli in the shape of Bangor City. They then overcame the subtle and not-so-subtle dangers posed by Red Star Belgrade and Bayer Uerdingen.

It had been an unbeaten run which took Atlético to the 1986 Cup Winners' Cup Final and they were led there by the polarising figure of Luis Aragonés, who was also head coach when they had reached the semi-finals in 1976/77. Remarkably, it was also Aragonés who started Atlético's run to the semi-finals in 1992/93, although by the time those last four games rolled around he had once again been unseated from his job by the impossible to predict, yet massively entertaining, Jesús Gil.

When Aragonés departed the Vicente Calderón in late January 1993, it was the sixth time he had relinquished the role of head coach of Atlético. In 2001 he would return for a seventh spell, with the club languishing in the Segunda División, and succeed in restoring them to the top flight. The contemporary version of Atlético would be built upon this foundation, with the club eventually breaking the Barcelona–Real Madrid duopoly on the La Liga title in 2013/14.

In 1992/93, however, Aragonés delivered Atlético a place in the quarter-finals but was not to be allowed to see if he could take them further. It was instead José Omar Pastoriza who oversaw the quarter-final victory over Olympiacos. He was also jettisoned by Gil before the semi-finals against Parma, into which Atlético were led by Ramón Heredia, an old team-mate of Aragonés from their playing days together for Atlético.

Against Parma, it was another case of what might have been for Atlético. Losing the first leg 2-1 at home, they travelled to Emilia-Romagna where a 1-0 victory meant that they were edged out by the eventual 1993 winners, on the away-goals rule.

While Atlético were the first, but by no means last, successful Spanish explorers in the Cup Winners' Cup, returning for their periodic and compelling attempts to win it again, over the border in Portugal there was only one winner of the Cup Winners' Cup.

The Cup Winners' Cup evaded the clutches of Benfica, who never even made the final, and FC Porto, who lost the 1984 final against Juventus, and it was left to Sporting CP to obtain Portugal's sole success in the tournament. It was through a stubborn resilience, perhaps never equalled in the Cup Winners' Cup, that they achieved this.

Requiring replays to overcome three of their five opponents, Sporting were pushed to 12 games, scoring 36 goals along their way to glory. Exactly half of those goals were scored in the second round against APOEL, of Cyprus, a club that in more contemporary times reached the quarter-finals of the Champions League during the 2011/12 season.

Incredibly, the scorelines in the two games between Sporting and APOEL were far from balanced. During the first leg at the Estádio José Alvalade in Lisbon, the home side were 16-1 winners. That's sixteen goals to one, as opposed to betting odds of 16 to 1 by the way. Mascarenhas, a phantom of a goalscorer who was usually notable for the amount of injuries he suffered as opposed to his undoubted talents when fit, scored a double hat-trick, while his strike partner, Ernesto Figueiredo, had to make do with just the one hat-trick.

APOEL, however, offered the only low hurdle for the entirety of Sporting's 1963/64 run. Even within this, the manner of APOEL's sizeable defeat simply added a polar eccentricity to the way Sporting's other ties would unfold.

Prior to APOEL, Sporting had seen off the Italian side, Atalanta, in the first round, a team led by the burgeoning talent of Angelo Domenghini. The Serie A side had won the Coppa Italia in 1963, a success that is still Atalanta's only major honour to date. As Italy's representatives, it automatically made them dangerous opponents for Sporting and it was something of a thankless task to have to travel to Bergamo, where the home side cruised to a 2-0 victory.

A professional job done by Atalanta, playing the waiting game until the final 15 minutes then picking off their goals from tiring opponents, it all fell apart for them in Lisbon. A 3-1 win for Sporting in front of a passionate congregation meant that, with two years still to go until the introduction of the away-goals rule, a replay was needed.

The replay took place in Barcelona, at the Estadi de Sarrià, the home of Español, a club that would never compete in the Cup Winners' Cup. Two closely matched sides, it would take extra time to split the difference. After 300 minutes of football, it was Sporting that was finally stubborn enough to persist their way to a 3-1 win.

It wouldn't be the last time the two would face one another in the Cup Winners' Cup, however. Sporting and Atalanta clashed in the 1987/88 quarter-finals, when neither side had won their respective domestic cup competition in 1987. Sporting and Atalanta had lost those domestic cup finals to Benfica and Napoli, respectively, who had also happened to win their domestic league titles.

That man Mascarenhas was one of the heroes for Sporting again. Scoring twice in Barcelona, he had also scored in Lisbon. Not always reliable as a rule, by the time they had overwhelmed APOEL, he was fast becoming the source of all Sporting's European prowess in the Cup Winners' Cup.

Sporting's prize for defeating Atalanta and APOEL in the 1963/64 vintage of the Cup Winners' Cup, was being drawn to face Matt Busby's Manchester United in the quarter-finals.

Towards the end of February, Sporting made their seemingly fatal trip to Old Trafford for the first leg. A Denis Law hat-trick and a goal from Bobby Charlton paved the way to a 4-1 victory that was thought insurmountable. Law's two second-half goals came from the penalty spot, the first of which was harshly awarded and, on an evening where the hosts were as profligate as they were prolific, Busby's side wouldn't have been flattered to have doubled their goal haul.

When Manchester United made the journey to Lisbon for the second leg, they did so within the slipstream of losing to West Ham United in the FA Cup semi-final, relinquishing their grip on the trophy and simultaneously assisting their opponents on a path that, of course, took them all the way to glory in the 1965 Cup Winners' Cup.

Manchester United's trilogy of FA Cup quarter-final games against Sunderland resulted in the trip to Portugal taking place a fortnight later than originally scheduled – domestic games taking precedence over European competition in this era. United were trying to shake off their FA Cup disappointment with a couple of days of sunshine, half an hour along the coast from Lisbon, in Estoril.

Naming an unchanged side from the one which had lost the FA Cup semi-final, and making sounds about going for more goals rather than protecting what they held, Manchester United's presence on the Iberian peninsula drew huge interest. Delegations of players, coaches and officials from both Benfica and Real Madrid made their way to the Estádio José Alvalade. The sense of reverence was added to when the holders, Tottenham Hotspur, sent a good luck telegram to their fellow First Division club.

While those who came to pay homage were not to be disappointed with the entertainment on offer, it was not delivered by the team in red shirts. It was instead Sporting, in their green and white hoops, who stunned those in attendance with a masterclass of a performance. The game was won by Sporting over the course of two fast starts: a 13-minute salvo at the beginning of the first half in which Osvaldo da Silva scored twice, followed by a ten-minute barrage at the beginning of the second half when strikes by João Morais and Geo Carvalho were added to by Osvaldo completing his hat-trick.

It was a devastating hour of football which rocked Manchester United to their very foundations, the opening goal coming after just two minutes, from the penalty spot, the fifth goal being almost caressed in, via a 30-yard free kick.

Not one of those occasions when suspicious glances could be cast upon the referee, Sporting were simply a force of attacking nature, even harshly having a third 'goal' disallowed before the interval. Not that this stopped their momentum. Geo scored their belated third goal with a beautifully low-struck shot from distance, while the fourth goal was slammed into the roof of the net by Morais. In fact, Sporting's margin of victory could have been wider as an open-goal opportunity was spectacularly put over the bar from six yards. Upon the full-time whistle, Sporting's delirious supporters swept on to the pitch to celebrate with their heroes, leaving a dazed Manchester United to wonder just what had occurred.

Olympique Lyonnais stood between Sporting and a place in the 1964 Cup Winners' Cup Final. After a goalless first leg at the Stade de Gerland, the second leg in Lisbon was almost as open and attacking as the game against Manchester United had been. On this occasion, however, Lyon kept pace with Sporting, opening the scoring through Nestor Combin, the Argentinian-born France international, who would go on to play for Juventus, Torino and AC Milan.

Trailing at half-time, Sporting were again quick out of the blocks after the restart. Within three minutes the game was level as Geo converted from the penalty spot. For the remainder of the game Lyon mounted a furious rearguard action, as Sporting created chance after chance, only to see them repelled. As a counter to this, Lyon sprang forward with sporadic attacks of their own, in the hope of snatching a winning goal.

With the game drifting to a 1-1 draw, it meant a replay was required, which was contested a fortnight later, in Madrid at the Metropolitano. Sporting edged the game 1-0 thanks to a well-taken goal from Osvaldo deceiving the Lyon defence when seemingly being ushered away from goal, only to spin and finish with speed and power.

When you consider Sporting's action-packed run to 1964 Cup Winners' Cup glory, made up of those closely contested battles of skill and stubbornness against Atalanta and Lyon, the 18-1 avalanche of goals against APOEL and their resounding comeback and dismantling of Manchester United, then the wonderful eccentricities of the final against MTK Budapest, make perfect sense. A sedate 2-0 just wouldn't have been acceptable.

That tumultuous 3-3 draw and a winning goal coming directly from a corner were the very least Sporting could do.

There is arguably no greater Cup Winners' Cup insult than that the 1964 final was the lowest attended major European final of all time. Yet those 3,208 spectators who were present at the Heysel Stadium were bathed in an extraordinary glow.

Despite the manner of their success in 1964, Sporting's achievement tends to be misted over to an extent by the legendary actions of Benfica, in becoming the first side not named Real Madrid to lift the European Cup.

After being crowned as the second kings of Europe, Benfica retained their title in 1962, going on to lose three further finals before the decade was over but, peculiarly, never lifting another European trophy beyond 1962 and failing to ever reach a Cup Winners' Cup Final.

All of this is part of a wider legend of the curse of Béla Guttmann, who footballing fables insist asked Benfica for a pay rise after delivering the 1962 victory, only to be rebuffed. Upon leaving the club immediately, Guttmann is believed to have stated that Benfica would not be champions of Europe again for 100 years.

Added to the storied history and mysticism of Benfica, the Sporting of 1964 are also overshadowed by the more contemporary European achievements of FC Porto, who became champions of Europe themselves in 1987, and again in 2004 under the polarising stylings of José Mourinho. Their most recent piece of European silverware is the 2011 Europa League trophy, won when they defeated Braga in Dublin in the first all-Portuguese major European final.

In European terms at least, Benfica somehow represent Portugal's early footballing history, while Porto represent Portugal's modern history. This is despite Benfica themselves reaching a Europa League Final as recently as 2014; remaining under the curse of Guttmann for another 48 years, they lost on penalties to Sevilla.

Amidst all this, Sporting may be forgotten, or simply ignored. Even the UEFA Cup Final they reached and lost on home soil, in 2005, was obscured by the blizzard of drama that was Liverpool's Champions League Final win against AC Milan in Istanbul, just one week later. Yet, Sporting will forever proudly remain the only Portuguese team to have won the Cup Winners' Cup.

As holders and having won the tournament at their very first attempt, in 1964/65 Sporting went out in the second round at the hands of Cardiff City, having received a bye in the first round. They returned to the Cup Winners' Cup four times during the 1970s, suffering first-round exits upon three of those occasions, but coming close to reaching the 1974 final at what would have been the expense of Magdeburg.

Beyond their 1988 rematch with Atalanta, Sporting graced the Cup Winners' Cup one last time in 1995/96, when they limped out early to Rapid Vienna. It was a sad way to bow out of a tournament they had illuminated in an almost anonymous way in 1963/64. Obscured by the achievements and the curses of others, Sporting's success in the Cup Winners' Cup should be a revered one.

With the final of the Cup Winners' Cup eluding Benfica, most notably in those semi-final losses, Porto provided Portugal with its only other appearance in the tournament's showpiece occasion. Living long in the shadows of both Sporting and Benfica, Porto suffered a 19-year title drought before claiming their sixth domestic league success in 1977/78, edging out Benfica in a dramatic title race.

Nothing but ordinary in their European endeavours up until this point, Porto's run to the quarter-finals of the Cup Winners' Cup, in the very same season, had been their best showing yet on the continent, a run that was ended by an Anderlecht side that was on their way to a third consecutive final. They would reach the quarter-final stage again in 1981/82.

Porto retained their league title the following season, in no less dramatic circumstances, and it was their forays into the European Cup in 1978/79 and 1979/80 that acted as invaluable lessons into the finer arts of European competition.

In the 1978/79 season, Porto travelled to Greece to take on AEK Athens, in the first round, where they succumbed to a hostile environment and capitulated to a 6-1 defeat. All of AEK's goals came in the first hour of the game. A spirited 4-1 win in the return leg wasn't enough to dig Porto out of the hole they had fallen into in Athens. Channelling the pain and storing a lesson learnt, they then undertook a covert campaign in 1979/80 that was short but vital to their development on the European stage.

Only going as far as the second round, Porto defeated the mighty AC Milan at the San Siro, after a goalless draw in the first leg at the Estádio das Antas. This was a significant result and they were beginning to grow up in European terms. In the second round, Porto beat the equally mighty Real Madrid 2-1, before heading to the Bernabéu for the second leg. Narrowly defeated 1-0, Porto went out on the away-goals rule.

Over the course of the following seasons, further salutary European lessons were taken from Grasshoppers, Standard Liège and once again from Anderlecht. By 1983/84, Porto had assessed all the positives and negatives they had encountered during their European studies and applied them to a first serious tilt at continental silverware.

In the tournament due to being beaten finalists in the 1983 Taça de Portugal Final, against a double-winning Benfica, who were led by Sven-Göran Eriksson, Porto's run to the 1984 Cup Winners' Cup Final very nearly floundered at the first hurdle. After they departed Yugoslavia with a precious away goal as part of a 2-1 defeat to Dinamo

Zagreb, Porto were made to sweat in the second leg, until Fernando Gomes made the belated breakthrough with only five minutes remaining.

The scoreline of 2-2, on aggregate, was repeated in the second round, against Rangers, when Porto once again were defeated away from home in the first leg 2-1, only to edge through with a 1-0 victory at home. It was with a sense of recent history repeating itself that Gomes scored the clinching goal at the Estádio das Antas.

A prolific striker, Gomes was in his second spell with Porto, having spent two seasons in the employment of Sporting Gijón. He would travel to both the 1984 European Championship and the 1986 World Cup with Portugal. He would score the goals to take Porto to the 1987 European Cup Final, only to heartbreakingly miss the biggest occasion of his club career, when sustaining a broken leg just days before the final against Bayern Munich.

Had it not been for the contributions of Gomes, they would have crashed out of the 1983/84 Cup Winners' Cup in the early exchanges of the tournament. Yet, the drama was far from over for Porto. Their coach, José Maria Pedroto – in his third spell in charge of the club – had to relinquish the role due to ill health, with his assistant António Morais assuming command.

Against Shakhtar Donetsk in the quarter-finals, Porto slumped to a 2-0 deficit in the first leg, at home, before a spirited fightback took the game 3-2. This still left them with the unenviable task of travelling to the industrial Soviet city of Donetsk for the return game. Trailing 1-0 and seemingly heading out on the away-goals rule, the rule that they had prospered through during the first two rounds,

Porto were saved by a goal from a former BBC Goal of the Season winner.

Mickey Walsh had won his Goal of the Season award in a Blackpool shirt in 1975, with a wondrous strike against Sunderland in a Second Division match. But by 1980 he was a Porto player, via a short stay at Everton and an injury-blighted spell with Queens Park Rangers. He would spend six years in the blue and white stripes of Porto, going on to extend his time in Portugal by playing for Salgueiros and Espinho.

Midway through the second half and just four minutes beyond conceding the opening goal of the game, Walsh climbed from the Porto bench to replace Rodolfo Reis. Within five minutes the Chorley-born Ireland international had had the desired effect. Reacting first to a rebound off the crossbar, Walsh headed home the goal which deflated Shakhtar and put Porto into their very first major European semi-final, forever earning himself hero status in the city of Oporto.

Riding the finest of lines to get this far, Porto were drawn to face the holders, Aberdeen, in the last four. With Porto still flying in under the radar to a degree, Aberdeen were seen by many as the favourites to go through, at a time when British teams were the benchmark of European competency across the entire continent.

When the two teams walked out to face one another in the first leg, at the Estádio das Antas, Aberdeen were part of a wave of British teams involved in the semi-finals of the various major European competitions. In fact, in 1983/84 there wasn't a major European semi-final taking place without the presence of a British team. With Manchester

United in action in the opposite Cup Winners' Cup semi-final, it made for the intriguing possibility of Alex Ferguson taking on Ron Atkinson's side, his future employers, in the final.

Gomes was the hero again for Porto, scorer of the only goal on an evening when their efforts deserved greater reward; it left all to play for in the second leg.

Repelling an incessant Aberdeen offensive which gave Ferguson's side most of the ball, yet few chances of substance, Porto expertly drew the sting of their opponents and sprang on the counter-attack whenever possible. It was a masterclass of a performance, topped with a goal of beauty. Within the circulating fog at Pittodrie, Vermelhinho, a left-winger by trade, skipped down the right wing, evading Aberdeen advances and leaving Alex McLeish for dust, before sending an arcing lob floating over the head of a bemused Jim Leighton and into his goal. Left with less than 15 minutes in which to concede three goals, Porto cruised into their first major European final.

Benefitting from the groundwork of Pedroto, while the 1984 Cup Winners' Cup Final was a bridge too far – beaten in Basel by a star-studded Juventus side, led by Michel Platini on the pitch and Giovanni Trapattoni on the touchline – it was a road which eventually took them to their European Cup glory of 1987.

Sadly, Pedroto wouldn't live to see that success. A hard-working but hard-living individual, he died in the early hours of 7 January 1985, at the age of 56, spending his final days smoking and imbibing the occasional spoonful of whiskey.

Portugal's part in the Cup Winners' Cup might not have been an all-encompassing one, but it was an eventful cameo that added some wonderful layers of drama and contributed massively to the tournament's overt quirkiness.

Back across the border in Spain, one of the great Cup Winners' Cup oddities was Real Madrid's failure to win the tournament. So dominant in the European Cup and their mid-1980s revival, instigated by back-to-back UEFA Cup successes, it remains an anomaly that can never be altered, that the Cup Winners' Cup proved to be elusive for *Los Blancos*.

Propelled into the tournament on only four occasions, Real made the final twice, in 1971 and 1983, where they lost to British opponents: firstly to Chelsea and then to Aberdeen.

In 1970/71 Real were four years beyond their sixth European Cup win, when they embarked upon their first ever Cup Winners' Cup campaign. Beaten at home by Wacker Innsbruck, and a loss away to Cardiff City, didn't cover the original kings of Europe in glory as they made their way to the semi-finals.

In the last four, Real came face-to-face with PSV Eindhoven, who were enjoying their first serious European run in the same 1970/71 season that Ajax won Europe's premier tournament for the first time, in succession to Feyenoord, who had been crowned as the Netherlands' first ever winners of the European Cup a year earlier.

Three years away from the Totaalvoetbal that Rinus Michels and Johan Cruyff peddled at the 1974 World Cup, PSV were a very genuine, emerging and yet still unwitting threat to Real's hopes. PSV came to within eight minutes of reaching the 1971 Cup Winners' Cup Final. A goalless draw at the Philips Stadion set up an uncomfortable evening of football for Real, in the second leg at the Bernabéu.

Taking their foot off the accelerator after Zoco opened the scoring ten minutes before half-time, it came as a shock to Real when Wim van den Dungen equalised for PSV just short of the hour mark. In possession of the away-goal advantage, it wasn't until Pirri struck in the 82nd minute that Real regained the destiny of the tie. Made to sweat over the course of the last few minutes, Real hung on to their place in the Athens final by the skin of their teeth.

As a testament to how Real were beginning to regress as a force in European competition – at least from the insanely high and impeccable standards set over the course of the first decade of pan-European tournament football – and as a considered nod towards the continued blossoming of PSV as a third megalith of football in the Netherlands, when the two sides were again drawn together the following season, PSV prevailed. The Dutch side's stirring second-half fightback meant success on away goals in the second round of the newly launched UEFA Cup. Having been fitful and inconsistent on the road to the final, Real were largely the better team against Chelsea, yet it took an injury-time goal from Zoco to send the game into extra time and, ultimately, Real on to the very last Cup Winners' Cup Final replay. The legendary Paco Gento, at the age of 39, had still been crucial to Miguel Muñoz's side.

Slow out of the blocks two days later, Real fell to a well-organised tactical game plan, plotted for them by Chelsea's Dave Sexton. Despite a strong last half hour, in which they brought the game to within one goal of levelling proceedings and forced Peter Bonetti into the sort of late heroics that had been beyond him for England in the previous year's World Cup quarter-final in León against West Germany, over the course of the 210 minutes played in the 1971 final, Real had perhaps contrived to lose rather than be a well-beaten team.

Defeated in the 1974/75 quarter-finals by Red Star Belgrade, on penalties, Real didn't appear in the Cup Winners' Cup again until the 1982/83 season. Unlike their run to the final in 1970/71, this time around there were no inconsistencies to be found. Real rolled through to the final in commanding form, only truly tested in the quarter-finals when they found themselves in one of those rare Cup Winners' Cup occasions when two of the unquestioned monarchs of European club football collided.

Drawn to face Inter Milan, the two games were played out in front of a combined attendance of over 170,000 spectators. Real rode their luck at the San Siro in the first leg when, on an electric evening, two giants of the game had to settle upon a 1-1 draw. Conceding first, Real did well to recover from a gifted opener. Gabriele Oriali sent a free kick through the Real wall and past a surprised Agustín. When Inter were denied a second goal, from Alessandro Altobelli, adjudged to have been in an offside position, it was an invitation back into the game that Alfredo Di Stéfano's team gladly accepted. To add insult to Inter's injury, Ricardo Gallego's equaliser midway through the second half was via an entirely stoppable shot that Ivano Bordon allowed to escape from his grasp to bounce agonisingly over his goal line.

Despite Inter's perceived injustices from footballing karma, they started the second leg well at the Bernabéu.

It was with a very typical Altobelli finish that *I Nerazzurri* took the lead. Elegant, yet gangling, he sidestepped his way into the Real penalty area and blasted the ball past Agustín. With four of the Inter line-up having had an on-pitch role in the World Cup Final, in the very same stadium, not much more than eight months earlier, Real could have been forgiven had they allowed the game to drift away from them, beaten by the vagaries of the mind. However, fortune continued to smile on the home side and it was with another free kick, which was directed straight through a defensive wall, that Real levelled the aggregate score at 2-2. This time, it was José Salguero who was the beneficiary of poor defensive organisation.

Inter must have felt that the game had gone full circle, in the most negative of manners. It is certainly hard to imagine that the form of Real's equaliser wasn't resting heavily on Inter minds five minutes later when the winning goal was procured by the predatory Santillana. At the back post he got on the end of a well-worked corner, with both Bordon and Fulvio Collovati being guilty of a lack of awareness and attention.

In the semi-finals, Real made heavier weather than necessary of getting past Austria Vienna, the 5-3 aggregate scoreline not doing enough justice to how hard Di Stéfano's team were made to work for their place in the final.

Yet, in the final was where it went wrong again for Real. Amidst the torrential rain of Gothenburg, where their supporters were outnumbered 10-to-1 by the travelling Aberdeen fans, they were always second best. Perhaps they were humbled by a combination of the weather, the away-game feel to the occasion, the belligerent demands of Alex Ferguson upon his Aberdeen players and even the weight of their own history, given 17 years had now passed since their last piece of European silverware. Whatever the reasons, in a defined game of men against boys, it was the boys who won it.

This was a Real side packed with world-class talent, many of whom had emerged from the 1981 European Cup Final with a runner-up medal, many of whom had taken part in the 1982 World Cup on home soil, and three of whom would play against France, in the 1984 European Championship Final at the Parc des Princes.

In comparison, in 1981, some of the Aberdeen line-up had only just left school and the concept of a first-team debut, let alone playing in a major European final, was something of a daydream.

For Real, it was a huge blow – one of four cup finals they lost in 1982/83 – to go alongside a third-place finish in La Liga. In a span of time when their domestic title would elude them between the successes of 1979/80 and 1985/86, they were often a hair's breadth from glory, only to be denied. An array of titles and cup finals, both at home and abroad, were agonisingly missed out on, until the Emilio Butragueño-inspired vintage dominated, at least domestically, from 1985 to 1990.

Real would compete in the Cup Winners' Cup on only one more occasion, again exiting at the quarter-finals, in 1993/94, this time to Paris Saint-Germain.

As for Di Stéfano, it was all a far cry from his Cup Winners' Cup experiences of three years earlier, when he led Valencia to success, blessed by the presence in his team of both Mario Kempes and Rainer Bonhof.

It could be suggested that Di Stéfano had fallen into the job at just the right time, when he returned to the Mestalla in the summer of 1979. Fresh from defeating Real Madrid in the final of the Copa del Rey, having earlier pulled off an incredible second-leg comeback in the last 16 against Barcelona, the foundations of their 1980 Cup Winners' Cup glory had arguably been laid by others.

This isn't to say Di Stéfano was a passenger in Valencia's victory; far from it. He had coached the club before, between 1970 and 1974, winning the La Liga title in 1970/71. The domestic double was narrowly missed out on when they were beaten in the final of the Copa Generalísimo by Vic Buckingham's Barcelona, in a spectacular 4-3 defeat.

The second of three separate spells as coach – Di Stéfano would later return to lead Valencia out of the Segunda División, after their stunning relegation of 1985/86 – in 1979, he had walked back into a club that had found away wins almost impossible to obtain the previous season.

Only marginally improving that problem, domestically Valencia struggled as the new season got underway. By the time they picked up their first league win of the campaign, at the sixth time of asking, they had already navigated a path into the second round of the Cup Winners' Cup.

Boldklubben 1903, of Denmark, had proved irritatingly stubborn opponents during a first leg that ended 2-2, in a game which was switched to the Idrætspark due to the star billing of the visitors and the legendary status of the man picking the Valencia line-up.

No mistakes were made in the return game a fortnight later; a 4-0 victory, inclusive of a brace from Kempes, eased Valencia into a second-round tie against Rangers, winners of the tournament in 1972 and beaten finalists on two other occasions.

Fumbling their way to a 1-1 draw at the Mestalla in the first leg, despite an almost vicious strike by Kempes from a free kick to open the scoring, it appeared that the advantage had been handed to Rangers and that a place in the quarter-finals was theirs to lose. Lose it Rangers did, however, as Valencia completely outclassed their Scottish opponents at Ibrox Park, Kempes chipping in with two more expertly taken goals. It was a win that set them up with an all-Spanish quarter-final against Barcelona, the holders.

Between the second leg of the Rangers game in early November and their trip to the Camp Nou for the first leg of the quarter-final, Valencia lost just twice during a 15-game run of La Liga fixtures. Finding consistency and climbing the table, those defeats were inflicted away at Athletic Bilbao and Barcelona.

While too much early ground had been lost to have any realistic hopes of working their way into the race for the title, their improved week-to-week performances had played them into the perfect form to be facing Barcelona in the Cup Winners' Cup in one of the rare occasions when two teams from the same nation faced one another in the tournament.

Just over nine weeks after losing narrowly at the Camp Nou in the league – Valencia's last defeat of any description – the two teams walked out to face each other once again, at the cathedral of Catalonian football. Just as in the league encounter between the two at the end of December, one goal settled the game, except this time the goal belonged to the visitors.

It was a stunning victory for Valencia and Di Stéfano, setting up an incredible night back at the Mestalla for the second leg, which at one point looked to be going Barcelona's way. However, the home side took control in the second half, eventually running out 4-3 winners on the night in a wonderfully open game.

Having excelled domestically in his first spell in charge of Valencia without making a serious impact upon Europe, it was maybe an aura of unfinished business which led to Di Stéfano finally adding a European title to his list of coaching honours, to sit alongside his litany of European achievements as a player.

In the semi-final, it was Nantes who stood between Valencia and the 1980 Cup Winners' Cup Final – the hypnotic skill and movement of the French side, up against the unstoppable determination of Kempes, at the Stade Marcel Saupin.

Largely the better team in the first game, Nantes took the lead in controversial circumstances. Denied when making enthusiastic claims for a penalty, they simply dusted themselves down and scored from the begrudgingly accepted free kick when the ball flicked off the head of the future French national manager, Henri Michel. Up against wave after wave of Nantes attacks, it took a certain belligerence to keep Valencia in the game. Kempes was just the man for the occasion, charging through on goal ten minutes into the second half and prodding the ball home in a manner that made it seem like it almost passed through the body of the Nantes goalkeeper, Jean-Paul Bertrand-Demanes, a goalkeeper so good he needed two hyphens in his name.

Ten minutes from time, however, Nantes got the winning goal that their performance deserved. Bruno Baronchelli brilliantly converted a reverse header after some bewitching play in the build-up.

Losing domestic momentum between the two games, it was a less sure-footed Valencia who welcomed Nantes to the Mestalla for the second leg. Initially thrown on to the back foot by their visitors, when Bonhof opened the scoring, it was a goal which came at the end of a swiftly executed and well-crafted move, tinged with some good fortune and against the run of play.

Despite the setback, Nantes continued to dictate the pace of the game. Unfortunate to have a goal disallowed, this was compounded when Valencia's second goal was massively deflected on its way into the net, via a hopeful shot, rather than one struck with unbridled conviction, from Javier Subirats. Still only one goal from completely levelling the tie when the second half began, the killer blow came courtesy of an outrageous volleyed lob by Kempes, just short of the hour mark. The man whose goals had won Argentina the 1978 World Cup added a fourth goal from the penalty spot. As one last slap to the face for Nantes, the foul that gifted Valencia their penalty was on the edge of the penalty area, rather than inside it.

The part Nantes played in this semi-final was worth more than a 5-2 aggregate defeat, and it was an unnecessarily wide margin of victory for Valencia when compared to how fine the lines had been between the two teams until the last half hour of the 180 minutes played. The Heysel Stadium and the Liam Brady-inspired Arsenal awaited Valencia in the final.

Embracing a season of attrition, for Arsenal the 1980 Cup Winners' Cup Final was their 68th game of a season that would stretch to 70 outings, inclusive of the 'traditional curtain raiser' to the English football season, the Charity Shield.

Promising so much but ultimately emerging from the campaign empty-handed, when Arsenal departed Brussels with shoulders slumped, it was just four days after they had lost the FA Cup Final to Second Division West Ham United. Over the course of their last two fatigue-laden league games they would fumble a UEFA Cup spot for the following season too, with a final-evening capitulation at Middlesbrough.

As far as 'after the Lord Mayor's Show' concepts go in football, the Arsenal vintage of 1979/80 possibly had no superiors. A fourth-place finish was usually more than adequate to clinch a place in Europe, but with West Ham swiping the FA Cup from under their noses, and the League Cup being picked up by sixth-placed Wolverhampton Wanderers, Arsenal were deprived of even the most minimal of end-of-season rewards.

The Gunners were in a great position to claim a cup double. They had defeated Liverpool in a four-game FA Cup semi-final marathon and claimed a 1-0 victory in Turin against Juventus in the semi of the Cup Winners' Cup. Young striker Paul Vaessen was the unlikely hero after the Italians had drawn 1-1 at Highbury in the first leg. Instead, during a ten-day span they lost at Wembley to West Ham, were beaten on penalties by Valencia in Brussels and then thrashed 5-0 on Teesside by Middlesbrough.

To add insult to injury, Juventus were so impressed by the skill of Brady in those Cup Winners' Cup semi-finals that they swooped for his signature that very summer. Within a year, Arsenal had also lost their other skilful Irishman, Frank Stapleton, when Manchester United took him off their hands.

At the Heysel Stadium most of the pre-match questions had been asked about Arsenal's strength of stamina, rather than their mental capacity to recover from their FA Cup Final defeat. A fitness test for David O'Leary had been passed on the morning of the game and the Arsenal manager, Terry Neill, sent out an ambitious line-up, with the more attack-minded Sammy Nelson returning at left-back in place of the more cautious John Devine, who had started against West Ham at Wembley.

Defying the effects of physical demands, Arsenal having played an astonishing 25 games more than Valencia during the 1979/80 season to this point, to the naked eye the 1980 Cup Winners' Cup Final was played out by two teams of equal fitness.

Starting brightly and fighting against their natural propensity to sit deep, Arsenal set out with a game plan to take the game to what they felt was a weak Valencia defence. This approach also had the secondary hope that by starving Kempes of the ball, the Spanish side might become frustrated. Despite Arsenal applying the early pressure, it was indeed Kempes who had the first decent chance of the game, powering forward in typical fashion when allowed too much space and forcing a fine save from Pat Jennings. A scare that provoked an outbreak of caution, after a sigh of relief Arsenal eventually ventured forward once more and it almost paid dividends. José Carrete was forced into a headed clearance off the Valencia goal line, just under the crossbar, after Stapleton directed a powerful header from an O'Leary cross which had Carlos Pereira, the Valencia goalkeeper, well beaten.

While some goalless major European finals have been desperately dull affairs, the 1980 Cup Winners' Cup Final didn't really fall into that category. Yes, tiredness crept in for both teams and the game slowed down in that wonderful way they used to before players were honed into human versions of Formula 1 cars. However, this was still the era when games drifting into extra time would descend to a near jogging pace, with socks being rolled down around the ankles and shirts untucked. Games that were ripe for the emergence of a dishevelled hero.

In the second half, the chances kept coming. Jennings made a vital, if somewhat fortuitous, stop from the advancing Bonhof, while for Valencia, Pereira threw out reaction saves to efforts from Brady and Alan Sunderland.

During the added 30 minutes, Sunderland had the ball in the Valencia net, only for it to be ruled offside. In circumstances that would not have been blinked at in the contemporary game, it wasn't Sunderland who was adjudged to have been in an offside position, but one of his team-mates instead.

Much of Arsenal's game plan worked to perfection. They continued to try to force Valencia backwards; they continued to carve out opportunities; and while Valencia still pushed forward, the dangers of Kempes were kept to a minimum. The free-scoring Argentinian scored nine goals on the way to Brussels but was largely kept quiet by Arsenal.

It was an open and expansive final, but it was one which defiantly belonged to the goalkeepers. Both Pereira and

Jennings were in a stubborn frame of mind and a penalty shoot-out became inevitable.

Never before had a European club final been decided by a penalty shoot-out. It delivered a dramatic finale that was frowned upon by many traditionalists, who yearned for the simpler days of replays and the noble tossing of coins to decide the winners of deadlocked football matches.

Kempes and Brady, arguably the two most talented players on the pitch – although Bonhof might well be happy to argue that point – were loaded up front by Valencia and Arsenal respectively. They were sent to lead by skilled example, to set the tone for those who would follow them. Of course, Kempes and Brady both missed, Jennings and Pereira continuing to stamp their authority on proceedings.

What followed was a masterclass of eight penalties. Some went for power, some went for placement, some went for power and placement. Only Ángel Castellanos came anywhere close to missing when his penalty, Valencia's fourth penalty, went in off the underside of Jennings's crossbar.

Through it all, the two goalkeepers dived correctly more often than not, while on several occasions they weren't far from getting a hand to what were very well-taken penalties. In the commentary box for the BBC, however, John Motson voiced his dismay that Pereira was regularly moving from his line before the kicks were taken.

At 4-4, and with five penalties taken by each team, the shoot-out rolled on to sudden death. Valencia handed the dreaded vote of confidence to Ricardo Arias; Arsenal presented the poisoned chalice to Graham Rix.

Arias's penalty was struck with enough weight, but there was dubiousness in the direction. Aimed too centrally for Valencian comfort, the ball skimmed beneath the diving Jennings who, had he dropped just a fraction of a second quicker, would have surely smothered it.

To Rix the ball went. On his walk up to the penalty spot he unsuccessfully tried to make eye contact with the retreating Jennings. Strolling onward, he dipped his shoulder and stuck out a left foot, side-footing an effort at an imaginary ball, as the match ball sat a yard or so ahead. It is hard to judge the confidence of Rix within this moment. Rix placed the ball on the spot, took a short run up and placed it better than Arias did with his penalty, but saw it pushed away by Pereira.

The overriding story of the 1980 final is the escalating torment of Arsenal, rather than Valencia's glory. There is a certain car-crash element about Arsenal 1979/80 that is simply hypnotic and impossible to draw the eye away from when it comes to the 1980 Cup Winners' Cup Final. Arsenal became the only team to complete a Cup Winners' Cup campaign unbeaten during all regulation play, yet not claim the trophy.

The trophy went to Valencia and Di Stéfano. Almost a 'pop-up' team in the Cup Winners' Cup, this was their second and penultimate season in the tournament. Returning as holders in 1980/81, where they fell in the second round to Carl Zeiss Jena, their only other sojourn had been a run to the quarter-finals in 1967/68.

Valencia's glory was hard earned and well deserved, yet they are classically symptomatic of the random nature of the Cup Winners' Cup. They won it 33.33 per cent of the times they took part yet, after their victory in 1980, they were only ever seen in the tournament one more time and not at all during the last 18 years of its existence. Valencia somehow creep under the radar of their own Cup Winners' Cup success; for them overcoming Barcelona almost feels more like the final.

In contrast, Barcelona were a near regular in the Cup Winners' Cup with their 13 appearances. Winners on four occasions, they were the tournament's most successful team and won it twice as many times as anyone else.

Reaching the final six times, Barcelona became synonymous with the Cup Winners' Cup, although it took them until 1992 to claim the European Cup. The UEFA Cup also eluded the *Blaugrana*, although they did win the Inter-Cities Fairs Cup three times, long before claiming their first Cup Winners' Cup.

So often, Barcelona slipped up at the business end of European competitions. In 1961, when they faced Benfica in the European Cup Final, Barcelona had been the favourites to win. Given their more recent achievements in the Champions League, it is strange now to consider that Europe's premier glory would not be theirs for a further 31 years. That curse was very real, however, and it seemed to roll on endlessly, as they either contrived not to win the La Liga title, or were forever denied it by those in the thrall of General Francisco Franco.

After winning the La Liga title in 1959/60, they won it only twice more before the construction of Johan Cruyff's 'Dream Team' after his return to the Camp Nou as coach, in 1988. In the era of only the reigning domestic champions and the holders taking part in the European Cup, Barcelona's opportunities to win it were scarce.

In 1975 Barcelona were beaten in the European Cup semi-finals by Leeds United, denied a place in a final that would have once again pitted Cruyff against Franz Beckenbauer, just a year on from them facing one another in the World Cup Final.

In 1986 against Steaua Bucharest, it was Terry Venables who led Barcelona to within a penalty shoot-out of winning the biggest prize of all, only to fail, the players freezing from 12 yards in one of the most wretched major European finals ever.

Through it all, and regardless of whether Barcelona being restricted to one La Liga title per decade throughout the 1960s, 70s and 80s was by conspiratorial design, or simply not being consistent enough, there was always the Cup Winners' Cup to take solace from: a warm embrace to be found.

After an early exit at the hands of Hamburger SV, in 1963/64, it was in 1968/69 that Barcelona were properly introduced to the tournament. Reaching the first of their six finals, at the St Jakob Stadium in Basel, they fell to a shock defeat to Slovan Bratislava.

It was a loss that added more questions regarding the temperament and the will of Barcelona to grasp their chances of European glory. To Benfica 1961, Leeds 1975 and Steaua Bucharest 1986, you can add Slovan Bratislava 1969.

With a bye obtained in the second round, Barcelona's route to the final was a predominantly sedate one. Lugano and FC Cologne brushed aside with ease, in the first round and semi-final respectively, it was the quarter-final that proved to be their most difficult assignment.

Taking on Lyn, of Norway, with both games peculiarly taking place at the Camp Nou, Barcelona won the first leg 3-2 in a game where caution was thrown entirely to the wind. Feeling the tie was over already, it came as a shock to the Catalan giants when Lyn shot into a 2-0 lead during the second leg. On the brink of an embarrassing elimination, it took two goals in the last 15 minutes from Gallego to save Barcelona's blushes.

Roundly expected to take the trophy, Barcelona surprisingly fell to a fearless Slovan Bratislava in the final. Uncomfortable with being the favourites perhaps, after building up an inferiority complex or a siege mentality in the face of Real Madrid's mooted position of domestic favourites, the boot suddenly being on the other foot can't have sat easily with them.

Away from their loss to Slovan, the striking thing about Barcelona's 1969 Cup Winners' Cup Final line-up was that one of them, Carles Rexach, went on to play in the 1979 final, at the same venue, the St Jakob Stadium in Basel, while another of them, Joaquim Rifé, would also be there a decade later, except as Barcelona's head coach.

In between those two finals was an early exit in the 1971/72 playing of the tournament. Intriguingly, this was a defeat under the leadership of their new coach, the legendary Rinus Michels. His new team went out to the team which until the previous summer had been led by his Ajax successor, Stefan Kovács.

Michels later laid the groundwork, with Johan Cruyff, for Barcelona to win the first of their four Cup Winners'

Cups. Although both had left the club before the 1979 win, they were the inspiration for the 1978 Copa del Rey Final victory over Miguel Muñoz's Las Palmas. A final where all four goals were scored in the first 27 minutes of the game, a game played at the Santiago Bernabéu, the venue that Muñoz had enjoyed so much success at, both as a player and a coach. Rexach scored two of Barcelona's goals in their 3-1 win.

The 1978/79 Cup Winners' Cup campaign was a thing of immense beauty. Taken for granted in many respects, because of the eventual winners perhaps, it offered up some outstanding football, threw out some wonderful games, gifted generous helpings of drama and conjured up moments of breathtakingly audacious skill.

Had the 1978/79 Cup Winners' Cup ended up with a suitably mysterious eastern European winner, then it would be held up in this book as the undisputed barometer of everything that was outlandishly nourishing about the tournament, rather than the 1980/81 version of the event.

In fact, that would probably also be the case had the final gone the way of Fortuna Düsseldorf, instead of Barcelona. An admirably 'eye of the storm' football club, Fortuna's fortunes have swung from one extreme to the other during the 40 years that have passed since they came so close to Cup Winners' Cup glory.

Conversely, there should be no ill will towards Barcelona for prevailing in the 1979 final. A hard-working and stylistically pleasing team, this wasn't the cartoon character that Barcelona could be accused of being today. This was a Barcelona that was less than four years beyond the death of General Francisco Franco; this was a Barcelona that still stood as a bastion of defiance against a regime that at best disliked it, and at worst actively supressed it.

All of that said, this was a Barcelona that excelled in style and flunked in substance. Without a strong enough constitution to stomach the long haul of winning La Liga titles, they were a daydreaming cup team. They still had that familiar sense of entitlement you would recognise today, but they lacked the stubbornness a team requires to insist upon winning league titles. For an English comparison at that time, they were mirrored by Manchester United.

Barcelona's run to the 1979 Cup Winners' Cup Final was one of extremes. While the first round and the semi-final were relatively formulaic, encompassing a comfortable victory over Shakhtar Donetsk and a routine progression past an overstretched Beveren, these sedate missions bookended second-round and quarter-final ties that were akin to wars of attrition.

In the second round, Barcelona had the unenviable task of facing Anderlecht. Finalists for the last three years, winning twice, in 1978/79 Anderlecht were the Cup Winners' Cup holders. The tournament had become their own personal fiefdom and Rob Rensenbrink was the king of all he surveyed.

During the first leg in Brussels, Barcelona were torn apart by a rampant Anderlecht. While the visitors were busy trying to keep an eye on Rensenbrink, François van der Elst did the damage. Anderlecht cut through Barcelona like a scalpel for their opening goal. It was a goal of élan and simplicity. It was a goal that Cruyff would have been proud of. In comparison, Anderlecht's second goal offered a different kind of allure. Ludo Coeck hit a vicious 30-yard screamer that the Barcelona goalkeeper, Pedro Artola, had little hope of stopping. As the cherry on the cake for the holders, Van der Elst guided in a third goal to complete a comprehensive 3-0 victory which left Barcelona on the brink of elimination.

Barcelona did have cause for complaint and frustration, however. They claimed desperately that Anderlecht's third goal should have been adjudged offside. Added to this, with the score at 2-0, they missed a golden opportunity to make it 2-1 when a flicked header struck the crossbar, only for the goal-bound rebound to strike almost the exact same spot.

They might no longer have had the genius of Cruyff to call upon, but Barcelona had shopped well for his successor. On the back of a string of outstanding displays at the 1978 World Cup finals, the Austrian international, Hans Krankl, had arrived at the Camp Nou, to be bestowed with the number 10 shirt.

With the continued presence of Johan Neeskens, Barcelona were not without inspiration of their own, willing and more than able to offer a riposte to the first-leg mauling that Rensenbrink and Van der Elst had administered for Anderlecht.

Krankl opened the scoring in the seventh minute, slamming home a venomous shot from an acute angle. The Camp Nou roared its approval and the game was now very much alive. Then seconds before half-time, Juan Carlos Heredia curled in a teasingly low effort between the left hand of the Anderlecht goalkeeper, Nico de Bree, and the inside of the far post.

Continuing their forward momentum in the second half, Barcelona looked like they were going to be repelled by Anderlecht's desperate defensive blanket until, with only four minutes left to play, Van der Elst was caught in possession by the Barcelona right-back, Rafael Zuvíria, who promptly weaved his way through the thick white line of banked Anderlecht players, to fashion himself a clear run on goal. Keeping his cool, Zuvíria slotted the equaliser in with the calm authority of a 30-goal-a-season marksman.

As unlikely a hero as the Barcelona right-back might seem at face value, when Zuvíria arrived at the Camp Nou, in the summer of 1977, he did so as a striker, from Racing Santander. He was actually well qualified for the situation he found himself in.

After the goalless stalemate of extra time, the game drifted to a penalty shoot-out. Under the sheer weight of pressure, amidst a cacophony of sound and a blur of colour, Anderlecht froze in front of the goal. There was only ever going to be one winner at the Camp Nou once Zuvíria had levelled the tie. Barcelona celebrated with a lap of honour, almost as if they had won the tournament there and then.

Ending the metronomic run that Anderlecht had enjoyed in the Cup Winners' Cup was a massive achievement, but to do it from a 3-0 deficit was hypnotic. Over the course of the two games, it was one of the greatest meetings of collective footballing minds that the tournament was ever blessed with.

A chasm of five months sat between Barcelona overcoming Anderlecht and them facing their quarter-final opponents. They played 14 La Liga fixtures during that span of time and to impress how unpredictable a side they were, while Barcelona could boast a 9-0 demolition of Rayo

Vallecano, a 6-0 drubbing of Celta Vigo, an away win in the Catalan derby against Español and victory in the El Clásico against Real Madrid, they also limped to defeats against the likes of Sporting Gijón, Racing Santander and Salamanca.

At this stage, Rifé wasn't even at the helm of the club. Barcelona were being led by Michels's immediate successor, Lucien Muller-Schmidt, a former Barcelona and Real Madrid player and French international, who had been brought in from Burgos.

In the quarter-finals, Barcelona were drawn to play Ipswich Town, as managed by the man who would lead the *Blaugrana* to their fourth and final Cup Winners' Cup success in 1997, Bobby Robson. The two teams had faced one another in the UEFA Cup third round the previous season when, with echoes of the comeback Barcelona would perform against Anderlecht, they had to overturn a 3-0, first-leg defeat, to eventually prevail on penalties at the Camp Nou.

It was with a sense of unfinished business and déjà vu that they went head-to-head again in the Cup Winners' Cup quarter-finals. In the first leg, which once again took place at Portman Road, David Geddis opened the scoring with a very English type of goal, involving a classic up-and-under of a cross and a challenge on the Barcelona goalkeeper that would have been laughed out of a Spanish stadium, before Esteban swiftly equalised, converting a ruthless counter-attacking move. Geddis then scored again for a 2-1 win, with all the goals coming within a 12-minute span, early in the second half.

Growing in confidence and stature, just two years away from lifting the UEFA Cup, Ipswich were a wiser team when they visited the Camp Nou for the second time. It still didn't stop Barcelona edging into the semi-final with a 1-0 victory, a scoreline that was enough to see them through on the away-goals rule.

While the semi-final, against Beveren, came to an eventual sedate conclusion, a 2-0 aggregate victory confirmed only by an 89th-minute goal from Krankl in the second leg, it was a tie filled with internal rancour. In the period between the first and second legs of the game being played, Muller-Schmidt was replaced by Rifé, as coach.

A 1-0 win in the first game, at the Camp Nou, antagonised the Barcelona powers that be. Taking a narrow lead to Belgium was deemed careless. Yet when that game was followed by defeat at relegation-threatened Celta Vigo, it was the last straw. Muller-Schmidt would return to Burgos before long.

Seemingly a popular decision with the Barcelona players, they responded with a 6-0 victory against Sporting Gijón, followed by their nervy yet trouble-free trip to Beveren to clinch their place in the 1979 Cup Winners' Cup Final.

Unbeaten under Rifé in the lead up to the final, it was with a feel-good factor that they headed back to Basel, a decade on from their loss to Slovan Bratislava there.

In a wonderfully open game, the pace was relentless. Tente Sánchez opened the scoring for Barcelona with only five minutes on the clock, a goal that came one minute after Fortuna had been forced to make their first substitution, when Gerd Zimmermann had to depart the pitch, replaced by Flemming Lund.

Just three minutes later, Thomas Allofs was the first to the ball in a goalmouth scramble after it bounced back off Artola. The younger brother – and strike partner – of Klaus Allofs, he prodded the ball past the Barcelona goalkeeper, creating a satisfying plume of chalk dust, when skidding over the powdered six-yard line. Merely eight minutes had passed, and the score was already 1-1, with Fortuna having lost a player to injury. Yet despite the lack of discipline that both teams had started the final with, there was no sign of the game settling into any sort of rut any time soon.

Having already lost Zimmermann, one of their centre-backs, Fortuna's injury woes continued, as in the 24th minute they promptly lost their right-winger too, Dieter Brei being replaced by Josef Weikl. Even if the game was to be confined to just the 90 minutes, it was a turn of events that left Fortuna with very little room for manoeuvre, when it came to further injuries.

Still the entertainment flooded forth, when Barcelona were awarded a penalty for a majestically late tackle on the fantastically talented Francisco Carrasco. Rexach placed the ball on the heavily powdered penalty spot, took his run up and, despite directing it reasonably well, saw it saved comfortably by the Fortuna goalkeeper, Jörg Daniel. Compensated a short time later when Asensi toe-poked home to put Barcelona ahead again, a sustained period of dominance followed that almost made Fortuna buckle. So it was completely against the run of play when Wolfgang Seel took advantage of a slumbering Barcelona defence to level the game once again at 2-2. With a plentiful number of chances during the second half for both sides to win the game, it almost defied football gravity to see no further goals added, and for the final to drift into extra time.

Given the beautiful nature of Barcelona's attacking play throughout their 1978/79 Cup Winners' Cup run, it was almost with a sense of disappointment that they got their third goal via a deflection. When Krankl added a fourth goal in the second period of extra time, taking the glory after some outstanding build-up play from Carrasco, there seemed no way back for the spirited Fortuna. Six minutes from time, however, the determined Seel netted again to make the scoreline 4-3.

It was with an outburst of unbridled joy and unrestrained relief that Barcelona embraced the full-time whistle. Their first Cup Winners' Cup success obtained, the St Jakob Stadium was awash with the red and yellow of Catalonia.

Strikingly antiquated, the stadium had terracing on three sides, a train track that was raised above the stand opposite the seated main stand upon which locomotives would rumble past, and a quaint cottage situated to one corner.

On the back of the high supplied by both teams in the 1979 final, UEFA decreed that the 1981 final was to be held at Fortuna's Rheinstadion, while the Camp Nou would host the 1982 final. Whereas Fortuna fell at the quarter-finals in 1981, thus fumbling their opportunity to reach a Cup Winners' Cup Final on home soil, there was no way that the Barcelona hierarchy were going to take no for an answer on their team's projected participation in their own major European final.

Making their exit, as holders, to Valencia in 1980, it was 1981/82 when Barcelona returned to the Cup Winners' Cup once again. Being handed an extra incentive to reach the 1982 final, given it was to take place at the Camp

Nou, added a darker edge to Barcelona's approach to the tournament. The concept, it seemed, was to make the final by any means necessary.

It was with a very eastern European flavour that Barcelona made it to the semi-finals of the 1981/82 Cup Winners' Cup. Botev Plovdiv, Dukla Prague and Lokomotive Leipzig were all dispensed with, although not without their irritations. Comfortable aggregate scorelines were offset by losing one of the legs to all three opponents. It was as if each of them had accepted that Barcelona were going to go through, but not without being administered a bloody nose in the process. In the quarter-final, Lokomotive even won at the Camp Nou, having lost in Leipzig 3-0.

Presiding over Barcelona's bid for a second Cup Winners' Cup was the outrageously successful Udo Lattek. Lattek had straddled the great 1970s West German football rivalry between Bayern Munich and Borussia Mönchengladbach, winning half of the Bundesliga titles on offer throughout the decade, three for Bayern and two for Mönchengladbach. Added to this, he led Bayern to their first European Cup success in 1974, and Mönchengladbach to the UEFA Cup in 1979, as well as to the 1977 European Cup Final in Rome, where they lost to Liverpool.

Despite everything he had achieved for Bayern, an inconsistent start to the 1974/75 season had irrationally cost him his job at the Olympiastadion. Legend has it that when Lattek approached the Bayern president, Wilhelm Neudecker, to discuss some vital changes he felt should be made, Neudecker told Lattek that he fully agreed changes were required, and that as head coach he was being sacked.

Lattek promptly resurfaced at Mönchengladbach for the 1975/76 season, as the replacement for the Barcelona-bound Hennes Weisweiler. Fitting in a frustrating two years at Borussia Dortmund before being offered the Barcelona job, he later returned to Bayern for yet more trophy-laden seasons, despite the manner of, and ill-feeling over, his earlier departure from the club.

In Catalonia, Lattek had been brought in as a prospective footballing spirit guide, to nurse the best out of the volatile, yet supremely talented, Bernd Schuster. And also to work in tandem again with the wonderfully skilful Allan Simonsen, whom he had previously crossed paths with at Mönchengladbach, where in 1977 Simonsen was named as the European Footballer of the Year.

Armed with an array of talent, both of a domestic and foreign nature, Lattek's Barcelona didn't really need the strong-arm tactics they took into their semi-final games with Tottenham Hotspur. Perhaps it was fuelled by the loss to injury of Schuster, but Barcelona's approach to facing Keith Burkinshaw's side was to get their retaliation in first, against opponents that weren't exactly synonymous with the fighting side of the game. Barcelona and Tottenham should have been well matched. An attractive and open set of games should have prevailed, but maybe that was Lattek's fear?

Barça's opposition could boast the services of Ricardo Villa, Glenn Hoddle, Mickey Hazard and, for the second leg, Steve Archibald, freshly returned from suspension. Tottenham were, however, deprived of the services of Osvaldo Ardiles. The Argentinian had returned to his homeland in the wake of the escalation of the Falklands

Conflict, which had begun five days earlier. But Tottenham had enough talent to compete with Barcelona on a level footing.

Barcelona, having led the La Liga table almost exclusively since the beginning of December, had begun to wobble, however. Over the course of the previous fortnight or so, they had lost three successive league games, which condensed their once six-point lead down to just one.

With Barcelona suddenly uncertain of themselves, at White Hart Lane the first leg wasn't for the faint of heart. If a Tottenham player skipped past one challenge, they were usually upended by the very next tackle. A free kick swung into the back post and, met by Graham Roberts, rescued the home side a 1-1 draw, after Antonio Olmo scored the opener with that speculative effort which slipped through the usually reliable grasp of Ray Clemence. This was the goal I mentioned being watched in conjunction with a plate of cheese on toast at the beginning of this book.

Lattek's men were savage at times, brutal at others.

At the Camp Nou, Simonsen scored the only goal of the return game, in the 46th minute. Barcelona had their place in the Camp Nou final, yet they also had a UEFA fine of £6,500 handed down for their part in the on-pitch rancour on display at White Hart Lane, the fallout of which saw Tottenham harshly fined £2,500.

At the 1982 Cup Winners' Cup Final, Barcelona were up against Standard Liège. In the same circumstances, in a contemporary setting, the biggest question would perhaps be whether Barcelona would hit double figures or not.

Just prior to the 1982 World Cup, however, football was a far less tilted battleground and while, even by the terms and conditions of the game 37 years ago, you might have thought Barcelona would win this one handsomely, that would fail to take in to account just how good Standard, and Belgian football in general were at the time.

While the Belgian national team are now enjoying a renaissance, it is something that doesn't walk together with a resurgence in fortunes, on a pan-European scale, of the country's club teams. When Roberto Martinez named Belgium's squad for the 2018 World Cup, there were more players plying their club trade in China than there were in Belgium. In fact, there was only one Belgium-based player in the 23-man squad Martinez selected to travel to Russia.

Put into context, when Belgium reached the final of the 1980 European Championship, not one member of Guy Thys's squad played their football outside of their home nation. The Belgian First Division was one of the strongest in Europe and it acted as a magnet to players from other countries. For instance, when the Netherlands walked on to the pitch at the Estadio Monumental for the 1978 World Cup Final, two of their starting line-up were Anderlecht players, with only one from Ajax.

Standard were led by the polarising yet godlike genius of Raymond Goethals. His team contained the substantial goalkeeping talent of Michel Preud'homme, the wonderful Eric Gerets in defence and the attacking threat of Arie Haan, recruited from one of Goethals's former clubs, Anderlecht. In the early 1980s Standard had successfully emerged from the long shadow cast by the 1976 and 1978 winners of the Cup Winners' Cup, their great rivals Club Brugge.

Winners of the Belgian First Division in 1981/82, eventually discovered to be in questionable circumstances, Standard headed to the Camp Nou on a high. Their first league title in over a decade, accusations emerged in 1984 that Goethals – with a nod towards future events at Marseille – had approached their last-day opponents, Waterschei, with an offer of financial gain should they go easy in the game, thus lowering the risk of absorbing any unwanted injuries for the Cup Winners' Cup Final, in and against Barcelona.

In front of a capacity attendance at the Camp Nou, one which was heavily stacked in Barcelona's favour, the 1982 final wasn't the foregone conclusion you would believe it to be.

Guy Vandersmissen stunned the congregation, opening the scoring for Standard in the eighth minute. Showing no signs of stage fright whatsoever, they continued to press forward, and it was Barcelona who were in danger of freezing instead. All of the home team's efforts were confidently dealt with by Preud'homme.

Forever the master tactician, Goethals, who took Anderlecht to both the 1977 and 1978 Cup Winners' Cup finals, was locked in a fascinating duel for supremacy with Lattek. Containing Barcelona with a relative ease, it was almost a shock when Simonsen equalised, in first-half injury time.

A peculiar season for Barcelona, a nervousness had been creeping in. Having thrown the La Liga title away with a hypnotic end-of-season capitulation, now here they were, threatening to lose the Cup Winners' Cup Final in their own back yard.

Added to the eccentricity on display, the next time Simonsen would pull on a football shirt for a competitive game, it would be for the English Second Division outfit Charlton Athletic. The limited number of foreign players allowed in La Liga meant he had to give way to the incoming Diego Maradona.

With Barcelona's equaliser coming so late in the first half, there was an understandable second-half lull to Standard's performance after the restart. When Quini put the *Blaugrana* ahead in the 63rd minute, the manner of the goal should have drained the remaining spirit from Goethals's team. Stemming from a free kick, both convincing and debatable in its awarding, taken quickly by Josep Moratalla, Quini was swift to collect, turn and convert in the penalty area for 2-1. It was a movement which was so rapid, it beat not only Preud'homme and his defence, but also a bewildered-looking referee and the reactions of the cameraman. Hard done by to an extent, Standard could have been forgiven for expecting the free kick to be taken again, even by the footballing principles of 1982.

For Quini, his winning goal was payback from karma herself. Kidnapped the previous March after scoring twice in a 6-0 victory over Hércules, with Barcelona once again well positioned at the top of the table in another bid to strike for rare La Liga glory, he was kept in captivity for 25 days during which the wheels fell off Barcelona's challenge, with Real Sociedad instead claiming the prize for the first time in their history. Quini and his team-mates eventually limped home in fifth place.

If Barcelona had expected Standard to lay down their arms at conceding a second goal, then they were in for a shock. Pushing up in high numbers, Standard had two decent shouts for a penalty, and were only repelled by the desperate defending of Barcelona, who were forced to rely upon sporadic counter-attacks to ease the growing pressure in their own penalty area.

It was with a pronounced sigh of relief that they reached the full-time whistle and collected their second Cup Winners' Cup. The potential indignity and trauma of losing a major European final on their own pitch had been averted.

As holders, in 1982/83, Barcelona contrived to exit the tournament in the quarter-finals, on away goals, to Austria Vienna. The addition of Maradona had been a spectacular yet destabilising one and Lattek soon made way for the arrival of César Luis Menotti. The Austrian side went on to face Real Madrid in the semi-final and the spectre of an El Clásico Cup Winners' Cup semi-final was sadly lost for ever.

One year later Barcelona fell at the same stage, this time against Manchester United. Barça crashed out at Old Trafford 3-2 on aggregate, having squandered a 2-0 first-leg advantage. The result was celebrated not only by Manchester United supporters, but also by those still holding a grudge about the method with which Barcelona had dealt with Tottenham in April 1982.

Competing in the Cup Winners' Cup for a stunning six seasons out of a seven-season span between 1978/79 and 1984/85, in the last of those campaigns Barcelona suffered an uncharacteristic first-round exit at the hands of the French club Metz, yet in the most outlandish style imaginable.

Barcelona won the first leg 4-2 at the Stade Saint-Symphorien, via goals that included a stunningly assured and precisely placed own goal by Luc Sonor – a player who wound down his playing days at Ayr United – and an outrageous effort from Ramón Calderé, which hit a divot around the six-yard line to provoke an exaggerated bounce beyond the Metz goalkeeper, Michel Ettore. The second of the goals Metz scored was a very late penalty, which at the time seemed no more than a consolation.

It was with four away goals in hand that Barcelona maybe felt a little too relaxed going into the return game at a sparsely populated Camp Nou. This sense of security can only have been increased by the fact that the opening goal of the second leg didn't arrive until the 33rd minute, and that when it did, it was a goal that belonged to Carrasco and Barcelona.

Six minutes later, however, Metz were ahead on the night. Two goals over the course of a 60-second span, the second of which was yet another own goal for the tie, this time by José Sánchez when he almost comically tripped over the ball, sending it into his own net, blew a hole in Barcelona's idle confidence. With Metz still in need of two goals to turn the game around, Venables and Barcelona probably weren't prepared to hit the panic button yet, surely feeling that more goals of their own were a realistic possibility.

As the game rolled on to the last 25 minutes, no further goals had been added and Barcelona's progression looked set to be a confirmed, but unnecessarily laboured one. But, suddenly, it all went very wrong for the home side. Another comedy of errors allowed Tony Kurbos in once again. Scorer of the first Metz goal of the game, he had set up a satisfyingly stereotypical 'Grandstand Finish'.

Level on aggregate, but with Barcelona shading it on away goals, there was a long time remaining to walk such a narrow tightrope. Metz, still going out as things stood, could play with a degree of impunity. Concede a goal and they would still need just one more of their own to take the game into extra time. There was a simple equation for the French side, regardless of what Barcelona did next. Score, or go out. For Venables's side the landscape had too many shades of grey. Plough forward for a goal and leave themselves more open to a sucker punch, or sit back, invite the pressure and hit on the counter-attack? The choice was to stick or twist essentially.

Given that for so much of the tie both Barcelona and Metz had repeatedly shot themselves in the foot, Metz's winning goal was one of great quality and boasted a fine interchanging of passes. Barcelona were left disorientated by it. Kurbos was once again on the end of the move, to complete his hat-trick.

Even in a world where Barcelona were at times their own worst enemy, this was a capitulation that couldn't have been any more 'Old Barcelona' if they had tried. It was entirely in keeping with the sweet and sour nature of their generational fortunes, since the dawning of the 1960s.

So unexpected was Metz overturning their first-leg defeat, that not one French television or radio station had picked up the second leg for live broadcast. With their previous two away days ending in 6-0 and 7-0 defeats to Bordeaux and Monaco respectively, French media being unable to buy into the chances of a Metz comeback was understandable. But it also made the fact that they missed out on covering one of football's greatest ever comebacks, a sobering lesson that just because something may seem to be a lost cause, it doesn't make it any less of a deserving cause to showcase.

After taking part in the Cup Winners' Cup six times in seven seasons, beyond their incredible defeat to Metz in 1984/85, Barcelona would appear in the tournament on just four more occasions.

On the next of those occasions Barcelona won it for the third time.

Johan Cruyff, having departed the club as a player one year prior to Barcelona's success in 1979, was now back, as head coach. In cutting his coaching teeth upon his third coming at Ajax, he had won the Cup Winners' Cup in 1987, defeating Lokomotive Leipzig in the final.

Cruyff's first two years as Barcelona coach were the footballing chemistry experiments that defined the future ethos and direction of the club, that planted the seeds of contemplation within the mind of Pep Guardiola. The way Barcelona continues to blossom to this very day is down to the works of Cruyff, between 1988 and 1991 in particular.

In 1988/89, Cruyff's first season at the helm of Barcelona, a job he took on the very same summer as Rinus Michels led the Netherlands to a long-overdue first major international title in the shape of the 1988 European Championship, he won the Cup Winners' Cup.

Everything that followed from that moment gave birth to a 'New Barcelona', a Barcelona that was no longer unsure of itself and its place in the world. The 1989 Cup Winners'

Cup Final was even a dress rehearsal for the night that their European Cup curse was finally lifted, at Wembley Stadium, three years later.

If there was a defined game where Barcelona shook the past from their system, then the 1989 Cup Winners' Cup Final was arguably the one. At the Wankdorf Stadium in Bern, Barcelona faced Sampdoria, continuing their extensive relationship with major European finals in Switzerland. It was also the very same venue where the club had lost the 1961 European Cup Final, against Benfica.

This was Barcelona setting the scene of a glorious future, while laying the ghosts of a tortured European past.

To get to Bern, Barcelona had to navigate their way past an eclectic set of opponents that wouldn't be allowed to get anywhere near a major European game with them now. Perhaps unwittingly, in 1988/89, football was on the cusp of huge change. The Iron Curtain was about to be flung open, borders were set to fall, and UEFA was to partitioning its most iconic clubs from the type of backwater riff-raff that played their football against picturesque mountain-terrain backdrops, or in hardened corners of grey Soviet industrial wastelands.

Breezing past Knattspyrnufelagio Fram of Reykjavik in the first round and labouring beyond Lech Poznan in the second round on penalties, they could only muster a 1-0 aggregate victory over AGF Aarhus in the quarter-finals. Scorer of that quarter-final clincher was an increasingly frustrated Gary Lineker. The prolific focal point of the Barcelona attack since signing for the club in 1986, he had arrived at the Camp Nou just as the best of the Venables era had effectively ended.

With Barcelona as La Liga champions in 1984/85 and beaten in the European Cup Final in 1986, Lineker was recruited after a stunningly prolific, yet trophy-free year at Everton. The Toffees narrowly missed out on the league and cup double which instead fell the way of Liverpool.

After a bright Barcelona flash of mid-1980s success under Venables, Lineker's presence in Catalonia coincided with a Real Madrid resurgence. *Los Blancos* won La Liga for five consecutive seasons from 1985/86, powered by the goals of Emilio Butragueño, the third-eye capabilities of Míchel and a supporting cast of luminaries such as Hugo Sánchez, Manolo Sanchis, Rafael Martín Vázquez and even, from the summer of 1988, the services of Barcelona cult hero Bernd Schuster.

While Real Madrid reasserted their domestic supremacy, Barcelona could only really take joy in the goals of Lineker. After Venables departed the Camp Nou following a poor start to what would be a 1987/88 season of internal division and rancour, they somehow won the Copa del Rey under the guidance of Luis Aragonés.

Cruyff, never shy of fielding players out of position if he felt it to be significantly beneficial to the collective, and perhaps even a distraction to the opposition, deployed Lineker on the right wing during the second half of the 1988/89 season. It was Lineker's last season in a Barcelona shirt.

Victim to a change of formation that meant fielding only one central striker, who would in turn be asked to take on greater responsibilities than being a simple, selfish yet utterly devastating goal-hanger, Lineker yielded the new sole central role to Julio Salinas. Biding his time until the summer of 1989, when he could assess his future better, Lineker took to the right wing for Cruyff despite his bewilderment to the request. It worked well, and he still chipped in with vital goals too.

Barcelona were faced with a glimpse of a crucial element of their near future in the semi-final: the CSKA Sofia side they were facing contained Hristo Stoichkov, scorer of both of CSKA's goals in a 4-2 win for Barcelona in the Camp Nou in the first leg. It was a pivotal moment, in which the well-being of both Barcelona's present and future was cemented in place.

While Stoichkov opened the scoring, it was Lineker who got the equaliser. The England striker would also score the opening goal of the return game in Sofia, on an evening when a 2-1 victory eased Barcelona into the final. Stoichkov once again got the CSKA goal.

With the Spanish domestic season not finishing until late June, the 1989 Cup Winners' Cup Final arrived while Barcelona still had eight league games remaining.

Despite Cruyff steadying the ship at the Camp Nou, there were still rumblings of discontent. The previous summer's power struggle between the president and the players had brought Cruyff back to the club, with an exodus of what were viewed as the most militant factions of the dressing room, inclusive of Schuster departing with the flourish of the ultimate riposte of joining Real Madrid, in retaliation.

Dealing with the expectancy levels of the Barcelona supporters was one thing, but watching his back when walking through the corridors of power at the Camp Nou was another. Having quelled the 1988 player uprising, the powers that be in the boardroom didn't want their authority challenged by a figure as strong as Cruyff.

Cruyff was brought in as a unifying figure, to take the heat off an unpopular board of directors. Conversely, Cruyff would have to succeed and succeed early in his mission to mould Barcelona in his own image. If he were to manage this, then he would take possession of the power himself.

Always a step and a half behind a dominant Real Madrid in the La Liga title race, the 1989 Cup Winners' Cup Final was critical in the development of what we see as the Barcelona of today. Standing in their way, however, were Sampdoria. Heading into their very first major European final they might have been, yet this was a Sampdoria just two years away from winning the Serie A title; this was a Sampdoria who were led on the touchline by the former Real Madrid coach, Vujadin Boškov, the man who took *Los Blancos* to the 1981 European Cup Final.

Inspired on the pitch by the attacking talents of Gianluca Vialli and Roberto Mancini, by the midfield dictatorship of Toninho Cerezo, the defensive solidity of Marco Lanna and Luca Pellegrini, plus the fine Italian goalkeeping of Gianluca Pagliuca, Sampdoria were also blessed by the presence of the former Barcelona midfielder, Víctor Muñoz, one of the players allowed to leave the Camp Nou in the summer 1988 squad clear-out.

Muñoz had been a vital part of the Barcelona team in 1981/82, but his absence through injury had denied him a place in that season's Cup Winners' Cup Final, and his loss to the team had arguably been the difference between Lattek's side winning and losing the La Liga title. He had also been in the Barcelona team that had lost the 1986 European Cup Final.

Lost within the shadow of them playing each other at the 1992 European Cup Final, the 1989 Cup Winners' Cup Final is something of a forgotten Cruyff masterpiece.

It was far too one-sided and cerebral a game, when you consider the calibre of the opposing players, and far too one-sided and cerebral a game, when you consider the shrewd knowledge of the opposing coach. Cruyff again deployed Lineker on the right wing and the decision paid early dividends.

Lineker, twisting and turning like a seasoned winger, created himself an acre of space in which to send over a fine cross to the back post, where it found the head of Roberto. He then sent the ball back across the face of goal, headed downwards, where it bounced back up from the turf to be met by the head of Salinas – the man who had been handed Lineker's job – who directed it into the Sampdoria net with only four minutes gone.

In many ways it was a goal that represented the old Barcelona passing the baton on to the new as, while Salinas represented everything about Cruyff's 'Dream Team'-to-be, Lineker played only three further games for the club beyond the 1989 Cup Winners' Cup Final. The middleman in that opening goal, Roberto, would also be gone within a year, to Valencia.

The goal disorientated Boškov's side. Stung early, it was an opening to the game that Sampdoria never recovered from. Yes, Boškov's side applied pressure to Cruyff's defence and they lived dangerously at times; yet in tactical terms the Dutchman had out-thought the proud Serbian.

It was eventually left to the substitute, Luis López Rekarte, to slide home Barcelona's second goal, in the 80th minute, hitting their opponents on the break and almost beating an Italian team at their very own game.

A lesson learnt, Sampdoria would return to the Cup Winners' Cup Final a year later, where they emerged as winners, following that by winning the 1990/91 Serie A title. As Sampdoria were drifting towards the finest moment of their history, as the spring of 1991 passed into the early summer months, Barcelona were once again preparing for a Cup Winners' Cup Final.

Having lost, as holders, to Anderlecht in the second round of the 1989/90 Cup Winners' Cup, Barcelona were again one of the field for the 1990/91 season after lifting the 1990 Copa del Rey, where they defeated Real Madrid in the final.

Seeing their way past the dangers that were posed by Dynamo Kyiv and Juventus, they were the favourites against Manchester United in Rotterdam for the 1991 Cup Winners' Cup Final despite being denied the services of their goalkeeper, Andoni Zubizarreta, and the strong midfield presence of Guillermo Amor, through suspension. However, in United's ranks was a player with a point to prove to Barcelona – Mark Hughes.

In a double blow for the Catalans, while Manchester United rose to the occasion, Alex Ferguson getting all his important calls correct, Barcelona compounded this by talking themselves out of playing to their own attacking strengths and instincts. At De Kuip, Manchester United were 2-1 winners, with Hughes proving his point by scoring both goals.

Given that Cruyff's 'Dream Team' began to deliver La Liga titles between 1990/91 and 1993/94, Barcelona's participation in the Cup Winners' Cup diminished over the seasons that followed their loss in the 1991 final, and they would be drawn into the tournament on only one more occasion before it was brought to an end in 1999.

As it was, Barcelona's final fling with the Cup Winners' Cup was to be a winning one, however. Sweeping past AEK Larnaca, Red Star Belgrade and AIK, it pitted them with Fiorentina in the semi-finals. A Gabriel Batistuta-powered Fiorentina.

No longer under the control of Cruyff, and with Bobby Robson loosening the apron strings a little, Barcelona were a liberated force in 1996/97. Playing like a late 1990s Nike advert personified, it seemed all Robson needed to do was massage a few egos and just set them free.

Ronaldo, during his only season in a Barcelona shirt, was simply unstoppable. Aided and abetted by Luis Figo, they were the most open, attacking and attractive side in Europe by a wide margin. Supported by the endeavour of Luis Enrique and the intelligence of Pep Guardiola, in the final they were only really missing the suspended Miguel Àngel Nadal – the uncle of the future tennis phenomenon, Rafael Nadal.

With the luxury of having Stoichkov and the Brazilian playmaker Giovanni amongst their substitutes, Barcelona went into the final in rude health. Even in the semi-final, when they carelessly drew the first leg at the Camp Nou against Claudio Ranieri's side, Batistuta scoring Fiorentina's equaliser in a 1-1 stalemate, Robson's side simply corrected themselves by going to the Artemio Franchi to obtain a convincing 2-0 win, thanks to first-half goals from Fernando Couto and Guardiola.

For Barcelona, there was a tidy degree of symmetry to the location of the 1997 Cup Winners' Cup Final. Having lost the 1991 final there, they were heading back to De Kuip to win their fourth and last Cup Winners' Cup. Putting their De Kuip wrongs of 1991 right in 1997 struck similarities in how Barcelona had returned to the St Jakob Stadium in Basel in 1979, having lost the 1969 Cup Winners' Cup Final there. Winners of the tournament four times, twice beaten in the final, they returned to the scenes of those defeats to lift the trophy there. Five years on from lifting the European Cup for the first time, it was a fitting way to say goodbye to the Cup Winners' Cup.

In Rotterdam, it was a 38th-minute penalty from Ronaldo that settled the outcome against the holders, Paris Saint-Germain. High hopes of a classic final sadly did not come to pass. The French side had overcome Liverpool in the semi-finals, but instead of being bold and brave in the final, boasting what was a talented team of their own with the Brazilian international, Raí, at the centre of everything they did, they opted for caution against Barcelona. It was an understandable move, yet utterly frustrating.

Barcelona were given passage into the 1997/98 Champions League, having been La Liga runner-up in 1996/97, the first season in which the top tournament was extended to multiple teams from individual nations. It was this that administered the fatal blow to the Cup Winners' Cup.

Barcelona would not be returning to the Cup Winners' Cup as holders. Not a unique situation in its own right, as upon other occasions teams had won the Cup Winners' Cup and their own domestic league title in the same season, thus heading into the following season's European Cup instead. But this was different as Barcelona hadn't won their domestic title. This was a defined downplaying of the Cup Winners' Cup. Being a runner-up in your domestic league now carried more weight than winning two of the three European trophies.

During the last decade of the Cup Winners' Cup the Iberian flavour that permeated the early years of the tournament continued to mature. In 1995 Real Zaragoza won in outlandish circumstances, while Real Mallorca reached the very last final in 1999.

Throughout the entirety of the Cup Winners' Cup no nation supplied more finalists than Spain did. From the dominance of Barcelona, to the perplexing inability of Real Madrid to win it, via penalty shoot-outs and last-gasp speculative lobs, with the added beauty of Portugal conjuring up a win with a goal scored directly from a corner, the Iberian peninsula brought nothing but awe and wonderment to the Cup Winners' Cup.

Chapter Five

Pre-Nouveau Riche Glories and a Very British Domination

IT WAS a time when Chelsea and Manchester City were backed by character rather than Russian oil-rich oligarchs and Emirati royals.

In the second half of the 1960s the teams from Stamford Bridge and Maine Road became serious contenders for trophies, on what was a wonderfully level playing field that English football had cultivated for itself.

During the 1960s, the First Division title was won by eight different teams, with no one club winning it more than twice. During the 1960s, the FA Cup was won by eight different teams, with only one club winning it more than once within that decade. The 1960s also gave English football its first European successes. Throw in a World Cup for good measure and this was a decade of variation that the likes of Sky Sports and BT Sport could only dream of being gifted.

When Manchester City won the 1970 European Cup Winners' Cup Final, beating the mysteriously named Górnik Zabrze – a team containing not one, but two z's – nobody in the UK got to see it. On the very same evening, the FA Cup Final replay was taking place at Old Trafford. Chelsea would defeat Leeds United in extra time, and the game was broadcast live by both the BBC and ITV. While the BBC had made moves to broadcast the Manchester City game, live from Vienna, the Football Association blocked them.

Had the BBC been allowed to show the 1970 Cup Winners' Cup Final, BBC Two being six years old at that point in time, then in a nation of only three television channels, the phrase wall-to-wall football would have been true to its word. Regardless, Barry Davies was sent to Vienna to cover the game, with highlights being shown the following night on *Sportsnight*. Ideal served with a plate of cheese on toast, of course.

With their contemporary financial, coaching and playing advantages, it is remarkable that the 1970 Cup Winners' Cup Final is still marked by being the only time Manchester City have reached a major European final. Manchester City only competed in the Cup Winners' Cup twice. On the back of beating Leicester City in the 1969 FA Cup Final, they gained entry to the 1969/70 tournament, and upon their success against Górnik Zabrze they returned the following season as holders.

Prior to that, you had to go back to 1956 for Manchester City's previous FA Cup win, which came four years before the birth of the Cup Winners' Cup. While beyond their 1969 win, they didn't lift the FA Cup again until 2011, long after the extinction of the Cup Winners' Cup.

The Cup Winners' Cup and Manchester City as a combination was a short-lived, yet successful, mirage. They won it at the first attempt and then fell at the semi-final stage in their final attempt. Led by the visionary and mildly eccentric Joe Mercer, assisted by the intelligent, yet arrogant, abrasive and ambitious Malcolm Allison, the competition represented the endgame of a glorious span of three seasons in which the Cup Winners' Cup was added to the First Division title, the FA Cup and the League Cup.

Still on the European frontier in 1969/70, Manchester City's very first continental campaign had been an abrupt first-round exit in the previous season's European Cup. Drawn to face Athletic Bilbao at the first hurdle of their Cup Winners' Cup adventure, it could have been another short sojourn.

Bilbao, coached by the former West Bromwich Albion striker and Wolverhampton Wanderers manager, Ronnie Allen, whom he would take close to the La Liga title in 1969/70, proved to be the perfect opponents, however.

Leading 2-0 and 3-1, Bilbao conspired to gift Manchester City a 3-3 draw at the San Mamés during the first round first leg, inclusive of their captain, Echeberria, scoring an own goal five minutes from time to complete Manchester City's comeback.

Winning the second leg 3-0, it was a result that Manchester City were made to work for, with all the goals coming during the last half hour. A closer game than the scoreline suggests, it was still a late flourish in which Mercer's side performed with style.

Troubled very little by Lierse, taking the second-round tie 8-0 on aggregate set up a quarter-final encounter with Académica, of Portugal. Physically demanding, trying to create openings against an agricultural approach to defensive play, Manchester City were left frustrated and bruised for most of the 210 minutes of football between the two teams. Académica had held on for so long that a third game was looking certain, until Tony Towers drove home when the ball dropped to his feet from what was yet another clearance.

It was a relieved Manchester City that embraced the final whistle, and they soon found themselves thrown together with Schalke 04 in the semi-finals. The least experienced of the four semi-finalists, in terms of European campaigns contested, there was no easy draw for Mercer's team. While the name of Górnik Zabrze might be retrospectively written off as a weak link, they were viewed at the time as the tournament favourites.

Nervousness crept into Manchester City's football during the first leg of the semi-final in Gelsenkirchen, yet the visitors weren't without chances to score. They just seemed to be taken by surprise when those chances presented themselves, leaving them unable to take them.

With not only a blizzard of attacking football being thrown at them, Manchester City had to cope with the inclement weather conditions too. A rotation of rain, snow and sleet making their task even more difficult, they did well to keep Schalke out until the 76th minute, when Reinhard Libuda set off on a determined, slaloming run, at the end of which he drove a powerful shot into Joe Corrigan's bottom right-hand corner. Wild celebrations ensued, including a pitch invasion by a very excited dog. A German Shepherd appropriately enough. The game finished 1-0, and Manchester City could count themselves fortunate that the second-leg mountain they had to climb wasn't significantly higher.

Back at Maine Road, it always had the prospect of being a very different game. This time it was Schalke who struggled in the glare of the spotlight. With only 30 minutes gone, Manchester City were 3-0 up, having cut through the Schalke midfield and defence with a ruthless simplicity. The West Germans seemed completely helpless. Within five minutes of the restart after the half-time break it was 4-0, Francis Lee's goal being added to those scored by Mike Doyle and Neil Young, with the latter scoring twice. The artistry in the fourth goal lay in a wonderful dummy, played by the referee during the build-up, which Sócrates would have been proud of. Colin Bell nonchalantly added the fifth goal before a final act of mercy was shown by Manchester City in allowing Libuda to snatch a very late consolation. A place in the final was theirs, and all Manchester City fans had to do was figure out how they were going to gain access to the game.

Basically, given the stance taken by the Football Association, the only way was to undertake the trip to Vienna. As the FA Cup Final replay descended upon their part of the country, around 4,000 Manchester City supporters departed for the Austrian capital.

Mercer and Allison were dealt worries of their own. The fitness of Mike Summerbee was a concern, as he continued to labour after picking up a leg injury during the League Cup Final. Added to this, the Manchester City managerial double act were organised and observant enough not to underestimate their opponents. Górnik might have been the first Polish side to reach a major European final, but they had destroyed Rangers, both home and away, during the second round. The warnings from Glasgow had been loud ones.

Summerbee was eventually assessed as not being fit enough to start the final, although he was named amongst the substitutes. The 18-year-old Tony Towers acted as his understudy, while as a defensive precaution, George Heslop operated as an extra centre-back.

As the players walked on to the pitch before kick-off, Davies had aired concern about Manchester City's need to keep Włodzimierz Lubański under control. Admirably, this is something that Mercer's team managed far better than Sir Alf Ramsey's England did during the qualifiers for the 1974 World Cup a short few years later.

Talented as they were, Górnik were slower than Manchester City to respond to both the weather conditions and the fact that they had suddenly found themselves on such an elevated platform. While some teams take to major European finals without a care in the world, to others they can feel like a weight bearing down on the shoulders.

Manchester City had already took the lead. A speculative low effort from Lee, which almost seemed like it was punched at goal by his right foot, from the left-hand angle of the Górnik 18-yard box, was parried by the goalkeeper, Hubert Kostka. The first man to the loose ball was Neil Young, the scorer of Manchester City's winning goal in the 1969 FA Cup Final. Prodding it into the empty net, he was the hero again for 1-0.

Absorbing the blow of losing Doyle to injury in only the 16th minute, Ian Bowyer stepped onto the saturated pitch as his replacement at the uncovered Prater Stadium. As the rains fell, in the commentary box for the BBC, Barry Davies lamented the torrential conditions.

Kostka might have been unlucky for the opener, but he was heavily to blame for Manchester City's second goal, which Lee procured shortly before half-time from the penalty spot. Racing to cut out the advancing Young, Kostka opted to confront the Manchester City left-winger as he entered the penalty area. It was an ill-advised decision and, unwilling to reconsider his actions, Kostka ploughed onwards and heavily into the oncoming attacker. It was as clear an unnecessarily gifted penalty as you are ever likely to see. Even then, Kostka was offered the chance of redemption as Lee's powerfully struck yet poorly directed penalty really should have been saved. Instead, it seemed to go straight through a goalkeeper who was falling in slow motion.

Stanisław Oślizło, the Górnik captain, reduced his team's arrears with just over 20 minutes to go. It was the least the sweeper could have done, since it was he who was caught in possession by Young, the incident at the very genesis of the move that led to Kostka giving the penalty away. It was the one and only moment that there was a lapse of Manchester City concentration. Despite there still being plenty of time to level the game, Górnik failed to produce an effort of substance and the Cup Winners' Cup was heading back to England.

In their bid to retain the Cup Winners' Cup, Manchester City crossed paths with Górnik again during the 1970/71 season. This time at the quarter-finals stage, it took three games to separate the two teams. The holders seemed charmed by the gods when they overcame a 2-0 first-leg defeat sustained in Poland; matching that scoreline at Maine Road, it took the tie into a play-off, in Copenhagen.

At the Idrætsparken there was a higher attendance for the play-off match between the two teams than there had been in Vienna for the previous season's final. At the third time of asking, Manchester City ran out 3-1 winners to progress to an all-English semi-final against Dave Sexton's Chelsea.

It wasn't only in the quarter-final that Mercer's side had ridden the fine line between winning and losing. While Honvéd were beaten relatively easily in the second round, it was in the first round that Manchester City's defence of the Cup Winners' Cup almost fell flat on its face at the first hurdle, against Linfield.

A lacklustre 1-0 win in the first leg at Maine Road, Bell scoring the only goal of the game with just seven minutes remaining, meant that Manchester City took only a narrow lead to Belfast for the return game.

With Linfield having put on an excellent defensive display in Manchester, it was doubtful that Mercer's star-studded side would make the same mistakes in Belfast. Instead of once bitten, twice shy, however, it was a case of twice bitten as Linfield won 2-1, leaving Manchester City to limp through on the away-goals rule. It was the game that brought Billy Bingham to the attention of English clubs.

The Linfield manager would soon be in charge of Everton, via a successful spell at Southport.

For Chelsea, they arrived at the semi-finals on a massive high, after a stirring quarter-final fightback against Club Brugge. When they were beaten in the first leg 2-0, at the Albert Dyserynck Stadion, by a team containing a young Rob Rensenbrink, Chelsea were left with a major task to reach the last four.

A 4-0 victory in the second leg, at Stamford Bridge, took the west London side through, however. Yet the scoreline masks how close the game was, as Chelsea needed extra time to see off the skilful Belgians. As the 1970s progressed, Brugge would mature enough as a team to reach the 1976 UEFA Cup Final and then the 1978 European Cup Final where, on both occasions, they were defeated by Bob Paisley's Liverpool.

A colour-clash of kits – with the two teams having varying shades of blue according to the 1970/71 scriptures of UEFA – meant that both Chelsea and Manchester City would be wearing their away strips for both legs of their semi-final showdown.

At Stamford Bridge, at the end of the first leg, Manchester City will have been reasonably satisfied with a 1-0 defeat. Derek Smethurst scored the only goal of the game, right at the start of the second half, getting on the end of a deep cross and shooting across goal, past Joe Corrigan.

Corrigan picked up an injury prior to the second leg, which brought his back-up, Ron Healey, into the team for the return game. It was a pivotal and cataclysmic moment in the tie. Shortly before half-time, Healey was under no pressure at all when he was presented with a clear catch from what appeared to be a wasted free kick by Keith Weller.

With one eye on where, and to whom, he was going to release the ball, Healey allowed it to slip from his grasp and, being positioned so close to his own goal line, it disastrously resulted in bouncing down and into his own net. One simple mistake, in the biggest game of his career. With the need for three second-half goals to reach the final, it was a comeback too far for Manchester City, and it was also the last game they ever played in the tournament. Instead, it would be Chelsea heading to Athens.

Largely impressive throughout their run to the 1971 Cup Winners' Cup Final, their first leg quarter-final defeat to Club Brugge had been the only blot on Chelsea's copybook, and their presence in Athens wasn't a surprise. Prior to the quarter-finals they had convincingly seen off the attentions of Aris Thessaloniki and CSKA Sofia.

A team renowned for both its flair and steel, they had been a club on the rise since the mid-1960s. They were gaining traction under Tommy Docherty, after initially being relegated under his stewardship in 1961/62, just as Manchester United would be in 1973/74. The confident Scotsman took Chelsea back up at the first time of asking, again, something he would emulate just over a decade later at Old Trafford.

When Chelsea returned to the First Division, fresh for the 1963/64 season, they did so as a team reborn. Over the course of the next four seasons, they only finished outside the top five on one occasion, and that was a campaign in which they reached the FA Cup Final, having reached the semi-finals for the two previous seasons. Amongst this span of near misses on silverware, there was also a run to the semi-finals of the Inter-Cities Fairs Cup, in 1966.

Falling short against Tottenham Hotspur in that 1967 FA Cup Final, new impetus and ideas soon arrived as the abrasive but tactically astute Dave Sexton succeeded Docherty during the early exchanges of the 1967/68 season.

Between Sexton taking over at Stamford Bridge, and Chelsea strolling out for the 1971 Cup Winners' Cup Final, the club never finished a First Division campaign any lower than sixth position. The trophies that had proved so elusive for Docherty, suddenly became obtainable under his successor.

Starved of the vital ingredient of good fortune under Docherty, perhaps Sexton had no such issues in this respect. When Chelsea won the FA Cup in 1970, it was akin to the wild Alaskan salmon swimming up the rapid stream. Leeds United were the better team for large swathes of both games, but Chelsea rode the waves and came on strong as the replay reached the business end of the second half. By extra time, a Chelsea winner seemed the only likely scenario.

This isn't to say that Chelsea were never in the 1970 FA Cup Final game until the last stretch. What they offered were sporadic flurries of both metaphorical and physical punches, before stepping back to let Leeds slug themselves into a standstill. It was a work of art, yet it also relied on luck. At Wembley, Gary Sprake, the Leeds goalkeeper, conceded a shocker of a goal to allow Chelsea back on to level terms at 1-1. Leeds led 2-1 until an 85th-minute equaliser, and had rattled the crossbar at one stage.

There were vague similarities between the 1970 FA Cup Final and the 1971 Cup Winners' Cup Final for Chelsea. At the Georgios Karaiskakis Stadium, just as Leeds had been a year earlier at Wembley, Real Madrid were generally the better team. However, with Chelsea leading 1-0, it took a late equaliser for the Spanish team to elongate the game to a replay. Even British media observers had extolled that no matter how cruel such a late denial of victory had been on Chelsea, Real hadn't deserved to lose.

Instead of Chelsea capitulating in the replay, it was Real who ran out of steam. A 2-1 victory was Chelsea's to claim, with Peter Osgood netting what proved to be the winning goal, in the 39th minute.

Unbeknown to those involved at Stamford Bridge, the 1971 Cup Winners' Cup Final marked the end of an era, rather than providing the hoped-for springboard to further successes, both at home and abroad.

Purveyors of the King's Road ethos, the Chelsea of Docherty and Sexton had become a magnet for the great and the good of the entertainment world, yet the party couldn't continue indefinitely. The League Cup Final was reached and lost in 1972, having earlier in the season carelessly drifted out of the defence of their Cup Winners' Cup in the second round. They were defeated by the Swedish side Åtvidabergs FF on the away goals rule, after defeating Luxembourg's Jeunesse Hautcharage in the previous round by the ludicrous aggregate scoreline of 21-0.

Within three years – and just four years after lifting the Cup Winners' Cup – weighed down by the poorly timed decision of building an overly ambitious new East Stand just as the world was consumed by an economic crisis that made materials both extortionately expensive, and at times impossible to obtain, Chelsea slid towards relegation. It was a stark fall from grace.

Chelsea's bid to be the stylish footballing face of London was a challenge to the established position held by Tottenham Hotspur. Wearing their hat at a jaunty angle, the goals of Jimmy Greaves, formerly a Chelsea player, had been a widely admired commodity and the focal point of a White Hart Lane collective that played their football with a swagger.

You could maybe suggest that when the two teams faced each other in the 1967 FA Cup Final, even though Tottenham prevailed, it was Chelsea who took the style baton from them and ran onwards with it.

In 1967/68, and undone by the away-goals rule, Tottenham made a second-round Cup Winners' Cup exit, to Lyon. It was a massive disappointment for Bill Nicholson's team, who had harboured grand designs of once again winning the trophy they had lifted in 1963.

The first English team to win a major European competition, Tottenham's success in 1962/63 was the final flourish of a three-season stretch in which they won the league and FA Cup double in 1960/61 and retained the FA Cup in 1962.

An outstanding and proud achievement, Tottenham were utterly dominant from beginning to end during their route to becoming the first British team to win a major European trophy. Avoiding being cast into the preliminary round, they were drawn into a 'Battle of Britain' tie in the last 16 against Rangers.

Eagerly anticipated, the first leg, at a packed White Hart Lane, was played out on Halloween, 1962. A marvellously open game, both teams were sitting at the top of their respective leagues, and they were fully committed to incessant, attack-minded football. Tottenham were 5-2 winners in a game that was far more even than the scoreline suggests. While the home side were able to take advantage of some of Rangers' defensive mistakes, Tottenham got away with a few of their own. One such error occurred when Dave Mackay back-heeled the ball in his own penalty area, completely taking his goalkeeper, Bill Brown, by surprise as it narrowly went wide of the post.

A wonderfully atmospheric evening, Rangers were backed by a vociferous following, but it was during a damaging 20-minute spell before half-time that the game ran away from them. Tottenham scored three goals in this period, one of which was by the Scottish international, John White, his second of the game.

Along with Mackay and Brown, White was one of three Scottish players in the Tottenham side. White was shockingly killed in July 1964, at the age of 27, when he was struck by lightning while sheltering under a tree on Crews Hill golf course, in Enfield, north London.

Holding a 4-2 half-time lead, although only one further goal was added in the second half the game remained an open and free flowing one. Rangers were unlucky not to score more goals, keeping Brown busy and striking the Tottenham crossbar.

By the time the return game took place, on 11 December, six days after it was originally postponed due to dense fog at Ibrox Park, the wave of goals that Tottenham had been riding prior to the first leg had ebbed away. Having scored 26 goals in the five games directly leading up to the first encounter, Nicholson's side had failed to score in the two games before travelling to Glasgow for the rearranged second leg. This was the culmination of a four-game span, in which they had scored only twice.

Without the kind of fluidity they had shown at White Hart Lane, Tottenham were left to fend off the constant stream of Rangers attacks, while countering on the break. Blessed by the return to fitness of White, having missed the previous two games through gastroenteritis, and opting to field the more bludgeoning goalscoring talents of Bobby Smith, ahead of Les Allen – father of the much- travelled future Tottenham striker Clive Allen – Nicholson's side might have struggled to make it through, had the game taken place on its original date.

White was a sporadic thorn in the side of Rangers, while Smith scored twice as Tottenham stunned Ibrox into an eerie silence, with a hat-trick of sucker-punch goals, to claim a 3-2 victory on the night and an 8-4 aggregate win that made the tie sound much more lopsided than it was. In a spirit of sportsmanship, the Tottenham players applauded the Rangers players off the pitch after the end of the game.

When the Cup Winners' Cup quarter-finals arrived in March, Tottenham were still leading the First Division, but had relinquished their vice-like grip on the FA Cup – Burnley, the team they had defeated in the 1962 FA Cup Final, had knocked them out in the third round. Future winners of the Cup Winners' Cup, Slovan Bratislava, lay in wait.

In Bratislava, Tottenham were picked apart ruthlessly in the first leg. With Europe still waiting for the legendary winter of 1962/63 to thaw, the nearby Danube river, rather than being a flowing torrent of untamed water, was frozen solid, and topped by a generous layer of snow. If Nicholson and his team had been hoping for a respite from the white and unnegotiable lands of home, they were left disappointed by the white and largely unnegotiable lands of Czechoslovakia.

Beaten 2-0; had it not been for the inspired goalkeeping of Brown, the scoreline would have been comfortably more than double that margin. Getting their tactics badly wrong, Tottenham were starved of a supply route to Greaves and Smith, as Slovan constantly closed on the man they considered to be the facilitator of Tottenham's attacking dangers, White.

Careless passes and sloppy defending, Brown was consistently exposed by the poor choices of his team-mates. Slovan, perhaps conscious that they hadn't scored as many goals as their pressure had deserved, ploughed forward in the final ten minutes on a muddy pitch that, viewed from overhead, would have looked odd when set within an almost entirely pristine white landscape.

With a string of late saves, inclusive of an outstanding double stop from L'udovit Cvetler and Ivan Mráz, Brown's exhaustive work almost set Tottenham up with the platform to snatch a completely undeserved away goal and narrower margin of first-leg defeat, when both Smith and Tony Marchi came close.

Nine days later, at White Hart Lane, the balance of power shifted from one end of the spectrum to the other. If it could be claimed that Slovan should have scored six in Bratislava, then the same could be said of Tottenham in north London.

In fact, Tottenham did score six. Despite the 6-0 scoreline, they were frustrated during the first half hour of the return game. Arguably too intense in their play, they almost fell further behind in the tie, with the woodwork being hit and Brown being called into action yet again. The tie completely turned, however, during a ten-minute stretch shortly before half-time, when Mackay, Greaves and Smith left Slovan punch-drunk, with a trio of quick-fire goals that put Tottenham in possession of a place in the semi-finals.

Another equally devastating second-half spell, from around the hour mark, brought with it three more goals: Greaves striking again, along with Cliff Jones and a rejuvenated White who, having been kept quiet in Bratislava, was now taking full advantage of those Slovan defenders that had shackled him so well during the first leg.

With a fixture backlog to slog through, as the winter finally thawed Tottenham were left with an avalanche of fixtures from early March onwards. In between facing Ipswich Town on Boxing Day and defeating West Bromwich Albion on 2 March, they played just three games. Within that period, they went over a month between fixtures. After playing only three games during the entirety of January and February 1963, Tottenham took on 14 fixtures throughout March and April. Amongst this run of games, they played three times in four days over the Easter weekend. Having led the title race for so long, a 1-0 loss to Everton dislodged them from the top of the table, just days before they travelled to Yugoslavia, to face OFK Beograd.

Temperatures far kinder in Belgrade than the ones they had encountered in Bratislava, Tottenham's players returned to White Hart Lane with a 2-1 victory which, when combined to their irrepressible home form, made them a near certainty to reach the final.

Perhaps learning the lessons of Bratislava, in Belgrade Tottenham were much more defensively attentive, something that became a compulsory issue during the last 35 minutes, after Greaves was sent off for his part in a physical exchange of views with one of the OFK defenders. Despite being down to ten men, with the half-time scoreline at 1-1, Terry Dyson stunned the home support by grabbing Tottenham's winning goal. Having provided a wonderfully intimidating atmosphere for the visitors, this second goal prompted the OFK faithful to turn on their own team. In what should have been difficult circumstances, due to the departure of Greaves, both the OFK team and supporters played straight into Nicholson's hands.

Back at White Hart Lane, it was with a display of silk and steel that Tottenham won 3-1 to ease into the 1963 Cup Winners' Cup Final. Physical enough to let the OFK players know that the dismissal of Greaves hadn't been forgiven, yet not rash enough to incur any new disciplinary problems, the power of Mackay, Jones, Smith and White was too much for the Yugoslavs to cope with, despite the absence of the suspended Greaves.

Rotterdam was the prize and a date with the holders, Atlético Madrid, for the most evenly matched thrashing ever administered in a Cup Winners' Cup Final.

Given that Tottenham became so known as a cup team during the decades to follow, lifting the FA Cup again in 1967, 1981, 1982 and 1991, that they never returned to a Cup Winners' Cup Final was almost an oddity.

In 1963/64 Tottenham went out 4-3 to Manchester United on aggregate, falling to a 4-1 second-leg defeat at Old Trafford, in which Bobby Charlton's 88th-minute goal was the difference between his team's progression to the quarter-finals and the need for a replay.

Beyond their early exit to Lyon in 1967/68, Tottenham's other three flirtations with the Cup Winners' Cup were ended with big head-to-heads. It was in 1982 that that harmless Antonio Olmo effort from distance squirmed through Ray Clemence's hands, in the first leg of the semi-finals, against Barcelona.

In 1982/83 Spurs were eliminated in round two by Bayern Munich, while their last Cup Winners' Cup campaign came to an end in the 1991/92 quarter-finals, narrowly exiting to Feyenoord.

Reaching and winning the final on one occasion, you can't help but feel Tottenham and the Cup Winners' Cup should have been far more entwined; that despite the tournament having expired 20 years ago, there is still somehow some unfinished business between the two. Unfinished business that can no longer be completed.

With West Ham lifting the Cup Winners' Cup in 1965, the English love affair with the tournament looked set to continue in 1966, when Bill Shankly's Liverpool made it to the final at Hampden Park.

Given a tough path to the final, Liverpool had been thrown together with the Italian powerhouse Juventus in the first round, turning around a 1-0 first-leg loss in Turin, with a 2-0 victory at Anfield. Navigating their way past the understated dangers of Standard Liège and Honvéd took Shankly's side into an all-British semi-final against Jock Stein's Celtic.

In Glasgow, a sole Bobby Lennox goal gave Celtic a slender 1-0 lead to take to Anfield for the second leg. On a resounding evening, when Celtic supporters were in huge numbers, Liverpool left it until the second half to make their fightback. Goals from Tommy Smith and a limping Geoff Strong saw them through to the final, past a team that would win the European Cup one year later. Strong had also been the hero against Juventus, yet he missed the final through injury.

Played out at a saturated Hampden Park, Glasgow was caught under a deluge in the build-up to the 1966 Cup Winners' Cup Final. With local residents opting to stay at home, and many people put off making the waterlogged trip to Scotland, it was only the truly dedicated that made the pilgrimage to the game. A final that really should have had Hampden packed to the rafters was instead reduced to an attendance that was just a shade under one third of the famous old stadium's capacity.

Borussia Dortmund as their opponents, Liverpool were up against a team that almost offered a mirror image of themselves. Tight, organised, fast, skilful and strong, yet not indulging in the glory of the individual, it was basically a rock vs a hard place.

Roger Hunt's equaliser cancelled out Sigi Held's opener, both goals coming during a seven-minute span just after the hour. The game subsequently drifted into extra time and it took a goal of outrageous misfortune, from Liverpool's perspective, to settle the outcome.

Shortly after the second period of extra time had begun, Tommy Lawrence raced to the edge of his penalty area to intercept the advancing Held. The ball ricocheted off his body and towards Reinhard Libuda on the right flank, who instinctively sent a looping effort towards Liverpool's unguarded net. Seeing this, and making a desperate attempt to clear the ball, the Liverpool captain, Ron Yeats, made ground; yet as the ball came down it struck the post, rebounding against Yeats and into his own goal, player as well as ball tumbling in the net for good measure.

It was a bizarre way in which to lose any game, let alone such a high-profile one, and is comparable to the overall silliness with which Arsenal would later lose the 1995 Cup Winners' Cup Final.

Liverpool would never come this close to winning the Cup Winners' Cup again. Joining Real Madrid in failing to win the tournament, they would only take part in it on another four occasions, their best effort being a run to the semi-finals in 1997.

As a further footnote, Liverpool clocked up their biggest ever win, in the 1974/75 Cup Winners' Cup campaign, when they defeated Strømsgodset IF of Norway 11-0 at Anfield.

With both Manchester City and Chelsea going on to win the tournament in 1970 and 1971 respectively, Liverpool's loss in the 1966 final was the only adverse result in a Cup Winners' Cup Final for an English club during that first decade of its existence.

North of the border it was a different matter, however. Celtic's angst at losing the 1966 semi-final would pale into insignificance a year later, when beating Inter Milan in Lisbon in the 1967 European Cup Final. While over at Rangers, they had lost the very first Cup Winners' Cup Final, in 1961, to Fiorentina.

It might have only been a ten-team tournament in 1960/61, but in the inaugural playing of the Cup Winners' Cup, Rangers were handed games against the forces-to-be that were Ferencváros and Borussia Mönchengladbach. Run close by the Hungarians, Rangers then obliterated Mönchengladbach 11-0 on aggregate. This set up an all-British semi-final against Stan Cullis's Wolverhampton Wanderers.

Seeming to wilt under the scrutiny of a deafening Ibrox, Wolves surprisingly froze, and they were unable to overturn the 2-0 first-leg loss, back at Molineux, three weeks later.

In what was the only two-legged Cup Winners' Cup Final ever played, Fiorentina proved too powerful and wily for Rangers. Losing the first leg on home soil 2-0 left the return trip to Florence a thankless task.

Experience stored in the memory banks, Rangers were back in the Cup Winners' Cup Final by 1967. Their opponents were Bayern Munich, in what was the Bavarians' first ever major European final.

Cast into the shadow of Celtic's success in Lisbon the previous week – part of what was an unprecedented quartet of major tournaments Stein's team competed in during the 1966/67 season – Rangers' defeat in 1967 is one that falls under the radar to a large extent.

At face value, it feels like the last insult of a devastating campaign in which their fierce cross-city rivals had ascended to immortality. Yet when you look beyond the surface, you find a Rangers team that came so close to their own slice of history.

In some respects, it isn't just the achievements of Celtic in 1967 that cast a shadow across Rangers' run to the 1967

Cup Winners' Cup Final. Rangers' eventual road to glory in the 1972 final draws the sting also, while there are nods of retrospective understanding because they were beaten by a mighty Bayern Munich side that boasted the likes of Sepp Maier, Franz Beckenbauer and Gerd Müller.

This only serves to draw a cloak of secrecy across the Rangers run of 1966/67, however. It shields from common footballing knowledge how deserving as finalists they were; it shields from common footballing knowledge how unfortunate they were in not lifting the trophy themselves. It wasn't a condescending case of how the spirited Scottish team pushed the West German footballing Cyclops to unfathomable limits. The Rangers of 1967 were more than a balanced proposition for the Bayern of 1967 to contend with.

Overcoming Glentoran in an evocative first-round meeting, in which the Northern Irish outfit held their visitors to a first-leg draw at packed-out Oval in Belfast, Rangers were simply too strong back at Ibrox, cruising through to the second round.

This was a Glentoran of great substance, however, and a year later they only narrowly exited the European Cup to Benfica on the away-goals rule, with the Portuguese giants going all the way to Wembley to face Manchester United. Added to this, Glentoran had previously proved stubborn opposition for the likes of Panathinaikos and Royal Antwerp.

Having navigated a way past the potential for upset with Glentoran, Rangers then faced a clearly defined task in the next round. To reach the quarter-finals they would have to find a way past the holders, Borussia Dortmund, conquerors of both Liverpool and West Ham United on the way to winning the tournament just six months earlier.

Dortmund's return to Glasgow was a volatile one, the holders opening the scoring with a controversial goal, a goal that the hosts felt should have been ruled offside. Rangers played the rest of the game in a state of vehement protestation. Channelling that sense of injustice positively, Rangers recovered to win the game 2-1, despite an increasingly physical slant to the evening. Putting in a very intelligent and stubborn performance during a goalless second leg, Rangers progressed to the quarter-finals, unseating the holders in the process.

This achievement was made even more astounding as, for the last 52 minutes of the second leg, Rangers were playing with just ten men after losing Bobby Watson to injury. With substitutes not allowed, Rangers' sense of injustice was again used positively.

Nursing the ignominy of a Scottish Cup exit at the hands of Berwick Rangers, European endeavour became a respite from domestic woes for Scot Symon's side. Real Zaragoza were waiting for them in the quarter-finals.

In a classic swing of fortunes, Rangers, having comfortably won the first leg at Ibrox 2-0, travelled to La Romareda for the return game. After 180 minutes, however, the aggregate score was level at 2-2. A further period of extra time failed to separate the two teams, despite Rangers being awarded a penalty that Alex Smith contrived to miss.

Riding their luck, the game drifted towards a coin toss. With Rangers having won the toss of a coin for the kick-off for both normal and extra time, Zaragoza might have felt that the law of averages would finally smile on them when it came to the coin toss to decide which of the two teams would advance to the semi-finals. If Zaragoza's tactics had been to 'play for the coin toss' it blew up in their faces. The law of averages did not apply on this occasion – when the Rangers captain, John Greig, called out 'tails', the outcome was indeed tails.

After the dramatic way they had reached the last four, Rangers' semi-final experience was a surprisingly sedate one. Winning both legs of their tie against Slavia Sofia 1-0, they would have won by a far wider margin had it not been for the inspired goalkeeping of the legendary Simeon Simeonov.

Completely in step with the theme of Rangers' travels across Europe in 1966/67, their task in the final was made as difficult as possible by a combination of luck and Symon's team selection.

Facing West German opposition again was going to be tough enough, but facing West German opposition in West Germany was always likely to be one ask too many. When you add to that, the conscious omission of the prolific goalscorer, Alex Willoughby – who had scored an incredible 17 goals in his previous 14 games – in favour of fielding Roger Hynd as a striker instead, a player who was a defender by nature, then arguably Rangers were neither assisted by the environment nor by their own manager's tactics.

With the Bayern supporters only having to travel 100 miles or so north for the final, to Nuremberg, despite the presence of a generous contingent of Rangers fans, the Städtisches Stadion was predominantly populated by Bavarians.

Never overwhelmed, however, Rangers were more than an even match for Bayern. Although it took 109 minutes to produce a goal, the 1967 Cup Winners' Cup Final was a wonderfully open and attacking game, with both teams creating opportunities.

Despite the consternation over the inclusion of Hynd, ahead of Willoughby, it was Hynd who came the closest to a Rangers goal, putting the ball beyond Maier and into the Bayern net, only to see his effort disallowed. It was a controversial decision, Maier having collected the ball in mid-air, only to spill it as he landed on the turf heavily, presenting it to Hynd who accepted the gift and prodded it into the empty net. While contact had been made between Hynd and Maier, it was a fair challenge for a ball in motion, Maier only losing possession of it as he landed and Hynd being a good yard away from the goalkeeper when it rolled towards him.

Franz Roth was the man to settle the issue, four minutes into the second period of extra time. A speculative ball played from the halfway line bounced kindly to him in the Rangers penalty area, where he managed to turn and hook it over the advancing Rangers goalkeeper, Norrie Martin. There was something brilliantly hypnotic to the move and finish, all accentuated by the composition of the ball, which was an Adidas Telstar. The 1967 Cup Winners' Cup Final was the first major European final to use the soon-to-be iconic ball.

Amidst the Bavarian celebrations upon the final whistle, there was also great respect shown towards the Rangers team for the part they played in the final. Two evenly matched competitors, it was by the slenderest of margins that it fell Bayern's way.

Another lesson absorbed, by the time Rangers returned to the Cup Winners' Cup Final for a third time, in 1972, they were more than ready to lift the trophy. They would also cross paths with Bayern again, en route to the Camp Nou.

In between Rangers reaching the 1967 and 1972 finals, Dunfermline Athletic had enjoyed their remarkable run to the semi-finals in 1968/69 and, with Celtic having reached another European Cup Final in 1970, when Rangers reached the 1972 Cup Winners' Cup Final it unwittingly stood as the marker for the end of an era.

Beyond Rangers' success, it would be 11 years before another Scottish team would grace a major European final; beyond Rangers' success, it would be 11 years before the Cup Winners' Cup was won once again by another British team. Another Scottish team at that.

Rangers' path to Cup Winners' Cup glory in 1971/72 was an arduous one. Thrown one serious set of opponents after another, while some winners of the Cup Winners' Cup were the beneficiaries of a weak field or a collection of favourable draws, Rangers enjoyed no such favours.

Navigating their way past Rennes in the first round, Rangers set themselves up with a second-round away tie against the 1964 winners, Sporting CP. As if a 6-6 draw on aggregate wasn't dramatic enough, the referee, Laurens van Ravens, ordered a penalty shoot-out, which was won by the home side.

Played out amidst varying degrees of devastation, bewilderment and nudges of elbows into ribs, it was while the dejected Rangers players were sitting in the visitors' dressing room that knocks on the door and guarded conversations started to escalate. Rumblings of discontent had started within small pockets of the Rangers party as soon as it became clear that the referee was organising a penalty shoot-out. After two brilliantly open and attacking games – Rangers had won the first leg at Ibrox 3-2 and Sporting the second leg 4-3 – it meant that Rangers held the advantage on the away-goals rule.

A chain of communication was then enacted as the Rangers manager, Willie Waddell, already having agreed with his captain, Greig, that they should be through to the quarter-finals, discussed the matter further with the Scottish pressmen that were knocking loudly on the dressing room door. Taking these concerns to the on-site UEFA staff, within minutes Waddell had returned to his players to confirm that Rangers hadn't been knocked out after all. From despair to delirium in the blink of an eye.

Why Van Ravens got it so wrong is open to interpretation. The popular retrospective explanation tends to be that it was down to the introduction of the away-goals rule. However, for the early rounds of the Cup Winners' Cup, the away-goals rule had been in operation since the beginning of the 1965/66 season. Instead, it may well have been with one eye on not making the erroneous suggestion that the game required a replay that Van Ravens insisted upon a penalty shoot-out. The penalty shoot-out was a far more recent introduction by UEFA to their tournaments, the previous season.

Confusion over, Rangers could put their European campaign into its winter hibernation, resuming in March when handed another difficult assignment against a tough, fluid and organised Torino side. *I Granata* would go on to finish third in Serie A, only one point behind the champions, their Turin city rivals, Juventus.

Just 24 hours after Wolverhampton Wanderers had faced Juventus on the very same pitch, in the UEFA Cup, it was Rangers' turn to face the bear pit of the Stadio Comunale.

With an aggressive streak that tested the fine lines of the laws of the game, it is fair to say that Rangers rattled Torino. Despite opting for a defensive set-up, it was the visitors who obtained the early lead, Johnston stunning the hosts after only 12 minutes.

Torino's equaliser was met by a fearsome roar and, although there was still half an hour to play, Rangers rode the storm to come away from Italy with a 1-1 draw on what was one of their greatest European nights. They completed a very professional job back at Ibrox, with a 1-0 victory, gaining a hard-earned place in the semi-finals.

In the last four, Rangers were reunited with Bayern Munich, both teams still harbouring survivors from the 1967 Cup Winners' Cup Final, Bayern just over two years away from the first of a hat-trick of European Cup successes, and having overcome Liverpool in the second round, on the way to meeting Rangers in the semi-finals.

While the semi-final draw handed Rangers the problem of playing against the best team left in the tournament, facing Bayern also had its blessings. With the alternatives having been Dynamo Moscow or Dynamo Berlin, at least the trip to Munich meant that Rangers avoided the logistics of navigating their way through the Iron Curtain. Also, with the first leg taking place at the compact and atmospheric Grünwalder Stadion, it allowed Waddell's men room for potential error, and the benefits of their own partisan backing at Ibrox, for the second leg.

Up against an incessant Bayern attack, Gerd Müller hit the crossbar with a header, long before Paul Breitner opened the scoring. Dropping deep however, Rangers largely restricted Franz Beckenbauer and his men to long-range efforts. Not that these efforts didn't pose Peter McCloy significant saves to make.

Employing classical European away tactics of their own once more, Rangers absorbed the pressure and shortly after the restart they stunned Bayern and their supporters into silence. A swift counter-attack resulted in Rainer Zobel eventually heading into his own goal, after a strongly struck cross from Colin Stein. An unsympathetic and jubilant Johnston dropped to the turf to celebrate with a prone Zobel. In possession of an unexpected away goal and back on level terms, Rangers became increasingly stubborn in their resistance. Bayern couldn't find a way through, while Rangers continued to indulge in the type of sporadic counter-attacks that lent a nervousness to Bayern's defence.

Within 22 minutes of the start of the return game, Rangers had effectively sealed their place in the 1972 Cup Winners' Cup Final. If the way they had worked their way past Torino had been stunning, then their achievement against Bayern was astounding. Not only was this a Bayern side that was on the way to European club football's biggest prize, in a thrice-repeated manner, but six members of their team would go on to help West Germany to European Championship glory just two months later, in Belgium.

Opening the scoring in the very first minute of the game, via an almost floating effort from distance by Sandy

Jardine, Rangers' second goal was a scrappier, but no less celebrated, moment. A poor punch from a corner by Sepp Maier was resoundingly thundered home by Derek Parlane.

Having made loud, but unjustified, complaints about the validity of Rangers' second goal, Bayern began to argue amongst themselves for much of the remainder of the game. Despite the standing and clear talent of Udo Lattek's team, it turned out to be Rangers' most comfortable home game of their entire 1971/72 Cup Winners' Cup campaign.

Barcelona's Camp Nou and Dynamo Moscow awaited.

The first side from the Soviet Union to reach a major European final, Dynamo Moscow had required a penalty shoot-out to sneak past Dynamo Berlin in their semi-final. With the legendary Lev Yashin, as their spokesman and part of the coaching team, making a plea to local residents to turn out in favour of the Russians, it was clear that they had concerns for what might be an almost exclusively pro-Rangers atmosphere for the game.

Only three flights and around 400 Dynamo Moscow supporters made the trip to Barcelona from the Russian capital, whereas a minimum of 20,000 Rangers supporters undertook the trip from Glasgow, over land, air and sea. It was nothing short of an invasion. While the streets, bars and restaurants of the Catalan capital were packed, the stands of the Camp Nou were not. In a game that might have been better served taking place at the more bijou Sarría instead, the 24,701 in attendance for the final simply rattled around a stadium built to house 110,000 spectators.

In a game that took elements from both legs of Rangers' semi-final encounters with Bayern, the 1972 Cup Winners' Cup Final offered Waddell's team both periods of domination and a near-apocalyptic defensive rearguard action.

Repelling the initial onslaught of Dynamo Moscow's attacking intent with the type of strength of challenge that they had dispensed to Torino, Rangers eventually found their range. It was Stein who made the breakthrough, running on to a long ball from Smith and bearing down on goal, hitting it high into the Dynamo Moscow net midway through the first half.

Ushering in a spell of Rangers confidence and Dynamo Moscow hesitancy, Rangers won the game with a goal each side of the interval. Five minutes before half-time Smith was again instrumental, as his flighted ball into the penalty area was met by the head of Johnston for 2-0. Four minutes after the restart an enormous kick downfield by McCloy bounced perfectly for Johnston to again be the hero, collecting it with his right foot, cutting onto his left and setting himself up to coolly slot the ball into Vladimir Pilguy's bottom left-hand corner. Rangers' players, coaching team and supporters were incredulous at being 3-0 up with less than 50 minutes played.

Perhaps still in a daze, in a game that was akin to a Rangers home tie and maybe feeling that Dynamo Moscow were unlikely to mount a fightback, the Russians were allowed back into the picture on the hour mark. A loose pass from Willie Mathieson was seized upon, instigating a turn of events that led to a tap-in for Vladimir Eshtrekov who, as a substitute, had only been on the pitch for two minutes.

With half an hour still to play, Rangers became edgy, and Jardine almost contrived to score an own goal, forcing his goalkeeper into a fine, low stop. Three minutes from time, Rangers did concede again, however. With the Rangers defence guilty of ball-watching, Dynamo Moscow walked almost unchallenged into the Rangers penalty area, until Aleksandr Makhovikov was presented with the choice of either going down, in a bid to win a penalty, or shooting. Makhovikov hedged his bets. Falling theatrically backwards towards the turf, he swung his boot at the ball. His fall making it rise upwards, the ball crashed into the Rangers net off the underside of the bar.

Their team nervously navigating the final few minutes, when the whistle was blown to mark the end of the game, Rangers fans swarmed onto the pitch in celebration. It was an unprecedented show of public disorder as far as the Spanish authorities were concerned, and in a country still under the control of General Franco, the long-repressed Catalans in attendance watched on in awe at the lawlessness unfolding on their own pitch. The trophy was presented in the Rangers dressing room, rather than in front of their ecstatic supporters.

With overtones of Manchester City and the 1970 Cup Winners' Cup Final, all of this unfolded without live coverage of the game being transmitted in the United Kingdom because Scotland were playing Wales at Hampden Park on the same evening in the British Home Championship. Fearing a loss of revenue through the turnstiles, a Scottish club playing a major European final was only seen in the form of late-night highlights. You could, however, watch the game live in Ireland. As it turned out, there were more spectators in attendance at the Camp Nou for Rangers' game than there were at Hampden for the Scotland game.

Not without a heavy degree of fallout, the aftermath of the 1972 Cup Winners' Cup Final centred around demands from Dynamo Moscow for the game to be replayed. The pitch invasion that engulfed the playing area upon the final whistle hadn't been the only encroachment. Fans had made it onto the pitch to celebrate Rangers' opening goal, while a minute from time there was a mini-invasion when a whistle blown was erroneously construed to be the full-time whistle. According to Dynamo Moscow, this was a deliberate act designed to halt the momentum that they had built up. While UEFA refused to agree to a replaying of the game, Rangers were banned from European competition for two years, eventually reduced to one.

Controversy abounded once again the following year. This time it was Leeds United, and this time it was controversy within defeat. A 1-0 loss at the Kaftanzoglio Stadium in Thessaloniki against AC Milan, was shrouded in rancour, amidst allegations of bribery.

Denied three strong calls for a penalty, one of which was a blatant swiping of Mick Jones's legs from under him, they were decisions which made a mockery of the innocuous challenge that led to the awarding of the free kick from which Milan scored the only goal of the game.

Leeds had gone into the game as the underdogs, despite their standing as one of the big hitters of English football. Their opponents, coached by the legendary Nereo Rocco, were sitting atop Serie A with only one game to play. Meanwhile, an arduous season for Leeds had seen a title challenge drift after an Easter Monday loss at Liverpool, a pain added to by a shock defeat to Sunderland in the FA Cup Final.

Team selection was also an issue for the Leeds manager, Don Revie. Captain Billy Bremner and striker Allan Clarke were both suspended, while Johnny Giles and Eddie Gray were injured. It all meant that the odds were stacking up against the English team. In all likelihood Milan would have been too strong for Leeds, but in the absence of Karl-Heinz Schnellinger, the ageing yet still massively influential defender, legend has it that *I Rossoneri* were unwilling to take any chances.

Greece was not only hosting the 1973 Cup Winners' Cup Final, they also supplied the match referee, Christos Michas. Michas's performance in this game led to a subsequent UEFA investigation and he was banned for life.

Of those who congregated for the match, the clear majority booed and barracked the Milan players when they set off on their lap of honour with the trophy after the game, instead applauding and chanting for Leeds. Outside the ground, spectators continued their chants and protests, while the Greek press turned on the referee, with the newspaper *To Vima* claiming it was obvious to the 500,000 watching on television in Greece that the result was unfair. Being allotted a game of such weight was of great pride to the nation, yet one of their own referees had brought the event into disrepute.

Leeds have worn the scars of both the 1973 Cup Winners' Cup Final, and the 1975 European Cup Final defiantly ever since. Both games owned dubious calls that went against Leeds, in games they subsequently lost.

West Ham United might have reached the final just three years later, but Leeds' defeat in 1973 feels like it represents the end of that era of British domination in the Cup Winners' Cup. During the first 13 years of the tournament, nine finals had a British participant.

That sense of expectancy of a British participant began to ebb away after the 1973 final. West Ham reached the 1976 final despite a domestic capitulation, and it would be a further four years beyond that when Arsenal made it to the final. The Cup Winners' Cup suddenly stopped being a British-influenced tournament, until Aberdeen and Everton took matters into their own hands in the mid-1980s.

Baton passed, over the following years the Cup Winners' Cup became the preserve of mainland northern Europe and those behind the Iron Curtain, as opposed to a new domination from Serie A, despite Milan's questionable victory in 1973 and final appearance in 1974.

A solace to Leeds fans it may or not be, but Milan went on to fumble the 1972/73 Serie A title when they lost at Verona four days later, on the final day, opening the door for Juventus to take the *scudetto*.

Intriguingly, had the 1973 Cup Winners' Cup Final gone to a replay, something Revie was happy to countenance, then the suspended Bremner and Clarke were cleared to play and were already booked on a Thursday morning flight to Greece to meet up with the Leeds squad. They would have made Milan's task much harder in a theoretical replay, a game that would have taken place 48 hours after the original game, and less than 48 hours prior to their title-deciding game at Verona.

Milan have remained silent on the subject of the 1973 Cup Winners' Cup Final but the smoke still circulates to this very day.

Fiorentina win the inaugural European Cup Winners' Cup, in 1961. The original trophy was only presented once, before being replaced by the more familiar versions from the following season.

Jimmy Greaves on target for Tottenham Hotspur during the 1963 final, at De Kuip against the holders Atlético Madrid, where they became the first British team to win a major European trophy.

Sigfried Held strikes from distance for Borussia Dortmund, past Liverpool's Tommy Lawrence at a saturated Hampden Park, on their way to victory in the 1966 final.

Gerd Müller attempts to turn the ball into the Rangers net during the 1967 final. Bayern Munich prevailed in Nuremberg, but the Scottish side had a good goal disallowed.

Manchester City's Mike Summerbee takes issue with the Schalke goalkeeper at Maine Road during the semi-final, second leg.

Policemen pose with the trophy in the name of guarding it, during Chelsea's 1971 victory parade after their win against Real Madrid in the replayed final.

Rangers celebrate their 1972 victory over Dynamo Moscow, when they were presented with the trophy in the Camp Nou dressing room, after the pitch was invaded by supporters.

The 1973 final was shrouded with controversy. Leeds United's Norman Hunter isn't the only transfixed observer, after he was sent off against AC Milan.

Magdeburg's Jürgen Sparwasser and Manfred Zapf lift the trophy after their deserved victory over Giovanni Trapattoni's AC Milan, at De Kuip, in 1974.

West Ham United's Pat Holland and Trevor Brooking drinking champagne, after defeating Eintracht Frankfurt in the 1976 semi-finals. Their European form flew in the face of a domestic capitulation.

Anderlecht's Rob Rensenbrink receives treatment, allowing West Ham a short respite during the 1976 final. Rensenbrink and François Van der Elst were at their devastating best in Brussels.

Georg Volkert and Rudolf Kargus parade the trophy in front of Hamburger SV supporters, in Amsterdam, after they beat the holders Anderlecht, in the 1977 final.

A train driver stops to watch some of the 1979 final, at the St Jakob Stadium in Basel between Barcelona and Fortuna Düsseldorf.

Klaus Allofs grabs a rapid equaliser for Fortuna Düsseldorf, with less than 10 minutes played of the 1979 final against Barcelona. The Hans Krankl inspired Barcelona eventually ran out 4-3 winners.

The Valencia team celebrate their 1980 victory over Arsenal, a final dominated by the excellence of two goalkeepers. Arsenal didn't lose a single game, in regulation time, despite missing out on glory.

The classic 'crack eastern European outfit', David Kipiani breezes past Carl Zeiss Jena's Gerd Brauer and Andreas Krause, as Dinamo Tbilisi claim their one major European trophy, in 1981.

*Allan Simonsen scores Barcelona's equaliser, in first half stoppage time, during the
1982 final at the Camp Nou, against Standard Liège. Within months, he was a
Charlton Athletic player.*

*John Hewitt wheels away to celebrate his clinching extra time winner for
Aberdeen, against Real Madrid, in a waterlogged Gothenburg at the 1983 final.
It was the first British success since 1972.*

Zbigniew Boniek makes his own luck to guide in the winning goal against FC Porto, in the 1984 final. Alongside the ultimately unfulfilled talent of Beniamino Vignola, they were the stars of the show.

Everton's Andy Gray in predatory pose as Rapid Vienna's nervous defence fear the worst during a one-sided 1985 final. How they might have fared in the 1985/86 European Cup is one of football's great what ifs.

Oleksandr Zavarov scores the opening goal in the 1986 final against Atlético Madrid. Dynamo Kyiv also won the tournament in 1975. Valeriy Lobanovskyi coached them on both occasions, while Oleh Blokhin played in both.

Marco van Basten and Frank Baum, the respective captains of Ajax and Lokomotive Leipzig, pensively await the outcome of the toss of the coin, to determine the kick-off at the 1987 final.

The peak of a meteoric rise, Rotterdam born Piet den Boer scores the winner for K.V. Mechelen in the 1988 final, against the holders Ajax. Mechelen were led by the former Ajax coach, Aad De Mos.

One of his last duties in a Barcelona shirt, Gary Lineker lifts the trophy after the Catalans defeat the rising Sampdoria in the 1989 final. Johan Cruyff adds to his 1987 success, when he was at the helm of Ajax.

Gianluca Pagliuca and Luca Pellegrini are ecstatic after Gianluca Vialli scores Sampdoria's second goal of the 1990 final, against Anderlecht.

Manchester United and Barcelona players prior to the 1991 final at De Kuip. In the first season of the return to European competition of English teams, after the ban in the wake of the Heysel Disaster, United's success was particularly impressive.

Wynton Rufer shares Werder Bremen's success in the 1992 final with the supporters, at the Estádio da Luz. It was Germany's first major European trophy since the reunification of east and west.

Alessandro Melli puts Parma back in front, against Royal Antwerp at Wembley in the 1993 final. The sparsely populated stadium did the event no favours, but Parma's football was wonderful.

David Seaman with the trophy after Arsenal defeated Parma in the 1994 final, in Copenhagen. Without the services of Ian Wright and up against a star-studded opposition, Arsenal defied expectations to win.

From pleasure to pain, David Seaman is caught out in iconic circumstances, by Nayim's late and outlandishly brilliant effort, which won the 1995 final for a talented Real Zaragoza, in Paris.

Bobby Robson and Ronaldo with the trophy after Barcelona defeated Paris Saint-Germain in the 1997 final. Their fourth success in the tournament, it was also the very last game they played in the Cup Winners' Cup.

Still Paris Saint-Germain's one and only major European success, Bernard Lama rides the shoulders of his team-mates and lifts the trophy into the Brussels night sky, after they beat Rapid Vienna in the 1996 final.

Gianfranco Zola scores the only goal of the 1998 final for Chelsea, just seconds after entering the fray as a second half substitute against VfB Stuttgart, in Stockholm. It came 27 years after first success in the tournament.

A special group photo containing a winner from all 39 teams to have won the tournament, to help mark the last Cup Winners' Cup Final, at Villa Park in 1999.

Lazio and Real Mallorca players walk out for the very last Cup Winners' Cup Final, in Birmingham. Pavel Nedvěd scored the winning goal for Lazio, the very last goal to be scored in the tournament.

Chapter Six

Forza Italia

CONSIDERING ITALY supplied the very first and very last winners of the European Cup Winner's Cup and, given that only English clubs won the tournament more times than Italian clubs, it seems ludicrous to suggest that Serie A underachieved in UEFA's second-born competition.

They kind of did though. Fast out of the blocks with Fiorentina in 1961, and Lazio being late to the party in 1999, it meant that over a 37-year stretch, the Cup Winners' Cup was *only* won by Italian teams five times.

During the heyday of the Cup Winners' Cup – between the sun setting on the 1960s and the bright new dawn of the 1990s – there were only two Italian successes, one of those being AC Milan's contentious win against Leeds United in 1973.

Consider also that Juventus won the competition only once and Inter Milan not at all, and the Cup Winners' Cup and Italy made for unusual bedfellows.

This, in part, was down to the way the Coppa Italia was viewed by the great and the good of Serie A. The *scudetto* and Europe have always been gods in this respect, and the Coppa Italia has too often been nothing more than an afterthought, a consolation, or even an irritation for some. Yet other nations managed to get over their ambivalence towards their own domestic cup competitions, to embrace the Cup Winners' Cup beyond.

Fiorentina were, of course, history makers, as the first winners and the first Italian beaten finalists. Fuelled by the goals of Gabriel Batistuta, they later rolled back the years in 1996/97, when they again made the semi-finals, where Bobby Robson's Barcelona would prove too strong for them.

Over the course of the last decade of the existence of the Cup Winners' Cup, Sampdoria, Parma and Lazio managed to up the Italian ratio of wins. In between, there were the grey areas of AC Milan's runs to the final in 1973 and 1974.

There was another Milan ingredient, however, and it bore striking similarities to the success Juventus enjoyed, in 1984. When AC Milan won the Cup Winners' Cup in 1968, they used it as a stepping stone to go on and win the European Cup the following year. A feat that Juventus also completed in 1984 and 1985.

Their first Cup Winners' Cup campaign, AC Milan's 1967/68 success was an integral element in their rise from a mild mid-1960s rut. Having lost to Real Madrid in the 1958 European Cup Final, and then going on to win the tournament in 1963, and with continuing domestic consistency, the 1965/66 and 1966/67 Serie A campaigns were uncharacteristically under par for them.

Catalyst to AC Milan's revival was Kurt Hamrin, the ageing Swedish international who was signed from Fiorentina, at which he had been part of their 1961 Cup Winners' Cup glory, and their run to the 1962 final as holders.

Teaming up in a forward line with the prolific Pierino Prati, and with the excellent support play of Angelo Sormani, Hamrin proved to be the missing piece of the puzzle. Supplied by the eternal talents of Gianni Rivera, kept secure by the midfield discipline of Giovanni Lodetti backed up by the defensive solidity of Karl-Heinz Schnellinger, Angelo Anquilletti, Roberto Rosato, Saul Malatrasi and a certain Giovanni Trapattoni, even when opposing strikers did manage to bear down on goal, they still had to find a way past Fabio Cudicini, the father of future Chelsea and Tottenham Hotspur goalkeeper, Carlo.

At De Kuip, in Rotterdam, at the 1968 Cup Winners' Cup Final, AC Milan were without the services of Malatrasi, however, instead forced to call upon the inexperienced Nevio Scala. Scala would only play 11 league games for them, before setting off on a nomadic playing career that would eventually see him pass through the club once again, during the 1975/76 season, after spells with Vicenza, Fiorentina and Inter Milan.

Scala would later go on to lead Parma to the 1993 and 1994 finals, joining his 1968 team-mate Trapattoni, in going from Cup Winners' Cup-winning player, to Cup Winners' Cup-winning coach.

As impressive as they would be at the business end of their run to success, AC Milan's path to the final wasn't without its obstacles. While Levski Sofia were easily brushed aside in the first round, both Vasas ETO Győr in the second round, and Standard Liège in the quarter-finals, gave Nereo Rocco plenty of headaches. AC Milan edged past the former on away goals, while the latter required a replay.

In the semi-final, AC Milan were handed a task to focus the senses, however, as they were drawn together with the holders, Bayern Munich. An all-West German final a distinct possibility, with Hamburger SV in the other semi-final, AC Milan were on a mission to stop that happening.

A packed San Siro played host to the first leg and, after a goalless first half, AC Milan emerged with renewed determination. Within six minutes of the restart *I Rossoneri* had their lead, procured in controversial circumstances when Sormani challenged Sepp Maier for the ball just as he was bouncing it inside his own six-yard box. As the television camera panned away towards the halfway line for the expected clearance from Maier, there was a sudden roar of approval from the home support, and an irate Bayern goalkeeper chasing upfield to remonstrate with Sormani, the referee, his own team-mates, and anybody who would listen to him.

In an environment where you weren't generally allowed to challenge the goalkeeper, Sormani's actions provoked the anger of the usually mild-mannered Maier, who had to be restrained from attacking the AC Milan goalscorer by Gustav Jung and Dieter Brenninger.

Amidst it all, the referee, Salvador Garcia, appeared to push over a protesting Rainer Ohlhauser, following that with a heated round of shouting and finger-jabbing with the Bayern coach, Zlatko Čajkovski. It was a hypnotic passage of something that looked like football, yet wasn't quite football.

Maier and Sormani would continue their war of words throughout the remainder of the game with Maier, at times, making exaggerated motions when in possession of the ball, and Bayern players increasingly encroaching upon Cudicini in the hope of exploiting the precedent which had been set. The message was that if a goal like that was good for AC Milan, then it was good for Bayern.

A wonderful finish from Prati made it 2-0. In a vaguely similar way to how the Bayern players would turn on one another against Rangers four years later, on this occasion the sense of injustice that the Bayern players felt seemed to blunt them during a second leg when there was still all to play for. A goalless draw and an Italian masterclass in containment saw Rocco's team into the Rotterdam final.

De Kuip, blessed with a far healthier crowd than would be present at the same stadium for the 1974 final, between AC Milan and Magdeburg, was the ideal setting for AC Milan's undisputedly greatest Cup Winners' Cup moment.

As a contest, the 1968 Cup Winners' Cup Final was over before it had really begun. There was only three minutes on the clock when Hamrin opened the scoring. A beautifully worked move that caught Hamburger SV cold, it was a goal that was at odds with the cagey stereotype of Italian teams. It was a goal of ruthless simplicity.

Just short of the 20-minute mark, Hamrin scored again. Collecting a throw-in from Anquilletti, he turned and headed for the Hamburger SV penalty area. Swerving past two uncompromising challenges, he slalomed to within shooting distance before striking the ball low and hard at Arkoç Özcan; it crept beneath the former Turkish international goalkeeper and over the line. This came just seconds after AC Milan had been denied a blatant penalty. Ironic, given Leeds' inability to be awarded a glut of penalties in the 1973 final. There might have been 70 minutes remaining, but there was no realistic way back into the game for Hamburger SV. Before the half-time whistle was blown, Sormani came close twice, while Hamrin should have completed his hat-trick.

It wasn't until the second half that Hamburger SV started to come into the game. Uwe Seeler, their biggest threat, and their captain, began to turn the tide when he created their best opportunity for Willi Schulz, which Cudicini did well to stop.

As the second half wore on, Cudicini was again left with an awkward save to make, this time from Seeler himself, when a shot from distance bounced right in front of the AC Milan goalkeeper, as he dropped to make the stop.

With Hamburger SV committing numbers going forward, they eventually started to leave exploitable gaps at the back. Hamrin came close with another attempt to complete his hat-trick, allowing self-interest to cloud his judgement perhaps, as Sormani was clearly visible and better placed; yet Hamrin kept hold of the ball and opted to go for goal.

Given a bumpier ride than had ever seemed possible in the 20th minute, AC Milan were relieved to hear the final whistle. A season in which they were Serie A's runaway champions, the 1968 Cup Winners' Cup Final was the perfect dress rehearsal for winning the 1969 European Cup in which they dismantled Rinus Michels's blossoming Ajax.

Maintaining a high stake in domestic matters, outside the confines of Serie A, AC Milan began to drift after their European glories of 1968 and 1969. Beyond their runs to the 1973 and 1974 Cup Winners' Cup finals, it would be a decade and a half before they again reached one of UEFA's showpiece events.

AC Milan's relationship with the Cup Winners' Cup was a peculiar one. After the 1974 final loss to Magdeburg, they would return to the tournament on only one more occasion, when they suffered an early exit during the 1977/78 campaign, to Real Betis. Their victory in 1968 worked as a springboard to greater glory in 1969, while their success in 1973 was dipped in high controversy. In 1974 it almost felt like karma was paying them a visit for a word or two about the wrongs of the previous year.

A decade beyond AC Milan's last Cup Winners' Cup Final, Juventus would reach their one and only Cup Winners' Cup Final. *I Bianconeri* would only play in the competition four times but each would be memorable. They would always be involved in a stellar showdown.

In 1965/66 Juventus failed to go beyond the first round, bowing out to Liverpool after erring on the side of caution in the first leg at the Stadio Comunale. Taking only a 1-0 lead to Anfield for the second leg, Liverpool won a wonderfully attacking game 2-0 in which early goals from Chris Lawler and Geoff Strong forced Juventus from their defensive cocoon in an attempt to chase a game that had gotten away from them.

Estranged from the tournament until 1979/80, Juventus came to within two minutes of reaching the 1980 Cup

Winners' Cup Final. In the semi-final, with an away goal in their favour and the second-leg score holding firm at 0-0, Arsenal stunned the Stadio Comunale when Paul Vaessen headed in a late winning goal after a burst of speed and skill from Graham Rix.

Juventus's last showing in the Cup Winners' Cup was in 1990/91 when they again made the semi-finals. In a blockbuster encounter with Barcelona, Juventus had appeared to be in control at the Camp Nou during the first leg. Pierluigi Casiraghi, against the run of play, had taken advantage of a defensive error to put Juve ahead.

This being Johan Cruyff's Barcelona however, a 20-minute second-half spell saw the home side score three times – two for Hristo Stoichkov and a spectacular goal from Ion Andoni Goikoetxea. It was an evening when Michael Laudrup was on a mission to show his former club exactly what he was capable of; yet it was one in which Juventus threw themselves forward when emboldened by scoring against the run of play.

In the return game at the Stadio delle Alpi, it was essentially Juventus versus Andoni Zubizarreta, as chance after chance presented itself to the home side. The most amazing aspect of the game was that it was an hour until Juventus broke through, when Roberto Baggio curled in a devilishly handsome free kick.

Try as they might, however, Juventus couldn't breach the Barcelona goal line a second time, the closest they came being when Toto Schillaci threw himself at a ball played across the six-yard box, missing it by millimetres, in a similar way to how Paul Gascoigne would come so close to scoring against Germany, in the Euro 96 semi-finals.

Two jaw-dropping games, witnessed by an aggregate attendance of almost 175,000 spectators, the Juventus–Barcelona semi-final in 1991 was one of the biggest head-to-head clashes the Cup Winners' Cup ever produced. They might have gone out at the semi-final stage but Juventus said farewell to the tournament in style.

Sitting between their semi-final losses of 1980 and 1991, however, came Juventus's 1984 success in the tournament. A year beyond their shock defeat in the 1983 European Cup Final and a year before the tragedy of the 1985 European Cup Final, the 1984 Cup Winners' Cup Final was arguably Juventus at their very best.

Amongst others, Juventus could boast the presence of Michel Platini at his peak, the goals of Paolo Rossi, the speed and skill of Zbigniew Boniek, the drive of Marco Tardelli, the defensive steel of Gaetano Scirea and Antonio Cabrini, and the immortal brutality of Claudio Gentile. A frightening prospect, Juventus had seemed invincible until Hamburger SV defeated them, in Athens, on what was meant to be a European Cup-winning farewell for both Dino Zoff and Roberto Bettega.

In their 1983/84 response, Juventus had a heavy degree of frustration to take out on Europe, along with the task of reclaiming the Serie A title from a troublesome and talented AS Roma. They were made to work hard for them, but Juventus successfully achieved both these targets.

Fending off Roma by just two points for the *scudetto*, in the Cup Winners' Cup Juventus steamrollered Lechia Gdansk 10-2 on aggregate, Boniek scoring the winning goal on his return to Poland in a tighter second leg, after

I Bianconeri had been in an imperious mood during a 7-0 first-leg victory.

Paris Saint-Germain offered Juventus a sterner second-round test. Not much more than a decade old, a club of convenience yet gaining in potency with each passing season, PSG were just two seasons away from their first French First Division title. They won their first major trophy in 1982 when they lifted the Coupe de France, retaining it the following year.

Just their second European campaign, PSG were learning fast. The French side took the lead thanks to Stefano Tacconi coming for a wonderful looping cross, only to collide with his own defenders, presenting Alain Couriol with the simplest of headers to make it 1-0.

Juventus were kept out until the 62nd minute when a perhaps overconfident PSG began to sleepwalk. A turn of speed, a swift one-two with Rossi, and Boniek was in on goal, where he clipped a clever finish beyond Dominique Baratelli and the legs of the despairing PSG defenders, lunging in the hope of making an interception.

Boniek celebrated his equaliser by skidding across the Parc des Princes turf towards the corner flag, and he would again be the key to Juventus taking the lead 14 minutes later. With a free kick to the left-hand side of the PSG penalty area and close to the touchline, Boniek weighted what seemed a medium-paced delivery towards the edge of the six-yard box. Meeting it almost in line with the back post was the head of Cabrini. Planted downwards, the ball bounced up for Baratelli to get a hand to it, only managing to push it onto his left-hand post from where it ricocheted into the PSG net. The keeper did well to get a hand to it at all; yet once he had, he probably should have kept it out.

Having come from behind, Juventus were once again undone by a looping cross into their penalty area. A scrappy exchange of attempted clearances eventually fell to the PSG substitute, Michel N'Gom, who blasted the ball home between the outstretched glove of Tacconi and his left-hand upright.

It was a goal that came in the 90th minute, levelling the score at 2-2, and it set up a massively anticipated second leg at the Stadio Comunale.

Embossed by a 0-0 scoreline, the result of the second leg doesn't do the game the historical justice it deserves. Just as open and as generous in attacking spirit as the first game had been, it was far from the dull goalless defensive blanket that is so stereotypical of Italian teams, when in possession of even the slenderest of advantages.

Ambling past FC Haka a little too sedately, it was two 1-0s that took Juventus into the semi-finals of the 1984 Cup Winners' Cup. The Serie A champions-elect had even had to wait for a 90th-minute winner during the first leg, a game that had been switched to Strasbourg so as to avoid the sub-zero temperatures of Finland in March.

If Juventus had been handed a quarter-final tie that left Trapattoni uncertain of how much velocity was needed to best approach it, then he was under no illusions as to the levels of focus his team required for the semi-finals. Manchester United lay in wait. Played out amidst another electric atmosphere, Juventus stunned the home support when Rossi scored via a massive deflection off Graeme Hogg, with only 14 minutes on the clock.

From there, Juventus were forced on to the back foot as their hosts launched wave upon wave of attacks. Alan Davies, on as an early substitute for John Gidman, netted the equaliser ten minutes before half-time with a goal that had a hint of handball during the frenetic build-up. It was Davies's first appearance since playing in the 1983 FA Cup Final replay.

The pace of the game unremitting, Frank Stapleton later struck an effort against the underside of the crossbar, while Boniek was struck on the head while waiting to take a corner, by a missile thrown from the crowd.

It had been as good a result as Ron Atkinson could have perhaps hoped for prior to the game. Shorn of the services of Ray Wilkins due to suspension, and without both Arnold Mühren and Bryan Robson through injury, it had been a makeshift line-up and formation that Manchester United had been forced to field.

A fortnight later in Turin, another game of immense drama took place between the two teams. Manchester United, once again able to call upon Wilkins, were still without Mühren and Robson. Juventus, fast, fluid and flowing, really shouldn't have had to rely upon such a late winning goal as the one they claimed in the 88th minute.

Boniek was again the generator, opening the scoring in the 13th minute with a lovely dink over the advancing Gary Bailey, having brushed off the determined attempts of Hogg. Despite conceding the goal, Bailey would produce one of his finest performances that evening at the Stadio Comunale.

Chief tormentor Boniek twisted Mike Duxbury inside out not long after opening the scoring, setting up a headed opportunity for Rossi that was deflected wide off Hogg's arm. A sort of 'Hand of Hogg' incident, it was one of those calls that could have easily been given as a penalty rather than the corner it resulted in.

For as long as the game was poised at 1-0, it always meant there was a chance that Manchester United could draw themselves back into the picture. While the loss of Stapleton was a blow, his substitute, Norman Whiteside, added a new threat. As the second half wore on, the visitors continued to absorb the pressure that Juventus were applying, tempering this with increasing counter-attacks.

Rossi was denied yet again by Bailey in a fascinating duel between striker and goalkeeper, after Mark Hughes had headed just over the crossbar a few minutes earlier. Understandably second best for most of the second leg, when Whiteside scored United's equaliser it was laced with good fortune.

Pushed into midfield, Paul McGrath was excellent over the course of both games, but at the Stadio Comunale he was completely unwitting in the way in which he set up the goal for Whiteside. Inside the Juventus penalty area, McGrath was twisting and turning, heading away from goal, when the ball broke to Whiteside for him to thunder it past Tacconi. With the tie level, the final 20 minutes were beset by nervous exhaustion for both teams. Bailey continued to perform heroics, saving at the feet of the marauding Boniek, while Tacconi was called upon more and more often.

When Juventus's winning goal arrived, it was Rossi again who swooped and, just as at Old Trafford, he benefitted from a huge deflection. This time the ball bounced off

Boniek, breaking to him with the goal at his mercy. Extra time had been within touching distance for Atkinson's men, but Rossi was clinical in his finish.

Basel's St Jakob Stadium was once again the venue of a Cup Winners' Cup Final, as FC Porto stood between Juventus and a third major European title. Upon the eve of their own glories, the Portuguese side were a significant last hurdle to clear.

A game beset by goalkeeping misadventure, all three goals could have been dealt with better. The opener was scored by Beniamino Vignola, a mirage of an attacking midfielder whose talent was often compared to the legendary Gianni Rivera, yet would never truly fulfil his undoubted potential. His performance in the 1984 Cup Winners' Cup Final was so dominant that he was widely expected to ascend to greatness in the famous black and white stripes; yet within 12 months he was being sent for a year back at Verona, where his career had started. By 1988/89, he was playing in a relegation campaign with Empoli, in Serie B.

It was a wonderful strike with which Vignola gave Juventus a 12th-minute lead. Collecting a through ball from Michel Platini around 45 yards from goal, he turned and carried it to the edge of the Porto penalty area. Travelling diagonally, he was closely shadowed by three defenders and when the left-footed shot came, it took the Porto goalkeeper, Zé Beto, who had edged across to secure his near post, completely by surprise. This, however, left an open target at the far post which Vignola was precise enough to hit, leaving Zé Beto motionless. Porto's equaliser wasn't long in coming. Just short of the half-hour mark, António Sousa hit a first-time effort which was hard and fast, yet also seemingly well covered by Tacconi. A combination of the ball dipping and Tacconi misjudging the flight meant that when it bounced off his six-yard line, the ball flew over the top of the sprawling goalkeeper. As with Vignola's goal, Sousa's also had the element of surprise, yet both were entirely stoppable.

During the last five minutes of the first half was when the outcome of the 1984 Cup Winners' Cup Final was decided. Again it was dictated by Vignola, again it was shaded by the actions of the two goalkeepers, and again Boniek proved to be the decisive hero. Calmly collecting a loose ball, roughly in the same spot as he had received it when setting off on his run to score the opening goal of the game, and having the presence of mind to skip out of the way of the immediate challenge to buy himself a little time to assess what was ahead of him, Vignola played the perfect lofted pass for Boniek to almost fall into. Under pressure from a Porto defender and with Zé Beto making an ill-advised dash from his line, Boniek collided with the ball taking it beyond the falling defender and wide of the goalkeeper. Dropping for him just right, Boniek was able to guide it into the unguarded net, before tumbling to the ground. Despite Porto protests, there was nothing Juventus were guilty of, apart from opportunism. Had Zé Beto stayed in his six-yard box he would have had an easy ball to scoop up.

Late as Juventus's second goal had been, Porto still had another excellent chance before the half-time whistle. Tacconi, however, made a wonderful double save, more than making up for his part in Sousa's equaliser.

Having reclaimed the lead, Juventus opted for containment during the second half. Dropping deep, they allowed Porto most of the ball, relying on the occasional counter-attack to relieve the increasing pressure. Despite their dominance, Porto could not find a way through. Trapattoni, having lost the 1974 final while in temporary charge of AC Milan, finally had his hands on the Cup Winners' Cup as a coach with Juventus. He had previously won the competition as an AC Milan player in 1968.

As with that AC Milan side in 1968, a year later Trapattoni was contesting a European Cup Final with Juventus. It was, of course, the ill-fated 1985 final, at the crumbling Heysel Stadium, where 39 spectators of varying nationalities, yet predominantly Italians, died in a horrific crush caused by rioting between both Liverpool and Juventus followers.

It was a disaster and tragedy that cast an indelible shadow across an era where *I Bianconeri* finally obtained the type of European glory they had so often been denied. No matter what domestic supremacy Juventus have enjoyed from generation to generation, their endeavours in Europe have usually met with frustration, certainly when compared to AC Milan's. That shadow which creeps across 1985 also shades 1984 in some ways. It is hard not to associate the two.

In a tournament which is frozen in time, the carefree, stylish, stubborn and arguably fortunate nature with which Juventus won the 1984 Cup Winners' Cup Final is one of the most evocative of all. It is impossible for me to watch the mildly grainy footage of the game without wondering how many of the 39 who didn't return home from the Heysel a year later were celebrating their team's success in Basel.

This is accentuated by the fact that Juventus, indeed, only competed in the Cup Winners' Cup in one further campaign. Although that run to the 1991 semi-final was powered by Roberto Baggio, it is their successes in the 1993 UEFA Cup, and 1996 Champions League – added to by reaching the final again in 1997 and 1998 – that defines the 1990s for Juventus.

All of this is, of course, aided by Sampdoria's achievements in reaching both the 1989 and 1990 Cup Winners' Cup finals. Juventus's run in 1991 is thus shielded for a multitude of reasons.

Beaten in Bern by Barcelona in the 1989 final, Sampdoria's run had been a meandering and vaguely unconvincing one. Reliant upon the away-goals rule to see themselves past IFK Norrköping in the first round, and Dinamo Bucharest in the quarter-finals, Vujadin Boškov's men also saw off our old friends Carl Zeiss Jena in the second round, and Mechelen in the semi-finals.

Contriving not to win at all on their travels, a trend that continued with their 2-0 defeat to Barcelona in the final, Sampdoria made it to Bern on the back of winning just three games. Blessed by being drawn to play the home leg second, in every round, the gods seemed to be smiling on Boškov and his men.

However, while the order of games was heaven sent, the teams they played weren't quite as easy as they appear. Dinamo Bucharest had reached the semi-finals of the European Cup in 1984, where their two games against Liverpool had been volatile affairs, laced with a broken jaw and angry police dogs, while Mechelen were the holders of the Cup Winners' Cup.

Added to this, Sampdoria played their first three home games away from the Stadio Luigi Ferraris, due to the renovations being made in preparation of the 1990 World Cup finals. Instead, they played those games at the Stadio Giovanni Zini, the home of Cremonese, some 115 miles from Genoa. It wasn't until the semi-final second leg that Sampdoria were able to enjoy the comforts of home.

Outclassed in the 1989 final by a more worldly-wise Barcelona, their 1988/89 Cup Winners' Cup campaign was only Sampdoria's second foray into European competition, having gone out of the same tournament in the second round in 1985/86. Despite the disappointment of losing the 1989 final, it acted as the perfect breeding ground to not only go on to win the 1990 Cup Winners' Cup Final, but also to reach the 1992 European Cup Final; a four-season peak that they had neither previously intimated they were capable of nor have since threatened to repeat.

Sampdoria were much more potent during their run to the 1990 final. Lessons learnt, they arrived at the Ullevi, in Gothenburg, unbeaten. They had also embraced the need to extend themselves when playing away from home. They won at Brann in the first round, and in Zürich, against Grasshopper in the quarter-finals, picking off crucial draws at Borussia Dortmund in the second round and AS Monaco in the semi-finals.

Gianluca Vialli was in rampant form, emerging from the tournament with seven goals. The last two of these settled the outcome of the final, while he also struck both Sampdoria's goals in Monte Carlo in the semi-final first leg.

Boškov, so often the runner-up, was finally the victor, although it still took extra time to get his team over the line in the 1990 final against an Anderlecht side that was looking to turn back the clock to their late 1970s Cup Winners' Cup glory days.

It was a game that had no right to drift into extra time, so one-sided was the Sampdoria performance. With desperate saves, goal-line clearances and defensive scrambles, Anderlecht defied their opponent's superiority to keep them out until the 105th minute, with Filip de Wilde in inspired form in goal for the Belgians.

Even in breaking the deadlock, however, Anderlecht almost thwarted Sampdoria, as De Wilde touched the initial shot on to his post, nearly reclaiming the ball as it bounced back to him, while prone on the turf. The loose ball was fair game but Vialli still had to make contact with the goalkeeper to bundle it over the line. Perfectly within the laws of the game, it was also a goal that could have easily been disallowed by a stricter referee.

It was past an exhausted Anderlecht defence that Vialli headed for the clinching second goal. A completely dominant performance that could easily have seen Sampdoria double, or even triple, their haul of goals.

It wasn't all about Vialli either. This was a win that galvanised a Sampdoria team that would go on to win the Serie A title in 1990/91. Partnered by Roberto Mancini, captained by Luca Pellegrini, their play generated by the midfield skill and determination of Giuseppe Dossena, Srečko Katanec and Attilio Lombardo, and protected in goal and defence by Gianluca Pagliuca, Moreno Mannini and Pietro Vierchowod, this was a beautifully designed and balanced Sampdoria side. This was Boškov at his most hypnotic.

With an eye on the Serie A title, Sampdoria slipped out of the 1990/91 Cup Winners' Cup in the quarter-finals to Legia Warsaw. The curse of the holders striking yet again. However, in winning it in 1990, Sampdoria became the second – and last – team to come back and lift the Cup Winners' Cup, a year after losing the final. Ironically, the team they beat in Gothenburg, Anderlecht, were the other to achieve that feat.

Sampdoria weren't the last Italian team to win the tournament, yet the success of Parma in 1993, at an under-populated Wembley Stadium, arguably marked the start line for the sprint finish to the demise of the Cup Winners' Cup, while Lazio's success in 1999 literally marked the very end.

Italy's relationship with the Cup Winners' Cup was a complex one. The second most successful nation in the history of the tournament, yet largely absent at the business end of it, at least during its core years throughout the 1970s and 1980s. Evading the clutches of Inter Milan, won once by Juventus, a success that falls within the long shadow of Heysel, AC Milan's perceived sleight of hand, Fiorentina's early association that never really grew, Sampdoria's use of the tournament as a springboard to their finest Serie A title-winning hour and the late moves of Parma and Lazio, Italian endeavour in the Cup Winners' Cup was predictably tinged with drama and pathos. Yet, also, as often seems to be the case when it comes to the home of Calcio, there was an overriding sense of them offering all, or nothing.

Chapter Seven

Robbie and the Purple and Whites, Plus Other Adventures Through the Low Countries

ROB RENSENBRINK came to within the width of a goalpost of true footballing immortality when he prodded a ball towards the unguarded Argentina net, from an angle, with only seconds remaining in the 1978 World Cup Final, with the score finely poised at 1-1. An inch or so to the right and Rensenbrink wouldn't only have scored the winning goal in the 1978 World Cup Final, he would have taken the golden boot with it too. Instead, Mario Kempes was the man who wrote his name into World Cup folklore, during extra time.

Eight and a half weeks prior to the World Cup Final, Rensenbrink had starred in his third successive European

Cup Winners' Cup Final. He had given a masterclass of a performance as Anderlecht reclaimed the trophy they had carelessly relinquished in the 1977 final to Hamburger SV.

Added to their victory over West Ham United, in the 1976 final, Anderlecht are the proud owners of a few pieces of Cup Winners' Cup history. They are the only team to have reached three successive finals; they were the first team to win a Cup Winners' Cup Final a year after losing at the same stage. Anderlecht are steeped in the history of the tournament.

Beaten in the 1970 Inter-Cities Fairs Cup Final by Arsenal, their victory over West Ham in Brussels had been a belated first European club success both for Anderlecht and Belgian teams in general.

Led to that first success by the controversial Hans Croon, a man who walked away from football at the age of 46 to join the Bahgwan movement, where he embraced the name Shunyam Avyakul, only to die two years later through injuries he sustained in a car crash. Croon was later outed for persuading some of the players under his control at VVV-Venlo to take performance-enhancing drugs.

When you consider Croon alongside Raymond Goethals leading Anderlecht to the 1977 and 1978 Cup Winners' Cup finals, the latter a man whose ethics were later called into question at Standard Liège, a man who was the head coach of Olympique Marseille when their 1993 bribery scandal erupted – albeit the charges were levelled at Bernard Tapie rather than Goethals – an understandable aura of surreptitiousness follows the history of Anderlecht. This is, of course, given added shade by the now uncontested charges of match-fixing during the

1984 UEFA Cup semi-final second leg between Anderlecht and Nottingham Forest.

Yet, none of the wrongdoings embossed on the CVs of Croon and Goethals were ever in relation to their Anderlecht dealings.

Despite the questionable side of Anderlecht, it is impossible for me to resist the allure of Rensenbrink, Haan and Van der Elst, hypnotic and resplendent as they were in that all-white strip with the three stripes of Adidas down the sleeves.

Fast, elegant, stylish, clinical and cool under pressure. So often excellent against their peers, dangerous against those seen as superior, Anderlecht could also be stubborn when they needed to be. When faced with Wrexham in the 1976 quarter-finals for instance, it took a strong constitution to navigate a way past a team playing in the Third Division of the English Football League, a team infused with the enthusiasm and hard-work ethos of a set of players who had been presented with the biggest games of their entire careers.

A year later, once again in the quarter-finals, Anderlecht faced a similar task against Second Division Southampton. Although Southampton could boast players of a higher calibre than Wrexham, inclusive of a strike partnership of Mick Channon and Peter Osgood, they were still a team struggling to escape the confines of the second tier of English football.

Southampton would end the 1976/77 season in ninth position, behind the likes of Blackpool, Luton Town, Charlton Athletic and Notts County; yet, on a mud bath of a pitch at The Dell, in the quarter-final second leg, they came to within a short few minutes of forcing the tie into extra time.

Anderlecht had won the first leg 2-0, on an evening in Brussels when Southampton had by no means played within themselves. With Goethals's men taking no heed of those warnings of a latent threat from the surprise FA Cup winners, Southampton launched a classic second-leg ambush of their opponents.

While it took the Saints an hour to break through, it was a goal that had been coming; Southampton having applied enough pressure on Anderlecht to see a first-half goal disallowed and a compelling shout for a second-half penalty waved away. When the first goal came it was a case of second time lucky, with a penalty finally being awarded and dispatched by David Peach. This was added to in the 78th minute, when the marauding Peach swung in the cross that Jim McCalliog eventually bundled over the line, after Channon had failed to make contact.

On the very same evening that Liverpool were completing their legendary European Cup quarter-final comeback against Saint-Étienne, Southampton were in with a fantastic chance of matching them at The Dell.

Maybe showing a little too much bravery in going for the winning goal within the 90 minutes, Southampton were caught on the break. Van der Elst was the hero yet again for Anderlecht; twisting and turning his way towards the Southampton penalty area, he evaded two challenges and rolled the ball into the bottom right-hand corner of Peter Wells's net.

It was exactly the type of fortitude that complemented Anderlecht's silken side perfectly. It is artistry to be able to weld bohemian styling to fighting spirit, yet this is what both Croon and Goethals managed to do, and it was a combination that was once again required in the semi-finals against Napoli.

A 1-0 first-leg defeat at the Stadio San Paolo in Naples came via a goal that was conceded in the last ten minutes. Anderlecht once more displayed their steely defensive side. They were marshalled by their captain, Erwin Vandendaele, a man who missed the 1976 final through injury and the 1978 final having moved on to a new challenge with Stade de Reims. It was one of footballing fate's cruel tricks that Vandendaele was denied a winners' medal in the Cup Winners' Cup, playing only in Anderlecht's defeat in the 1977 final.

Anderlecht opted for pure football in the second leg, when goals from Jean Thissen and, of course, Van der Elst saw them through to a second successive Cup Winners' Cup Final. The pre-Maradona Napoli would have to wait another 12 years for their own moment of European glory, when they lifted the 1989 UEFA Cup.

At the Olympic Stadium in Amsterdam, Anderlecht would find themselves frustrated by the stubbornness of Hamburger SV, and one of the greatest opportunities for the Cup Winners' Cup to be retained was lost. With four Dutchmen in his line-up, it was a bitter blow for Goethals and his Anderlecht side.

One month beyond losing the 1977 Cup Winners' Cup Final, Goethals's Anderlecht were presented with their last shot at obtaining silverware for the 1976/77 campaign. Having been muscled out of the race for the Belgian First Division title by their great rival Club Brugge, the two teams faced one another in the Belgian Cup Final. Throwing everything they could at each other, Anderlecht and Brugge shared seven goals, Brugge only holding the lead when they scored the last goal of the game. Having led 2-0 and 3-1, the 4-3 defeat was hard to stomach for Anderlecht. The former Derby County striker Roger Davies scored not only Brugge's equaliser for 3-3, but also the clinching goal. It was one of the finest domestic cup finals ever.

Brushing off their disappointment, Anderlecht seized the chance to have another shot at the Cup Winners' Cup with both hands. Belgian club football at its peak, while Brugge reached Wembley for the 1978 European Cup Final, to face Liverpool – having contested the 1976 UEFA Cup Final against the very same opponents – Anderlecht went the distance in the Cup Winners' Cup for the second time.

Strong in club football, Belgium were also on the brink of blossoming on the international scene again, after their failures to qualify for the World Cups of 1974 and 1978, and the 1976 European Championship, on all three occasions being stopped in their tracks by the Netherlands. In 1980, however, they reached the European Championship Final, fuelled by the rich seam of European club success which was led by Anderlecht, and ably supported by the near misses of Brugge. By 1982 Standard Liège were also making their presence felt.

While the modern rebirth of the Belgian national team is a joy to see, more so with their excellent retro kits, there will never be another rise at club level quite like the one that was enjoyed in Brussels, Bruges and Liège during the second half of the 1970s and the first half of the 1980s.

In 1977/78, Anderlecht again missed out on the Belgian First Division title, this time by one solitary point. While domestic matters continued to torment them, Europe brought solace. Their run to the 1978 Cup Winners' Cup Final took them past Lokomotiv Sofia, Hamburger SV, Porto and a Twente side that had reached the UEFA Cup Final only three years earlier, and could boast the services of Arnold Mühren and Frans Thijssen.

Lokomotiv Sofia and Twente were despatched in the first round and semi-final respectively, while Hamburger SV and Porto offered greater headaches. In the case of the former it was revenge that was in Anderlecht minds, against the team that had taken the Cup Winners' Cup off them in Amsterdam.

Strengthened by the signing of Kevin Keegan, Hamburger SV should have been able to build spectacularly on their 1977 Cup Winners' Cup success. But losing as many Bundesliga games as they won, and in a highly congested mid-table demolition derby where sixth and 12th places were separated by only four points, Hamburger SV limped in a disappointing tenth.

This didn't mean a thing, however, when Anderlecht and Hamburger SV faced one another, not much more than five months after they had contested the trophy in Amsterdam. Goethals's side returned to Brussels, from the first leg at the Volksparkstadion, with a 2-1 victory. Rensenbrink was pivotal to their performance. Advantage gained, it was still a nervy evening back at the Constant Vanden Stock, where a 1-1 scoreline brought Hamburger SV to within one goal of forcing extra time, Keegan and Van der Elst locked in a personal duel for supremacy.

In the quarter-final, Porto inflicted a 1-0 first-leg defeat on Anderlecht, their only loss of the tournament, and the 3-0 second-leg win which took them through wasn't the formulaic result it might appear. The game was still poised on a knife edge until Frank Vercauteren scored Anderlecht's third goal with only seven minutes remaining.

At an ebullient Parc des Princes, the 1978 Cup Winners' Cup Final was a one-sided event. Anderlecht's 4-0 victory equalled the biggest winning margin the final of the tournament would ever know.

It would be all too lazy to suggest that Austria Vienna weren't good enough. This was a team that would supply six players to Austria's 1978 World Cup squad; this was a team that lost only one game on their way to the final, being asked to go behind the Iron Curtain on three occasions, twice prevailing via penalty shoot-outs, navigating one round on away goals and conceding only one goal more than Anderlecht did, to reach Paris. They were also spearheaded by the Uruguayan international, Julio Morales, a man who had played in the 1970 World Cup semi-final against the Brazil of Pelé, Jairzinho, Tostão, Gerson, Rivellino and Carlos Alberto.

Their nation's first major European finalist Austria Vienna might have been, yet that Anderlecht were able to sweep away such potentially stubborn opponents was nothing short of stunning. The pre-1978 World Cup Rensenbrink, at the very zenith of his powers, was simply unstoppable. He scored twice, with Gilbert Van Binst netting the other two goals. It was one of the most complete performances a European final has ever been graced by, comparable to AC Milan's deconstruction of Johan Cruyff's Barcelona in the 1994 Champions League Final.

Anderlecht's run of three successive finals is one of the standout elements of the Cup Winners' Cup. They came to prominence and then ebbed away, before again reaching the final in 1990. There is a touch of the 1971–73 Ajax about the Anderlecht of 1976–78. The former inspired by Cruyff, the latter by Rensenbrink, a player who was shockingly allowed to escape the net of the biggest clubs of his homeland, to instead play in Belgium. Ajax were already spoilt for choice when he departed DWS Amsterdam, while Feyenoord, despite showing an interest, stalled and missed out.

Goethals watched his side dramatically lose their grip on the Cup Winners' Cup, during that incredible Barcelona comeback in the 1978/79 second round, before departing Anderlecht for a year in Bordeaux, then taking charge at São Paulo.

It was after his surprise spell in Brazil that Goethals returned to Belgium, and into the wide-open arms of Standard Liège, where he finally won the Belgian First Division titles that had eluded him at Anderlecht. Tainted by belated controversy, it was in the build-up to the 1982 Cup Winners' Cup Final that he was alleged to have made his suggestions and initiations of bribery towards players of Waterschei, bidding them to go easy, with Standard Liège's trip to the Camp Nou on the horizon.

Standard's achievement in reaching the 1982 Cup Winners' Cup Final remains a forgotten pleasure. Shielded by Barcelona being expected to win, and clouded by the Waterschei controversy, the quality of that Standard side becomes lost in contemporary translation.

Easily seeing their way past Floriana and Vasas SC in the opening two rounds, their performances in the quarter-final against the ever-maturing Porto, and in the semi-final against the holders Dinamo Tbilisi, were the type of masterclasses that Goethals's Anderlecht would have been proud of. As far as the Cup Winners' Cup was concerned, he had picked up with Standard where he had left off with Anderlecht. It was with a loud sigh of Catalan relief that Goethals's men fell narrowly short of pushing the 1982 Cup Winners' Cup Final into extra time.

As Anderlecht were preparing themselves for the 1977 Cup Winners' Cup Final, KV Mechelen were preparing themselves for life in the Belgian Second Division. Relegated at the end of the 1976/77 season, it was four years before they returned to the top flight, only to go straight back down again at the end of the 1981/82 campaign.

Bouncing back up again in 1984, the next two seasons offered Mechelen lower-table respectability yet gave absolutely no indications about what was about to unfold. Having been crowned Belgian champions three times in the 1940s, they had led a yo-yo existence between the top two divisions for three decades until their unexpected late 1980s renaissance.

Ambitions were steadily rising, however. The signing of Michel Preud'homme from Standard was as inspired as it was shocking. With Erwin Koeman influencing the midfield, things began to click for Mechelen. In 1986/87 they finished as runner-up to Anderlecht in the title race and won the Belgian Cup for the very first time, defeating RFC Liégeois in the final. It was Mechelen's first major honour in 39 years and it took them into European competition for the first time.

There are meteoric rises and there are meteoric rises. When Mechelen won the 1988 Cup Winners' Cup Final, they did so on the back of another near miss of the Belgian First Division title; they did so just four years after gaining promotion back to the top flight; they also did it by beating the holders, Ajax, in the final, before taking from them their star striker, John Bosman, who would then score the goals that led Mechelen to the league title in 1988/89.

It was an incredible series of events.

Just as incredibly, Ajax, the previous year, had become the first Dutch club to reach a Cup Winners' Cup Final, when they overcame Lokomotive Leipzig. Unbeknown at the time, they would be the only Dutch club to ever reach a Cup Winners' Cup Final.

The abject and collective underachievement of Eredivisie clubs in the Cup Winners' Cup was one of the tournament's greatest oddities. Feyenoord were beaten semi-finalists in 1981, 1992 and 1996, while PSV Eindhoven lost in the last four in 1971 and 1975. Twente had, of course, also made it to the same stage in 1978.

As remarkable as Mechelen winning the 1988 Cup Winners' Cup was, Ajax were as doomed as Liverpool were against Wimbledon three days later in the FA Cup Final. Both would sleepwalk their way to their respective defeats.

Shorn of some of the players responsible for winning them the tournament in 1987, along with the loss of Johan Cruyff as coach, it was another pillar of Ajax's dominant early 1970s vintage that led them into the 1988 final, Barry Hulshoff.

In the Mechelen dugout, however, there was another former Ajax man, Aad de Mos, who had been in charge at De Meer when Ajax rashly eased Cruyff the player to the exit door in 1983, from where he took himself to

Feyenoord where he won the domestic double to complete his on-pitch career.

De Mos was left short-changed by Ajax – two Eredivisie titles and a KNVB Cup was not enough to impress a demanding football club, it seemed. His arrival at Mechelen in the summer of 1986 coincided with the club shooting for the stars.

Not short of motivation, Mechelen were provided with an early gift at the Stade de la Meinau in Strasbourg. Ajax's Danny Blind was sent off in the 16th minute. With three Dutch players in their line-up, a former Ajax coach with an axe to grind and the outrageously talented Eli Ohana at their disposal – a man often referred to as the Israeli Ruud Gullit – Mechelen were a dangerous proposition for a young but gifted Ajax side, who were led on the pitch by the ageless Arnold Mühren.

Many of the Ajax line-up would go on to greatness. A 19-year-old Dennis Bergkamp was on the bench and he would be thrown on by Hulshoff just minutes after the Rotterdam-born Piet den Boer scored the only goal of the game in the 53rd minute.

A shocking yet inevitable outcome, Mechelen's success was born of determination and carried out in the face of, at the very least, a caricature of the embodiment of all that is good about Ajax. Under the radar for the entire distance, Mechelen's run to the final had been a measured one, during which they defeated an array of good, but not exceptional, opponents. Dinamo Bucharest, St Mirren, Dinamo Minsk and Atalanta had all been dispensed with.

To prove they were no flash in the pan, Mechelen reached the semi-final as holders in 1988/89, inclusive of beating Anderlecht convincingly in the second round. Even when they fell to Sampdoria in the last four, they went into the final 20 minutes of the second leg leading the tie, before Vujadin Boškov's men came on strong. De Mos and his players were left to console themselves with their league title.

Remaining competitive over the following seasons, domestic cup success evaded Mechelen, thus denying them a return to the Cup Winners' Cup. They did come close, however, losing both the 1991 and 1992 Belgian Cup finals, the second of which was lost on penalties against a Royal Antwerp side that went on to reach the 1993 Cup Winners' Cup Final.

While Royal Antwerp still stand as the last Belgian club to reach a major European final, Mechelen are to this day the last Belgian side to win a major European final. Three decades have now passed since the madness of Mechelen and that sums up the way football's landscape has grotesquely altered. How the once-level playing field has been tilted so far out of proportion that only the strongest can prosper. Of all the major European trophies to be presented since the Cup Winners' Cup came to an end, half of them have been handed over to Spanish teams.

Belgian brilliance in the Cup Winners' Cup was offset by the nonsensical underachievement of the Netherlands. When it came to this tournament, the power base of the Low Countries wasn't to be found in Amsterdam, and certainly not in Rotterdam or Eindhoven, but instead over the border in Brussels and, briefly, in Mechelen.

Chapter Eight

Everton 1985

A MIRAGE in European competition, Everton are a complexity. Prior to winning the European Cup Winners' Cup in 1985, they had no discernible pedigree on the continent. Their only other brush with the Cup Winners' Cup had resulted in a second-round exit to Real Zaragoza during the 1966/67 season.

Besmirched by a track record of early European exits, Everton's run to the quarter-finals of the European Cup in 1970/71 had been their best showing, up until setting sail upon their 1984/85 Cup Winners' Cup campaign.

Blessed by the famous 'School of Science' midfield triumvirate of Alan Ball, Colin Harvey and Howard Kendall, it was a frustrated Everton that slipped out of the competition at the hands of Ferenc Puskas's Panathinaikos. In a season when the final took place at Wembley Stadium, it was a careless turn of events for the team from Goodison Park. To compound issues, three days after exiting the

European Cup, they lost an FA Cup semi-final to Liverpool at Old Trafford.

It was a Merseyside derby in which the tectonic plates of football shifted dramatically. Everton, runaway champions less than 12 months earlier, had seemed to be set to dominate the 1970s. Four members of the Everton team that won the 1969/70 First Division title also went to the 1970 World Cup finals, as part of Sir Alf Ramsey's England squad. Had Gordon West, the Everton goalkeeper, not declined the opportunity to travel, then it would have been five of them.

At the 1971 FA Cup semi-final, Everton had the team of established stars while much of the Liverpool team was inhabited by players who were on the eve of glorious careers. The mountains the Liverpool players would climb were largely ahead of them, whereas Everton's players had seen it all and almost done it all.

Having led 1-0, Everton yielded to a 2-1 defeat. While the 1971 FA Cup Final would ultimately be beyond Liverpool, the semi-final worked as a springboard to the Anfield club's incredible successes to come. As for Everton, they began to unravel.

Standing aside, watching Liverpool go on to glory after glory, both at home and abroad, Everton could only rue their missed chances and the dismantling of their team that started the decade with such a powerful sense of intent.

As Liverpool swept up the trophies, Everton tried to regenerate. They came close, under both Billy Bingham and Gordon Lee, the men who followed in the footsteps of Harry Catterick, the manager that built the 'School of Science'; the man who won Everton two league titles and an FA Cup.

Bingham should have won the league title for Everton in 1974/75, when having put themselves in a commanding position, the wheels fell off during the run-in. Lee meanwhile put together a team that sat on the periphery of success. A League Cup Final was reached, two FA Cup semi-finals were lost, and there were two seasons of league consistency that brought with them UEFA Cup qualification. Everton were close, but not quite close enough during those seasons.

Frustration finally bubbled over in the 1980/81 campaign. A promising start in the league fell by the wayside, while another hopeful FA Cup run ended in the quarter-finals against Manchester City. It was a defeat that represented the straw that broke the camel's back. Drained of spirit, Lee and Everton parted company in the summer of 1981, undone by only the finest of margins between success and failure.

Kendall returned to the club, initially as player-manager. Over the course of his first two and a half years in the job, improvements were negligible. Bit by bit, however, he began to assemble the components that would arguably create Everton's finest ever team.

Legend has it that Kendall's future turned on a League Cup quarter-final draw at Oxford United, in January 1984. Sitting in 18th position in the First Division at the time, Everton had won only twice in the league since mid-November and there was a definite restlessness amongst their supporters. A priceless FA Cup third-round victory had been obtained at Stoke City a week and a half earlier, while a draw at Oxford in the League Cup was a fifth game without defeat. Rather than Kendall and Everton turning their fortunes on the pivot of one game, that encounter at the Manor Ground was part of a wider corner being navigated.

Beyond that mythical evening at Oxford, Everton lost just five of their remaining 31 games of the 1983/84 season, one of those being the League Cup Final replay, to Liverpool. After the tremors of the previous four years, this was a very different Everton. They would make two trips to Wembley and lift themselves to a very creditable seventh-place finish.

After overcoming Stoke in the third round, the FA Cup was quite kind to Everton. They breezed past Gillingham, Shrewsbury Town and a relegation-threatened Notts County to reach the semi-finals, although a replay had been required to see off Gillingham.

In the semi-final, at Highbury, Everton went head-to-head with Lawrie McMenemy's Southampton. A team that would eventually finish runner-up to Liverpool in the First Division, a team packed with star names, it made for a difficult afternoon for Kendall and his players. Adrian Heath scored a 117th-minute winner, to stop the game drifting to a replay and to take Everton to their first FA Cup Final for 16 years.

Blessed by the exit of the tournament by all the other traditional big names of English football, Everton were left with the awkward Watford to face in the 1984 FA Cup Final. Fast, organised and not without skilled players, Graham Taylor's men had been First Division runners-up the previous season, their very first season of top-flight football. The UEFA Cup had been embraced and Watford were becoming accustomed to big games.

Incredible as it might seem now, this was a match of two evenly balanced opponents; in late February, they had shared an incredible 4-4 draw at Vicarage Road. At Wembley, with only one player on the pitch with a major winners' medal to his name, it was always going to be a case of who would blink first.

Watford did the blinking and the FA Cup belonged to Everton. An instinctive finish from Graeme Sharp and a controversial second from Andy Gray – the goals coming shortly before and shortly after the half-time interval – earned Everton their first major trophy since that 1969/70 First Division title. With it came a place in the 1984/85 Cup Winners' Cup. It would mean the return of European football to Goodison Park for the first time in five years.

Given their previously uneasy relationship with European competitions, Everton started true to form. They very nearly tripped themselves over in the first round, against University College Dublin. A goalless draw in the first leg, at Tolka Park, was compounded by an equally lacklustre performance at Goodison, where Everton ended the game grimly holding on to a 1-0 lead having been in very real danger of conceding what would have been a tournament-ending away goal.

A lesson learnt and with Everton shaking off the early season lethargy, Internacionál Slovnaft Bratislava proved to be of little threat in the second round. A 4-0 aggregate win was enough to put Kendall's side into the quarter-finals, the Cup Winners' Cup going into cold storage for the next four months.

Locked within a tense title race with Tottenham Hotspur and in the quarter-finals of the FA Cup, the

Toffees would be forgiven for having other things on their minds going into their games against Fortuna Sittard. If they were distracted, however, they did a remarkable job of masking it. A 5-0 aggregate stroll saw Everton into their first ever major European semi-final.

If the draw to this point had been kind to Everton, the semi-final task they were handed was a completely unenviable one. Bayern Munich stood between Kendall's men and a first major European final.

With Rapid Vienna and Dynamo Moscow contesting the other semi-final, the Everton and Bayern Munich tie took on the image of the de facto final, and as usual, Bayern walked a slender line between confidence and arrogance.

An accomplished performance in the first leg, at the Olympiastadion, meant that Everton returned to Merseyside with a goalless draw. One of those results that is both very useful and very dangerous, it left Kendall and his players nursing the upper hand yet skating across a thin sheet of ice. Concede an away goal and Everton would need to score twice. They were circumstances that generated the type of European electricity that Anfield has been so fabled for. This was Goodison's finest night and as with all great European nights it involved a stunning comeback, Everton having conceded the much-feared away goal.

With Bayern opting for a physical approach, to counter the perceived British style of play, Everton didn't need to out-think the Bavarian club. Bayern, having had their last four European campaigns ended by British teams, out-thought themselves. In the 37th minute, however, it looked like Bayern had got their tactics just right. Neville

Southall pulled off two fine saves within 60 seconds of one another, only to see the second of those saves converted by Dieter Hoeneß when the ball broke to him kindly after Southall blocked Lothar Matthäus's initial effort when put clean through on goal. The silence within Goodison was deafening.

Regaining their composure at half-time and with Bayern perhaps too sure of themselves, Everton were level on the night within three minutes of the restart. A long throw from Trevor Steven was flicked on by Gray and there was Sharp to guide in the equaliser. Atmosphere recharged, Everton continued to apply layer upon layer of pressure on Bayern. Responsible for so much outstanding passing football throughout the 1984/85 season, it was conversely a more agricultural route that got them back into the semi-final second leg.

A long throw and a flick-on having undone Bayern for Everton's first goal, it was again Steven propelling a throw-in towards the near post that provoked their second. This time, the usually outstanding Jean-Marie Pfaff came for a ball that he simply wasn't going to reach. Largely blocked by his own defenders, the ball bounced to a disbelieving yet ecstatic Gray who prodded the ball into Bayern's unguarded net.

Leading 2-1 but knowing that a further goal for Bayern would see their opponents through on the away-goals rule instead, it wasn't until the 86th minute that Everton made the tie safe. When that third goal came, it was one of breathtaking simplicity, and it was a goal that was far more in keeping with the style they had been playing for most of the season.

After supplying the throw-ins that led to Everton's first two goals, it was apt that it should be Steven who was on the end of a flowing counter-attack which swept from Paul Bracewell, to Kevin Sheedy, to Gray and on to Steven, from where he lifted it over the advancing Pfaff and into the Gwladys Street End goalmouth. Goodison was in a state of near self-combustion.

Everton's season arguably peaked at that very moment. Already sure of their place in the FA Cup Final, ten points clear at the top of the First Division after Tottenham had faded from the title race, and with a Cup Winners' Cup Final that looked set to be an idle coronation, Everton won their next four league games to complete the formalities of their first league title success for 15 years.

All focus was switched to their two cup finals. At De Kuip, in Rotterdam, after their opponents put up spirited first-half resistance, Everton ambled past the collection of faded genius and limited next-generation players that Rapid Vienna had, to field in the 1985 Cup Winners' Cup Final.

Rapid might have been blessed by the presence of Hans Krankl and Antonin Panenka, but with their combined ages fast approaching 70, they simply didn't have the legs to carry them, or the talent surrounding them, to trouble Everton. What Rapid really needed was Zlatko Kranjcar to play the game of his life.

Rapid, massively outclassed, were left chasing shadows and it was a minor miracle for the Austrian side to repel Everton for almost an hour. Gray had already had a first-half strike harshly disallowed, when he opened the scoring at the second time of asking.

When it eventually came, Everton were gifted their breakthrough. Sharp, seizing on a badly misjudged back pass by Rudi Weinhofer, managed to compose himself near the byline, inside the Rapid penalty area. Ignoring the invitation to go to ground he instead picked out Gray, unmarked in vast quantities of space, who directed the ball into the back of the empty net.

As soon as Everton had the lead the spectre of Rapid maintaining their stubborn effort long enough to nick a goal of their own was gone. Chance after chance fell their way and the inspired Steven was only denied by a smart save from Michael Konsel, the Rapid goalkeeper. It was merely a temporary reprieve, however, as Steven made it 2-0 not long after, profiteering at the back post when the Rapid defence allowed a Sheedy corner to bounce across their six-yard line unchallenged. Sheedy had had to physically remove a photographer who was obstructing his run up.

They had been organised in their approach to the game, yet Rapid had still given goals away. Everton had also needed to be ruthless enough to capitalise upon the gifts that were bestowed upon them. Yet, just as the outcome of the game appeared to be settled, Krankl made it 2-1 with the best goal of the game, rounding Southall and stroking the ball home after an intelligent turn from Kranjcar.

A belated flash of what Rapid might have brought to the game, a tense finish was averted when a few seconds later Sheedy put the result beyond any lingering doubt. With its roots very much of a route-one variety, a long clearance by Southall was headed onwards by Gray; yet, from Sharp collecting the ball and deftly laying it off for Sheedy to run on to, Everton's third goal became a work of art. Taking one touch to steady himself, Sheedy then powered the ball into the back of the Rapid net via the underside of the crossbar.

This is where Everton pass into the realms of the hypotheticals. Beaten in the FA Cup Final by Manchester United and denied a unique treble, they were still heading into the 1985/86 European Cup. The Heysel disaster stopped that happening, however, and it gave birth to a million hypotheses as to how Kendall's Everton were halted from ruling the European game for the foreseeable future.

We'll of course never know, but the 1985/86 European Cup wouldn't have been easy to win. Everton were placed in the draw for the first round of the 1985/86 European Cup, to provide numerical balance to proceedings, as were Manchester United in the hat for the first round of the Cup Winners' Cup. Everton were drawn to face Anderlecht, with the second leg hypothetically at Goodison.

A talented side on the pitch, and little more than a year on from Anderlecht purchasing a UEFA Cup semi-final victory over Nottingham Forest, this would not have been an easily navigated tie. Had Everton progressed, then the route Anderlecht took would have pitted Everton against Bayern Munich, once more, in the quarter-finals, Steaua Bucharest in the last four and Terry Venables's Barcelona in the final.

For a team with a traditionally uneasy relationship with European competition, my view is that Everton might well have gone the distance in the 1985/86 European Cup, but they would have been equally capable of falling at the first hurdle to Anderlecht. They'd have likely been all or nothing, with very little in the way of middle ground. Meanwhile, any prolonged success would have been down to the vagaries of momentum. In the same way as Leeds United, Derby County, Nottingham Forest and Aston Villa had risen then ebbed away, Everton did the same, with Arsenal being the next in line to rise. Football's cyclical nature will always be.

Everton returned to the Cup Winners' Cup one last time, in 1995/96, where they were narrowly knocked out in the second round by Feyenoord. A strong side, enhanced by the arrival of Andrei Kanchelskis, they could have come close to glory again had they plotted a path beyond the second round. It represented a return to type, a return to the pre-1985 European campaigns that Everton used to endure. Every European adventure they have set sail upon since has been laced with unfulfilled potential, an aura of what might have been. Would 1985/86 have been any different?

Turning back the clock themselves, Rapid Vienna went on to reach the 1996 Cup Winners' Cup Final, where they were beaten by Paris Saint-Germain.

Chapter Nine

West Germanic Tendencies and French Fancies

NO NATION has a more awkward relationship with European club football than France. If you could sum up the concept of Brexit within the medium of major European football competitions, then you would do no better than to point at France's stunning lack of success.

The French league system failed to supply a European Cup Winners' Cup finalist until Monaco lost the 1992 final against Werder Bremen. Granted, prior to that, there were some near misses, none more pronounced than Bordeaux, who lost their 1987 semi-final to Lokomotive Leipzig in that marvellously insane penalty shoot-out. Yet it is truly nuts to consider that France's sole success in the Cup Winners' Cup was so belated that it came just three years before the tournament expired, and still to this very day, remains one of only two occasions when a French team has won a major European tournament.

Put into further context, the French national team has won twice as many major international tournaments as France's clubs have won major European tournaments.

Responsible for some of football's very finest elements and for some of football's brightest ideas, it is incredible that their clubs have failed so resolutely. Just like Manchester City, Paris Saint-Germain's only success in European terms remains the one solitary Cup Winners' Cup that they procured.

PSG finally won the Cup Winners' Cup in 1996, two years after losing in the semi-finals. The following year, they became the eighth and last team to return to the final as holders, only to lose it. Despite the disappointments, they could at least point to their moment in the spotlight, to their moment of glory.

Others weren't so lucky. Monaco were comfortably beaten by Werder Bremen in the 1992 Cup Winners' Cup Final. Arsène Wenger led them past both Roma and Feyenoord, after coming to within a hair's breadth of facing Tottenham Hotspur in the semi-finals instead of Feyenoord. Blessed by the presence of Emmanuel Petit, Rui Barros and George Weah, Wenger had talent to spare, with Lilian Thuram and Youri Djorkaeff on the bench. Fortune still deserted them in the final, however, and the newly reunified Germany had their first European club glory instead.

It felt like both Monaco and French club football had once again been jilted at the altar, in the same way that AS Saint-Étienne had been in the 1976 European Cup Final, and Marseille likewise 15 years later.

Djorkaeff's father, Jean, was part of the Olympique Lyonnais side that narrowly missed out on reaching the 1964 final. Djorkaeff senior played all three of France's games at the 1966 World Cup in England and would later proudly watch on as his son collected a winners' medal in 1998.

With FC Nantes comfortably beaten by Valencia in the semi-finals in 1980, by the time Bordeaux came to within 12 yards of the 1987 final, they were only the third French side to reach the last four. While the final remained elusive for French teams, Bordeaux's run did mark the beginning of a wave of concerted efforts to win the Cup Winners' Cup by their compatriots.

Marseille made the semi-finals the following year. Monaco did the same in 1990, almost as a dry run before making the 1992 final. Within this there was an irony that, while French clubs were edging closer and closer to a first major European success, their national team were beginning to labour. After the peaks of the 1984 European Championship and their runs to the semi-finals of the 1982 and 1986 World Cups, *Les Bleus* went into a sharp decline, failing to reach the 1988 European Championship and the World Cups of 1990 and 1994.

In 1992, Monaco were undone by goals from Klaus Allofs and Wynton Rufer, at another sparsely populated final, this time at the Estádio da Luz. Fast approaching his 36th birthday, Allofs had been part of the Marseille side that made the 1988 semi-finals and had been in the Fortuna Düsseldorf team for the 1979 final, scoring their first in that beautifully swaying 4-3 defeat to Barcelona. Allofs had also captained the FC Cologne side which lost the 1986 UEFA Cup Final to Real Madrid. To him at least, the 1992 Cup Winners' Cup Final was the just reward of a long career of near misses on the European stage.

It was a game cast within an eerie shadow, however. A beautifully hot Lisbon day, an open-plan stadium and an echoey sound from a crowd that totalled not much more than 16,000.

It was played out just 24 hours after 18 people had lost their lives at the Armand Césari Stadium in Bastia, when a section of a temporary stand collapsed shortly before the scheduled kick-off at the Coupe de France semi-final between SC Bastia and Marseille.

Impossible to countenance that it didn't play a contributory factor, Monaco failed to rise to the occasion that was presented to them. Werder Bremen had trodden water through a mid-table Bundesliga campaign, the first to be played after the end of the DDR-Oberliga at the end of the 1990/91 season, while Wenger's team had been the only other contender for the French First Division title, when in pursuit of Marseille. The time had seemed nigh for Monaco. However, uncharacteristic mistakes gifted Bremen their glory, with Petit badly at fault for the second goal of a 2-0 defeat.

The 1991/92 Coupe de France was not completed. Monaco, who had already reached the final and had been awaiting the outcome of the Bastia–Marseille game, would go on to represent France in the 1992/93 Cup Winners' Cup. Their hearts perhaps not fully being in the task, they exited the tournament at the second hurdle, to Olympiacos. It would be the last time Monaco graced the Cup Winners' Cup.

A Champions League Final was reached by Monaco in 2004, and as recently as 2017 they reached the semi-finals of the same tournament. Yet the 1992 Cup Winners' Cup Final remains the one that truly got away for a club that still awaits a first major European title to call their own.

Marseille, a year later, finally broke the hoodoo when they defeated Fabio Capello's AC Milan in the 1993 Champions League Final in Munich. As belated a victory as it was, it was also shaded by the bribery scandal that would erupt domestically for the club. Luckily enough, Paris Saint-Germain's late charge on the Cup Winners' Cup gave French football the untainted success it so badly needed.

PSG were losing semi-finalists in 1994, having been edged out by Arsenal over two games that introduced David Ginola to an English audience. They followed that up with a run to the semi-finals of the Champions League in 1994/95, where they were outclassed by Louis van Gaal's fast-paced, skilful and progressive Ajax.

It was all part of a fast learning curve for PSG and, despite the sale of Ginola to Newcastle United, Luis Fernández – one quarter of France's legendary *Carré Magique* – crafted a side that could finally ascend to European glory.

In the 1995/96 Cup Winners' Cup, PSG swept past Molde, Celtic, Parma and Deportivo La Coruña on their way to the final. The only reversal they sustained upon that odyssey was a 1-0 quarter-final first-leg defeat at Parma, something that was rectified during a dramatic second leg when, at 2-2 on aggregate, PSG had been trailing on the away-goals rule against Nevio Scala's star-studded line-up. It was with stubbornness that PSG prevailed, thanks to the second of two penalties converted by the hypnotic Raí.

On paper, PSG's route to Cup Winners' Cup glory largely seems one of difficult tasks being easily fended off. Yet, it wasn't only Parma that made them sweat. Molde, in the first round first leg, led 1-0 until the 72nd minute, thanks to a goal from the ever-progressing Ole Gunnar Solskjær. A late flurry of PSG goals at the Molde Stadion and a comfortable second leg at the Parc des Princes saw them through.

In the second round first leg, Celtic acquitted themselves well in Paris, with only a 1-0 deficit; it set up a hugely anticipated evening at Parkhead. Instead of Celtic rolling back the years however, PSG strolled to a 3-0 victory.

Impressively assured, beyond their massively significant quarter-final success over Parma, PSG beat Deportivo La Coruña 1-0, twice, to facilitate their passage into their very first major European final. They faced Rapid Vienna, the 1985 beaten finalists. Rapid had seen off Feyenoord in the semi-finals after earlier completing a stirring second-leg extra-time fightback against Sporting CP in the second round, coming back from 2-0 down.

At the King Baudouin Stadium in Brussels, PSG's 1-0 margin of victory did no service to just how one-sided the 1996 Cup Winners' Cup Final was, despite Fernandez losing the services of Raí after only 12 minutes.

Bruno N'Gotty – 2005 Bolton Wanderers Player of the Year-to-be – was the scorer of the only goal of the game, with a well-struck, low-flying and slightly deflected free kick just before the half-hour mark. A final that falls beneath the radar, it perhaps came down to the lower-calibre opposition, despite them twice being finalists in the Cup Winners' Cup. The low-scoring nature of the game also did it no favours. Nor does the fact that PSG went on to lose the 1997 final to the Barcelona of Ronaldo and Luis Figo. When an achievement is succeeded by something exceptional and iconic, then it soon becomes forgotten.

French clubs made a huge breakthrough in 1996. The problem was, however, that they didn't seem to know what to do once they had reached the peak of their surprisingly arduous mountain. A third major European trophy still eludes the clubs of Ligue 1.

In a world of footballing yin and yang, you would have thought that anything that France struggled with, West Germany would have mocked from across the border with an annoying sense of superiority. Given that Werder Bremen's 1992 victory essentially belongs to a unified Germany, it is stunning to consider that West Germany's last Cup Winners' Cup success came in 1977, when Hamburger SV defeated Anderlecht. Two years later, Fortuna Düsseldorf became the last West German finalist, when they lost that sumptuous 1979 final in Basel against the Hans Krankl-inspired Barcelona, 4-3.

West Germany's first and last Cup Winners' Cup finals were separated by 14 years. Their first and last successes in the tournament were separated by 11 years. Rather than having a defining movement, it almost feels that West German clubs were the substantial bystanders in the wider stories of the clubs from other nations. West German clubs could be cast as 'Best Supporting Actor'. In Germanic terms, the east was where it was when it came to the Cup Winners' Cup.

The first West German team to reach a Cup Winners' Cup Final were 1860 Munich, under the wonderfully storied Max Merkel. They were part of the legend of West Ham United winning the tournament in 1965, while Borussia Dortmund were there in 1966 as the first team Liverpool faced in a major European final. Dortmund's subsequent erosion as a team of intent, to the point of being relegated from the Bundesliga in 1972, assists in this concept.

Dortmund didn't build upon 1966, despite being the winners, while Liverpool, a decade later, went on to repeatedly win the European Cup, albeit after a seven-year gap between major trophies until 1973.

When Bayern Munich prevailed in 1967, it was detached enough from their 1974–76 European Cup hat-trick for them to feel unrelated to one another, despite Sepp Maier, Franz Roth, Franz Beckenbauer and Gerd Müller going on from the 1967 side to the 1974–76 side. Rangers were beaten in the 1967 final, the second part in the trilogy of their finals that eventually took them to success in 1972. It makes the 1967 Bayern Munich seem like they were a building block towards Rangers' greatest moment.

Similarly, when Hamburger SV were defeated in the 1968 Cup Winners' Cup Final, they were arguably a stepping stone for AC Milan, when *I Rossoneri* went on to win the 1969 European Cup. Even within their victory of 1977, Hamburger SV sat right in the middle of Anderlecht's three successive finals. Hamburger SV became the property of Anderlecht in this respect. A new story began for Hamburger SV, from the summer of 1977, that started with Kevin Keegan and ended with them winning the 1983 European Cup Final.

The exploits of Fortuna Düsseldorf, in 1979, were the final glorious curtain on the West German tendencies for the Cup Winners' Cup, at its most pronounced level at least. Never again would a team from the nation of West Germany reach a Cup Winners' Cup Final.

It all acts as a peculiarity. There was a West German presence in four successive Cup Winners' Cup finals, 1965 through to 1968; four finals, four different West German teams, yet the roles they all played in the paths travelled by other teams makes it easy to miss this as being a collective West German rise which, of course, it really was. Four finals: two won, two lost.

This coincided with the continued rise of the West German national team. In 1966 they reached a second World Cup Final, and they would go on to dominate the 1970s. Added to Bayern's three European Cups, Borussia Mönchengladbach would likely have won two of their own in the very same decade, had it not been for Bob Paisley's Liverpool.

Despite the way they were largely support acts, along the way to their respective finals, for all four West German sides that reached those 1960s Cup Winners' Cup finals, wonderment occurred. The 1965 semi-final was fought out between 1860 Munich and Nereo Rocco's Torino in a tie that took three games to settle and one that would have gone the way of the Italians had it been contested after the implementation of the away-goals rule. The comradeship between the supporters of West Ham and 1860 Munich was also a fabulous occurrence at a game that garnered an attendance for a Cup Winners' Cup Final that was eclipsed only once, in 1982, at the

Camp Nou, when Barcelona played the final in their own back yard.

A year later, Borussia Dortmund had to overcome Atlético Madrid, the holders West Ham United, and then Liverpool in the final, to complete one of the toughest runs to Cup Winners' Cup glory, which offset the fluke manner of their winning goal at Hampden Park.

Bayern Munich, in 1967, when keeping the Cup Winners' Cup in West German possession, almost succumbed to a second-round exit at the hands of Shamrock Rovers. Having played out a 1-1 draw in the first leg at Dalymount Park, the return game at the Grünwalder Stadion saw Bayern fly into a two-goal lead within the first ten minutes, thanks to strikes from Dieter Brenninger and Rainer Ohlhauser. Rovers kept their composure and during a four-minute span shortly before the hour mark they shockingly levelled the game through goals from Bobby Gilbert and Liam Tuohy, Tuohy being the Irish club's player-manager.

With Bayern in danger of going out on the away-goals rule, it wasn't until the 86th minute that they were bailed out by the winning strike of Gerd Müller. At the very same stage of the tournament, Rangers were unseating the holders, Borussia Dortmund.

Made to sweat profusely by Shamrock Rovers, the 1966/67 Cup Winners' Cup insisted upon being a hard-earned first European success for Bayern, as Rapid Vienna provided yet more stubbornness in the quarter-finals, while in the final Rangers were a closely matched foe, who were unfortunate not to win it themselves.

To complete this 1960s quartet, Hamburger SV's passage to the 1968 Cup Winners' Cup Final was also fraught with overly complicated and unexpected scares. After comfortably overcoming both Randers Freja and Wisła Kraków, life became difficult during the quarter-finals, when they relinquished a 2-0, first-leg advantage against Lyon, four years on from the French side having beaten Hamburger SV at the very same stage of the very same tournament.

At 2-2 on aggregate, both sides having won their home tie 2-0, Hamburger SV and Lyon were sent into a play-off match, where the West Germans prevailed, at 2-0 yet again. In a season of inconsistencies, Hamburger SV laboured to 13th place in the Bundesliga in 1967/68, seemingly saving their very best for Europe.

Cardiff City, however, fancied their semi-final chances. Cardiff, like Hamburger SV, finished 13th in their respective league campaign. Theirs though was in the English Second Division, having obtained their participation in the 1967/68 Cup Winners' Cup via Welsh Cup glory in 1967.

Plundering their way past Bayern Munich-botherers Shamrock Rovers, along with NAC Breda and Torpedo Moscow, and armed with the Liverpool star-to-be, John Toshack, Cardiff travelled to Hamburg in a fearless frame of mind. Going into the first leg, at the Volksparkstadion, Hamburger SV were on the back of three successive Bundesliga defeats, yet seen as the favourites to progress to the final. All the pressure was on the West German side and it was intensified when Norman Dean stunned the hosts, opening the scoring after only four minutes.

This in turn provoked an almost ceaseless and relentless Hamburger SV attacking response. Bob Wilson – no, not the Arsenal one – the Cardiff reserve goalkeeper, produced the performance of his career. In something which was akin to a prototype of Jan Tomaszewski's gravity-defying acrobatics against England at Wembley in 1973, Wilson kept Hamburger SV at bay with a combination of outstanding agility, amazing reflexes and outrageous good fortune. Eventually, Cardiff and Wilson were breached, midway through the second half, when Helmut Sandmann thundered home Hamburger SV's equaliser from point-blank range. No further goals would be added, and Cardiff returned the principality with a barely believable 1-1 draw.

Yet, in that way that football can give kindly with one hand, only to snatch cruelly with the other, Wilson was at the centre of the goal that took Hamburger SV to the 1968 Cup Winners' Cup Final. A looping and seemingly covered effort from Uwe Seeler, who had missed the first game through injury, managed to squirm from Wilson's desperate grasp to bumble over the Cardiff goal line. It was a winning goal which came shortly after Cardiff had scored the goal that looked set to take the tie to Scandinavia for a play-off match. A painful experience for the Cardiff team and their devoted followers, it was the culmination of a wonderfully open game that Hamburger SV shaded, 3-2.

In the 1968 final, AC Milan, Serie A champions-to-be, were simply too strong. Hamburger SV would have to wait another nine years before they could lift the Cup Winners' Cup. When they did so, they won it in style. Easing their way through to the semi-finals, it was with a stirring second-leg, last-four fightback in which they overcame Luis Aragonés's Atlético Madrid that they claimed the opportunity to defeat Anderlecht in the final.

Losing the first leg 3-1 at the Vicente Calderón, Hamburger SV turned it all around back at the Volksparkstadion in the first half hour of the second leg. All the goals of a 3-0 victory were procured within 28 minutes of the start, a blizzard of goals that began in the 19th minute, when José Luis Capón put the ball past his own goalkeeper, Miguel Reina. Hamburger SV enjoyed a nine-minute goalscoring storm.

In Amsterdam, at the Olympic Stadium, Hamburger SV stubbornly bided their time. They remained compact enough not to allow Rob Rensenbrink, François van der Elst, Arie Haan and Peter Ressel the space to run amok, while simultaneously winding down the clock to a point of the game where nervousness could begin to creep into Anderlecht's play. When the breakthrough came, it was, predictably, an avoidable goal that Anderlecht conceded. A penalty was awarded: one of those penalties where the two teams meet in the middle somewhere, via a lazy, almost tired challenge being made by the defender, and the attacker accepting the invitation to go to ground. Georg Volkert thundered home the penalty, and press photographers encroached upon the pitch to snap their visual records of the celebrations. There were only 12 minutes left.

It was ten minutes later when Felix Magath removed any remaining doubts over the outcome, getting himself on the end of a quick breakaway to prod the ball past Jan Ruiter for 2-0. Hamburger SV, while not as aesthetically pleasing as Anderlecht, were justifiable winners on an evening when the West Germans' hard work and endeavour trumped the Belgians' whimsical, yet perhaps arrogant, expectation of victory.

Two years later, in 1979, Fortuna Düsseldorf became West Germany's last Cup Winners' Cup finalists. It was a run that began and ended with a 4-3 scoreline. A first-round first-leg 4-3 victory away to Universitatea Craiova and their 4-3 loss, in the final, to Barcelona in Basel, bookended an impressive run for the team that claimed the DFB-Pokal as their own as the tail end of the 1970s met the start of the 1980s.

Beaten finalists in their domestic cup competition, to a double-winning FC Cologne, in 1978, Fortuna followed that up by winning it in 1979 and 1980. This was a Fortuna team of purpose when they reached the 1979 Cup Winners' Cup Final. It was with an equal sense of adventure and misadventure that they came so close to glory.

Beyond the first round, Fortuna bludgeoned their way to a 3-0 first-leg win in the second round against Aberdeen, before contriving to very nearly throw it all away at Pittodrie, where Alex Ferguson's side clawed their way back to within one goal of levelling the tie.

Away goals were required in the quarter-final to dispense with Servette, while in the semi-final Baník Ostrava offered a sense of déjà vu when, in a similar way to Aberdeen in the second round, the Slovakians almost turned a first-leg 3-1 deficit completely on its head, fighting their way to 2-1, to leave them one goal short of forcing the tie into extra time.

For Fortuna, the 1979 Cup Winners' Cup Final would ultimately be one of football's great 'what if' moments. A tumultuous game that swayed back and forth, Barcelona were joyous, yet relieved, to hear the final whistle.

Nobody could have foreseen in 1979 that by the time a Bundesliga team once again reached the Cup Winners'

Cup Final, West Germany would have been reunited with East Germany. Nobody could have foreseen that the last two Germanic Cup Winners' Cup finalists before reunification would be from the east: Carl Zeiss Jena in 1981 and Lokomotive Leipzig in 1987. Along with Bayern Munich's run to the 1985 semi-final, the only other West German team to come anywhere near a Cup Winners' Cup Final was Bayer Uerdingen in 1986, when they reached the same stage.

Such a pillar of not just European, but global football, West Germany's grey areas when it came to the Cup Winners' Cup were as surprising as those of Italy. As for France, there is something vaguely reassuring about their contemporary struggles with major European tournaments, when compared to their European struggles of the past.

The more things change in football, the more they stay the same.

Chapter Ten

Welsh Endeavours

CARDIFF CITY'S run to the semi-finals of the 1967/68 European Cup Winners' Cup was the best run made by a team from within the United Kingdom, apart from those of England and Scotland. Having put themselves to within touching distance of facing the great AC Milan in the final, a Milan vs Cardiff 1968 showpiece event is perhaps the most tantalising of hypothetical scenarios to be denied the tournament.

It is, however, debatable whether that was Cardiff's finest moment in the Cup Winners' Cup. Three years later they faced the mighty Real Madrid in the quarter-finals, with the first leg at a packed Ninian Park. Brian Clark scored the only goal of the game, with a towering header from a cross supplied by the talented yet fragile 17-year-old Nigel Rees. Not much more than a year later, Rees had been released by the club, drifting off to play for Bridgend Town and later taking part in an unsuccessful trial to return to Cardiff, when under new management.

To put Cardiff's victory into further context, if that could possibly be needed, Real Madrid had won at the Camp Nou just a few short weeks beforehand. Defying the balance of play, it wasn't until the second half at the Santiago Bernabéu that Cardiff relinquished their lead. Even then there was a stroke of luck involved, as Manuel Velázquez took advantage of a punched clearance by the Cardiff goalkeeper, Jim Eadie, which fell straight onto his right foot, from which the midfielder rifled in the aggregate-equalising goal.

Real Madrid's winning goal then came just two minutes later, a goal which was unashamedly route one in nature; a long clearance from the goalkeeper, a flick-on and a neat finish from the Paraguayan international, Sebastián Fleitas. The remainder of the game was played out upon the knife edge that one goal for Cardiff would be good enough to go through on away goals. They never really looked likely to score it, however.

Like a duck to water, Cardiff had also reached the quarter-finals in 1964/65 before bowing out to Real Zaragoza. It all made for a six-year span that encompassed one semi-final and two quarter-finals. They would never rise to such European heights again.

Before the epic odysseys of Cardiff, other Welsh teams had ventured into the Cup Winners' Cup, taken there by the wonderful perk of Welsh Cup success. Not until the 1995/96 season was the Welsh Cup out of bounds to Welsh teams that were part of the English league system. While an understandable move, considering that the League of Wales had been launched in 1992, it was a sad day when the mystical portal that took the likes of Cardiff, Swansea

City, Wrexham and Newport County into European competition was shut. Romance suffered a blow, as at one point these had been teams capable of the occasional and spectacular upset.

Swansea Town as was, took Wales's first faltering steps in the Cup Winners' Cup, during the 1961/62 season, falling at the first hurdle to Motor Jena, the East German team that would eventually take the name Carl Zeiss Jena. It was, however, the exploits of Bangor City, in 1962/63, that really set the ball rolling for Welsh teams, when they famously defeated Napoli at their bijou Farrar Road ground, 2-0 in the first round first leg, thanks to goals from Roy Matthews and Kenneth Birch.

Playing in the Cheshire League, the Bangor side was inhabited by part-time players. Inclusive of a handful of engineers, a stonemason, a caretaker, a company director, a grocery rep, a schoolmaster and a brewer, pitted against the Serie A outfit, it should have been the biggest mismatch the Cup Winners' Cup ever conjured up.

When the first leg took place, Napoli were still a week and a half away from the opening day of their league campaign. Bangor caught them cold. The first goal came shortly before half-time and when it did arrive it was a well taken one by Matthews that Napoli would have been proud to have called their own. It was also not Bangor's first effort at goal. The breakthrough was a belated one. A contentious second-half penalty, converted by Birch, gave Bangor their 2-0 victory.

In the return game, it was a determined Napoli who flung themselves at Bangor in the Stadio San Paolo. However, it was a stubborn Bangor that stood up to

Napoli and they came within six agonising minutes of going through. The 3-1 scoreline would have taken Bangor through on away goals had the game been played a short few seasons later. Yet, in 1962 it meant a replay was required.

That replay would take place in front of a healthy crowd at Highbury, where again Bangor would give Napoli another sleepless night. The Neapolitans were made to wait until the 85th minute to obtain their winning goal. Over the course of the three games played, Bangor had produced a set of the finest performances from a British team in European competition, forever scorching their name upon the psyche of the club that Diego Maradona would later grace.

Bangor were made to wait 23 years to return to the Cup Winners' Cup; yet when they did, for the 1985/86 season, they once again made headlines. Defeating the Norwegian outfit Fredrikstad FK, on away goals in the first round, thanks to a goal by Everton Williams, they were then drawn against Atlético Madrid in the second round.

This is where the Cup Winners' Cup was at its most beautiful: world-beating players tipping up in random picturesque backdrops in the Welsh valleys, or over the North Sea on the Emerald Isle. Ubaldo Fillol, who played in and won the 1978 World Cup Final, who shared pitches with the likes of Diego Maradona and Mario Kempes, was there at Farrar Road, the home of Bangor City, on 23 October 1985. Atlético Madrid might have comfortably prevailed, but the fact that Bangor City were there in the first place was a footballing wonder. It was the same for Merthyr Tydfil in 1987/88, when they hosted Atalanta.

A rush of further Cup Winners' Cup qualifications came for Bangor during the 1990s, some of them before the expulsion from the Welsh Cup of those inhabiting the English leagues, but by then the escalating proliferation of the former communist states had brought in the need for a preliminary round which the Welsh clubs struggled to get past. The giant names and the enormous clubs were placed just out of reach of the small clubs that sat amidst the hills. It was a move that contributed to the dilution of the character that made the Cup Winners' Cup what it was.

When it came to Welsh endeavour in the Cup Winners' Cup, it was a double-sided coin. While the likes of Borough United were allowed their 15 minutes of fame and Bangor were magical, Cardiff weren't the only team from the principality to shoot for the stars.

You had Newport County's run to the quarter-finals in 1980/81. John Aldridge would never get to play European football in a Liverpool shirt, yet he did in the colours of Newport, and they came perilously close to making the last four. Cardiff might have had their golden period, a final narrowly denied them; Swansea City might have clocked up a 12-0 win against Sliema Wanderers in 1982/83, before bowing out to Paris Saint-Germain; Wrexham, however, was where the consistency lay.

From defeating FC Zürich in their first European excursion – a Zürich team that would reach the semi-finals of the European Cup in 1977 – to facing off against Manchester United in the autumn of 1990, Wrexham rarely short-changed the Cup Winners' Cup on the occasions they paid a visit to the tournament.

Desperately unlucky not to reach the quarter-finals in 1972/73, seeing a 3-1 second-round first-leg advantage against Hajduk Split eroded in the second leg, to go out on away goals, the Racecourse Ground quickly became an electricity conductor on European nights.

Certainly, when it came to Wrexham's great 1970s runs, what is most startling is just how close they came to clearing the hurdle they eventually fell at. If 1972/73 and Hajduk Split was amazing, then 1975/76 and Anderlecht simply stunned the senses completely. Rob Rensenbrink, François van der Elst and company: yet still Wrexham went toe-to-toe with an Anderlecht side that was on the cusp of legendary status.

Other stirring nights at the Racecourse Ground came, inclusive of defeating the winners of the 1974 Cup Winners' Cup in 1979/80, Magdeburg, and narrowly going out on away goals in 1986/87 to Real Zaragoza.

The greatest of the lot came in September 1984, however, against FC Porto, just four months beyond them having contested the 1984 Cup Winners' Cup Final against Juventus. The sad part was that the Racecourse was not much more than a quarter full. Jim Steel scored the only goal of the game – a player who would retire from football aged 32 to follow his dream of being a policeman – to set up an intriguing return tie in Portugal.

Seemingly being swept away by a vastly superior team, Wrexham were 3-0 down inside 38 minutes. Something bewildering was afoot, however. By half-time Wrexham had scored two goals of their own and were in possession of the away-goal advantage. Jake King, a defender, was Wrexham's unexpected hero.

A shocked Porto were made to wait until just past the hour mark to edge ahead again, the prolific Paulo Futre surely breaking Wrexham's resistance. Two seasons further down the line, Porto would be on their way to lifting the European Cup, but in early October 1984 they were just about to be hit by one of the biggest sucker punches in their proud history.

Barry Horne, an often-uppity midfield presence who would later go on to score the goal that saved Everton from Premier League relegation in 1994, plundered Wrexham an 89th-minute strike that levelled the aggregate score at 4-4, to take them through on the away-goals rule. It was an incredible turn of events and Wrexham were rewarded with a second-round tie against AS Roma, who six months earlier had come to within a penalty shoot-out of winning the European Cup in their own stadium.

Far from embarrassing themselves, Wrexham escaped the Stadio Olimpico with only a 2-0 deficit. The second leg, bringing Sven-Göran Eriksson to the Racecourse Ground, armed with players of the calibre of Falcão, Bruno Conti, Francesco Graziani and Giuseppe Giannini, also went the way of Roma, 1-0.

While FC Petrolul Ploiesti would be Wrexham's last opponents in European competition, in 1995/96, their last huge Cup Winners' Cup night came five years earlier when they faced Alex Ferguson's Manchester United, in the 1990/91 second round, after defeating Lyngby BK. It unwittingly marked the end of an era.

For the last three contests of the Cup Winners' Cup, the Welsh representative came from the League of Wales. Instead of Wrexham, Cardiff City or Swansea City, in

1996/97 it was Total Network Solutions that rode into battle for the principality. With their own stadium, The Recreation Ground, not meeting UEFA standards, the ironic twist was that Wrexham's Racecourse Ground would instead be used for the game. A 1-1 draw ensued against Ruch Chorzów, before Total Network Solutions were dispatched 5-0 in the second leg in Poland.

Cwmbrân Town, the inaugural winners of the League of Wales, ventured forth in 1997/98, having lost the 1997 Welsh Cup Final to the double-winning Barry Town, shipping ten goals over the course of their two games against FC Naţional Bucharest. In more recent times they have plummeted to the fifth level of the Welsh football pyramid where they now find themselves occupying the Gwent County League Division One. A salutary tale of how financially fragile League of Wales clubs were from the very beginning.

Fittingly perhaps, it was left to Bangor City to bring down the Cup Winners' Cup curtain for Wales. Some 36 years after their heroics against Napoli, they fell at the qualifying round to FC Haka having acquitted themselves as well as they maybe could have hoped. It had been eight long years since a Welsh side had cleared the first hurdle in the Cup Winners' Cup. A sad, yet understandable, way to complete their last lap of the tournament given the way the sands of UEFA had been shifting.

It wasn't a spirit of the random that was confined only to Wales either. The Cup Winners' Cup spotlight intermittently fixed itself upon Northern Ireland too. Fabio Capello was in the AS Roma team that was held to a goalless draw by Ards, at the Belfast Oval in the autumn of 1970. A year later, Manchester City had to rely upon the away-goals rule to see off the threat of Linfield. At Windsor Park, in September 1971, Distillery faced Rinus Michels's Barcelona.

There was a marvellous random-generator effect in process. Imagine a contemporary era in which Lionel Messi strolled out to play at Farrar Road, or the Belfast Oval. There simply was no cocoon for the great and the good of football during the lifespan of the Cup Winners' Cup. Anything really was possible. In for a penny, in for a pound.

This gloriousness continued apace. Glentoran reached the quarter-finals in 1973/74, where they were dismantled by the Borussia Mönchengladbach of Berti Vogts, Rainer Bonhof, Uli Stielike, Herbert Wimmer and Jupp Heynckes, having navigated their way past Chimia Râmnicu Vâlcea and SK Brann. It was the greatest Cup Winners' Cup run by an Irish team and, despite chasing shadows during the first leg in Belfast, Glentoran worked tirelessly to restrict Hennes Weisweiler's team to a 2-0 win, before being overrun during the return game.

These games gave a troubled Northern Ireland some much-needed respite from what was often the horrors of day-to-day life. A shining positive that brought the great and the good of football into an unlikely environment.

Ards, having already faced Roma, and greatly admired for their style of play, were completely overwhelmed by PSV Eindhoven in the 1974/75 first round, 14-1 on aggregate, inclusive of a 10-0 drubbing in Eindhoven. While there was a star-studded element to these fixtures, sometimes the results were brutal.

Other giants paid a visit. Coleraine faced both Eintracht Frankfurt and Tottenham Hotspur; Ballymena United went head-to-head with Torino and Anderlecht; Glentoran took on Paris Saint-Germain. Elsewhere, in more neighbourly spats, intriguing ties were enjoyed by Carrick Rangers against Southampton, Crusaders against Newport County and Derry City against Cardiff.

On not one occasion did the footballing gods smile upon the Northern Irish, yet unforgettable experiences were bestowed upon those who took part, or simply watched on in awe.

A similar story can be found over the Irish border where, to go along with Shamrock Rovers' wonderful scaring of Bayern Munich, Dundalk gave Tottenham palpitations and later faced Johan Cruyff's Ajax, University College Dublin winded Everton, and Barcelona and Torino paid visits to Shelbourne and Limerick respectively.

Domestic cup competitions were notoriously full of surprise heroes, of David vs Goliath encounters; so it somehow made perfect sense that Bangor City were defeating Napoli, that Ards were frustrating Roma and that Shamrock Rovers were coming close to glory against Bayern Munich.

Nothing less would have sufficed.

Chapter Eleven

Ferguson at the Double

LEFT TO the penultimate chapter, as a Liverpool fan procrastinating over writing about Sir Alex Ferguson's two victories in a tournament that eluded my own team of choice, there were times when I mused over finding a way in which to absorb 1983 and 1991 into other chapters of this book.

To gloss over them maybe. It would have done his achievements a disservice, yet at times I was having so much fun putting this homage together that it was a disservice I was more than willing to make. At my most mischievous, the thinking was: why bring down the tone?

Blithely sweeping past Ferguson's achievements was never truly on, however. No matter what scarf I wave above my head on big European nights, no matter which partisan tribe I belong to, I am a football fan in general too. I watched in awe as his Aberdeen overcame Real Madrid in Gothenburg in 1983; I watched on in respect and with a heavy degree of envy as he took his Manchester United to glory against Barcelona in Rotterdam in 1991.

I used to work in Manchester. In the comically named Dumplington to be precise. I started out there, on Trafford Park, a good few years before the Trafford Centre was built, just a few short months after Manchester United's European Cup Winners' Cup success. There was no 24-hour supermarket at that point in time; there was no nearby rugby league stadium; there were no hotels, no artificial indoor ski slope, no dinosaur-related novelty golf course, no drive-thru Starbucks. Just a substation and the nauseating aroma of the adjacent sewerage works, that locals referred to as 'The Chod Factory'.

Things came and went, but the smell of poo lingered throughout the decades of regeneration and progress. What a time to saunter into Manchester on a daily basis, just as Liverpool relinquished the knack of winning trophies as a god-given right, only for Manchester United to be bestowed with it. Stick was liberally given, while the wit sharpened and the skin thickened. Behind enemy lines essentially, I've largely remained impervious to wind-up merchants and banter ever since.

Through it all, good friends were made. Tolerations were arrived at. Impromptu games of football were played while work was supposed to be taking place. Paul McCartney's 'Pipes of Peace' resonated in the background and it got to the point where many of my workmates were genuinely pleased for me personally when I went to Istanbul for the 2005 Champions League Final. It was both touching and a devilishly clever way for them to channel their pain of Liverpool becoming champions of Europe for a fifth time too.

Endless conversations about football took place and the similarities became increasingly evident. As much as the two cities rival one another, there are an uncomfortable amount of mirror images when they look at each other.

Accused of harking on about the past too much, talking of glories gone in the absence of victories present, it was always interesting when introspection kicked in for my hosts. At the peak of their late-1990s and first decade of the new millennium powers, Manchester United fans of a certain age also, surprisingly, yearned for the character-filled 1980s. Sky even managed to ruin football for at least one generation of their supporters, despite the relentless collection of trophies. From one workmate, confessions were made that the Cup Winners' Cup win of 1991 meant more to him than the Champions League win of 1999 did. No matter what the club, it is always those early successes of an era that make the biggest and longest-lasting impact. The point of genesis.

What Manchester United's run to the 1991 Cup Winners' Cup Final lacked was a sense of genuine peril, a sense of danger. In a field of qualifiers that included not only Barcelona, but Juventus, Sampdoria, Bobby Robson's PSV Eindhoven, Dynamo Kyiv, 1. FC Kaiserslautern and Steaua Bucharest, Ferguson's men managed to avoid them all as they picked their way through to Rotterdam. Even the evocative possibility of Ferguson having to return to Pittodrie to take on his former club, Aberdeen, was sadly swerved.

Pécsi Mecsek, Wrexham, Montpellier and Legia Warsaw were the hurdles that Manchester United cleared to reach the final showdown with Johan Cruyff's Barcelona. That long-propagated theory, harboured by rival supporters, that the team from Old Trafford always get an easy draw? This was the birth of that concept.

There were hidden dangers, however. Hidden dangers can at times be easier to fall for than the clear and present ones. Montpellier travelled to Old Trafford for the first leg of the quarter-final, returning to the South of France with an away goal and a 1-1 draw. A game with an eventful start, Brian McClair opened the scoring in the first minute, only for their unlikely FA Cup-winning hero, Lee Martin, to put the ball past his own goalkeeper seven minutes later, when under no discernible pressure.

For Montpellier, without the services of the outrageously talented Carlos Valderrama, but boasting the commanding presence of the future Manchester United defender, Laurent Blanc, it was the jet-heeled Jacek Ziober that gave Ferguson his biggest headaches.

After such a fast start to a game that was the real European deal, after their sedate meanderings in Hungary and north Wales, Manchester United encountered an evening of frustration, unable even to take advantage of an extra man when Pascal Ballis was sent off within minutes of the restart for the second half.

Suddenly vulnerable, Manchester United's next two Cup Winners' Cup games were away from home, away from the weight of Old Trafford's intense expectation. Perhaps lulled into a false sense of security, maybe their balance upset by the loss to suspension of Ballis and the return of Valderrama, Montpellier failed to make the most of the hard work they had put into the first leg.

Having knocked both PSV and Steaua out in the previous two rounds, Montpellier's path to the quarter-finals had been in stark contrast to Manchester United's. With English teams only just returning to European competition, the ground lost over the course of the previous five seasons meant that Ferguson's hopes of reaching the semi-finals were widely deemed to be speculative at best.

With the pressure switching to Montpellier, however, Manchester United took full advantage of a shocking goalkeeping error from Claude Barrabé when he allowed a 40-yard free kick from Clayton Blackmore to trickle through his grasp and over his goal line. With this gift being presented deep into first-half stoppage time, it was a stunned Montpellier that returned for the second half. Within a short few minutes it was 2-0, thanks to a penalty from Steve Bruce, one of a remarkable 19 goals he scored during the 1990/91 season.

Into the hat for the semi-final draw, the only downside for Manchester United was the loss to suspension, for the first leg, of Bryan Robson. They were entirely compensated for this, however, by evading both Barcelona and Juventus and instead being paired with the easier option of Legia Warsaw.

Legia, struggling towards the foot of their domestic league and without the services of both their captain and their first-choice goalkeeper, went into a surprise 37th-minute lead, thanks to the weaving sense of adventure of Jacek Cyzio. It was a goal that was totally against the run of play. The vociferous euphoria engendered by the wonderfully partisan home support only lasted for one minute though. McClair silenced them when, at the end of a scrappy passage of play, he mishit the ball into the Legia net. Wind taken from Legia's sails, the second half was one-way traffic and it came as no surprise that Mark Hughes and, yet again, Bruce put the tie way beyond their hosts.

Having looked in danger of exiting the tournament at the end of the quarter-final first leg, when European football returned to Old Trafford for the semi-final second leg, it was almost a foregone conclusion that Manchester United were heading into the 1991 Cup Winners' Cup Final. A flat 1-1 draw saw Ferguson's team over the line.

By the time Rotterdam rolled around, a cautious optimism had circulated amongst the Manchester United team. An unease seemed to be gripping Johan Cruyff and his Barcelona team. With Zubizarreta suspended, and without Amor, they also had to absorb the blow of being shorn of the services of the injured Hristo Stoichkov. Added to this, the looming shadow of a determined Hughes was unsettling for them too. Hughes's time at Barcelona had been a largely difficult experience and he was grinding his axe.

After Ron Atkinson had taken them so close to the 1984 Cup Winners' Cup Final, there was the added element that Manchester United also had a heavy degree of unfinished business with the tournament. The comparative ease of their route to the 1991 final was arguably a rebate from karma for throwing both the Diego Maradona-led Barcelona and the Michel Platini-powered Juventus at them in 1983/84.

As a Liverpool fan, observing from afar, there was an inevitable feel that fate was dictating this one. Everything was falling into place for Manchester United, while it was all unravelling for a Barcelona team that should really have been unstoppable.

In a first half that was akin to a courtship dance, shoulders were dipped and moves were made. Shadows were boxed, but no compelling punches were landed. A classic it was not. The more the game drifted along, the more the likelihood of a Manchester United win increased. Barcelona were sleepwalking towards defeat.

Goalless at half-time, goalless as the hour mark was surpassed, the last 20 minutes were lumbering into view when the deadlock was broken. In a game where both teams were waiting for the other to blink first, Manchester United took matters into their own hands. Chances began to fall their way, earned by being the braver team.

McClair almost benefitted from disarray in the Barcelona defence, caused by the erratic nature of Zubizarreta's stand-in, Carles Busquets – father of future Barcelona star Sergio Busquets. Lee Sharpe came close and Hughes was increasing in prominence. With only a quarter of the game remaining, the tide was only flowing in one direction.

When the opening goal came, Busquets was largely at fault. A free kick was angled into the Barcelona penalty area by Robson and the keeper came for a ball he was never going to reach. Changing his mind partway there, he left a sizeable part of his net attractively unguarded. Bruce was first to the ball with a well-directed header towards the far post. His header goal bound, Hughes forced it over the line, depriving Bruce of his moment of supreme glory. Both would claim the goal; Hughes would be awarded it.

Seven minutes later, there was no ambiguity over the scorer of Manchester United's second goal which most certainly belonged to Hughes. Charging through the centre and with calls for an offside flag ignored by the linesman, the former Barcelona man took the ball past the advancing Busquets. But, with his touch being a heavy one, it left the Welshman with a narrowing angle on goal and the convergence of a desperately back-pedalling Barcelona defence to contend with. Left with one shot at glory, Hughes caught up with the ball, hit it first time, with power, and it flew into the Barcelona net for 2-0.

Rather than concede the final there and then, Manchester United's second goal provoked a Barcelona fightback. Five minutes later, Ronald Koeman struck a wonderful free kick that Les Sealey almost got to, setting up a thrilling last ten minutes.

An end-to-end climax, it became a game of punch and counterpunch. The real Barcelona had finally awoken, their dominance defied by Manchester United to stop their goal being breached for a second time, although Cruyff's side did have a goal harshly disallowed. There was also a late goal-line clearance.

Despite the late and almost intolerable pressure that was applied by Barcelona, Manchester United had chances of their own to make it 3-1. Amongst it all, Nando was sent off after bringing down Hughes. When the final whistle came it was met with delirium on the pitch, along the touchline and in the stands. The 1991 Cup Winners' Cup Final was the definitive stepping stone to the rest of Manchester United's honour-laden decade. It was the night that they grew up; the night they found their inner belief.

They would return to the tournament as holders, where their second-round exit to Atlético Madrid in 1991/92 marked Manchester United's last games in the tournament. The return of league titles to Old Trafford for the first time since 1967 meant that they became part of the Champions League furniture instead.

Integral to the evolution of Ferguson's Manchester United, eight years earlier his Cup Winners' Cup success with Aberdeen, in 1983, had been one of validation of the team he had built at Pittodrie. It was also a success that put him firmly on the radar of not only clubs south of the border, but across the rest of Europe too.

Joining Rangers as a player in 1967 after they had contested that year's Cup Winners' Cup Final, Ferguson never kicked a ball in anger in the tournament. Instead, his first flirtation with it came in 1978/79, his first season in charge of Aberdeen, having inherited the job from Billy McNeill, who had returned to Celtic in succession to Jock Stein.

A club in a healthy position, Aberdeen had finished runner-up to Rangers in the Scottish Premier Division in 1977/78, also losing out to them in the Scottish Cup Final. Ferguson, meanwhile, had impressed by taking St Mirren back into the top flight in 1976/77. When he took the job, Ferguson became Aberdeen's fourth permanent manager in just three years.

Grasping the chance to test his capabilities in European competition, Ferguson managed to plot a path past Marek Stanke Dimitrov, before Aberdeen went out narrowly in the second round to eventual finalists Fortuna Düsseldorf.

Further lessons were taken on board over the following seasons, together with the domestic successes that started to flow their way after they took the 1979/80 Scottish Premier Division title. The biggest of these European lessons was given by Bob Paisley's Liverpool, in the 1980/81 European Cup.

In 1981/82 the signs of what was to come the following season began to bubble to the surface. In the UEFA Cup, Aberdeen beat Bobby Robson's Ipswich Town, the holders, in a spectacular pair of first-round games. They would go out narrowly to Hamburger SV in the last 16. Bundesliga champions-to-be, Hamburger SV were a team that went on to reach the 1982 UEFA Cup Final; Hamburger SV were a team which had reached the 1980 European Cup Final and would win the very same tournament a season later. They contested three major European finals in four seasons. That Aberdeen pushed them so close was a testament to just how good Ferguson's team really was.

Aberdeen were part of what was christened 'The New Firm', alongside Jim McLean's Dundee United. The hegemony of Scottish football, so taken for granted by Celtic and Rangers, was challenged in the most beautiful of ways.

By the time Aberdeen reached the 1983 Cup Winners' Cup Final at the end of Ferguson's fifth season in charge at Pittodrie, they were a team that were perhaps as synonymous with the near misses they had had with success, as they were with what they had won.

While they had followed up their 1979/80 league title success with victory in the 1982 Scottish Cup Final, prior to that they had lost two further semi-finals. They had also been beaten in back-to-back Scottish League Cup finals and they were Scottish Premier Division runners-up in the two seasons directly after winning the league.

As Aberdeen headed to Gothenburg, they were still in with a slender chance of winning a treble. A title-deciding day, in a three-horse race, lay three days beyond facing Real Madrid, and a week later was yet another Scottish Cup Final.

Dundee United's aesthetically pleasing artistry would land them their first league title, and they made wonderful yet unrewarded efforts across Europe; but the metronomic consistency and will to persevere belonged to Aberdeen. Within this, Celtic tried to keep order and Rangers slipped into mediocrity. The Old Firm was beginning to look its age when compared to this vibrant dawning of The New Firm.

Playing all in red and challenging for trophies, Aberdeen should have appealed to my senses. They did appeal to my senses in many ways and they certainly had my respect, but there was something angrier about Aberdeen, when compared to Dundee United, which is where my 1980s soft spot lay when it came to Scottish football: the vivid orange-and-black kits, the strange oversized TSB advertising hoardings in the corners, Paul Sturrock's and Eamonn Bannon's propensities to hit what seemed to be weekly screamers into the top corners of the nets of what were all-too-suspecting visiting goalkeepers.

Given a preliminary-round tie to navigate, Aberdeen's run to the 1983 Cup Winners' Cup Final was one of extreme contrasts. Brushing aside Sion in that extra initial hurdle, the subtly dangerous Lech Poznań in the second round, and Waterschei Thor in the semi-finals, quite effortlessly, their games against Dinamo Tirana in the first round and Bayern Munich in the quarter-finals were where the tensions lay.

A character-building goalless draw was obtained in Tirana, when Aberdeen took a precarious 1-0 lead to the Albanian capital in the first round – the early banana skin being duly avoided in the late September sun.

It was Bayern Munich, however, that offered the requisite legendary home European night of mysticism that all great continental adventures must have. Less than a year since they had contested the 1982 European Cup Final against Aston Villa, still boasting the presence of Paul Breitner and Karl-Heinz Rummenigge, this was a member of football's aristocracy. The goalless draw that Aberdeen departed the Olympiastadion with was just reward for how prepared they had been upon their arrival.

At Pittodrie, a wonderfully open game was provoked when Klaus Augenthaler gave Bayern an early lead. Unprepared for a quick free kick, Aberdeen were exposed when Breitner rolled the ball to the unmarked Augenthaler, who promptly powered it in from distance. It was a fantastic strike, but one which was gifted by the acres of space Bayern were allowed.

Undeterred by the away goal they had conceded, Aberdeen launched themselves forward. Alex McLeish saw a header bounce off the crossbar, and Neil Simpson crashed one over the top when a little more composure might have made Manfred Müller work. Amidst it all, Breitner played the marvellously Machiavellian villain, snapping at Gordon Strachan whenever possible, trying to rile Aberdeen's prime generator of chances. It was gamesmanship at its most ugly, yet utterly fascinating to watch. Another Aberdeen opportunity came from a free kick awarded for one such occurrence.

Aberdeen's pressure eventually told, however, when, with little more than five minutes remaining of the first half, Simpson bundled the ball over the Bayern goal line. Before the interval arrived, Aberdeen could have been ahead. A reasonable shout for a penalty was ignored when Peter Weir stayed on his feet rather than opting to go to ground, and in the ensuing bedlam the ball eventually hit the top of the crossbar again.

With Aberdeen starting the second half in the same frame of mind as the first half ended, Müller continued to be the busier of the two goalkeepers. So, it was entirely against the run of play that Bayern reclaimed the lead just beyond the hour. When it came, however, it was another outstanding finish, this time from Hans Pflügler. With the need now for two goals, Aberdeen were edging towards exiting the tournament.

Still Aberdeen created chances. A brilliant cross was met by a powerful header from Weir, which was stopped on the goal line. In their desperation, many Aberdeen fans celebrated, thinking, or simply hoping, that the ball had crossed the line.

When the equaliser did finally come, it was laced with genius. From being poised over a free kick, Strachan and John McMaster then both ran past the ball, fooling the Bayern defence that they'd miscommunicated with one another over who would be taking it. As the two players ambled back to the ball, the distraction was just enough to allow Strachan to float over a quick cross that McLeish flicked past Müller for 2-2.

With 15 minutes remaining, it set up a dramatic finish; yet not even Aberdeen could have expected to be ahead just one minute later. With Pittodrie still crackling in the wake of the equaliser, the stadium went ballistic when Eric Black's looping header was brilliantly saved by Müller, only for it to drop kindly to John Hewitt who planted the ball onto the turf and through the keeper's legs into the back of the net. It was a wave of emotion that saw Aberdeen over the finish line on what was Pittodrie's greatest night. Black and Hewitt would, of course, be the heroes again before the season's end.

At the Ullevi, in Gothenburg, everything was conducive to an Aberdeen win. The conditions were on their side and most of those who had made the trip to the 1983 Cup Winners' Cup Final were on their side. The saturated and unforgiving outpost of the further reaches of northern Europe was the great leveller for Real Madrid.

Sometimes you just know. Some cup finals are a foregone conclusion before they begin due to the chasm between the two protagonists; some cup finals are more ambiguous, when the competitors are closely matched. There are other finals, however, when there is a calm authority that nothing is going to stand in the way of a team. Aberdeen were that team, in Gothenburg, in 1983.

Black opened the scoring in the seventh minute. A short time later Juanito levelled the game from the penalty spot. So much rain had fallen that, as the ball hit the back of Jim Leighton's net, the water that had settled on it sprayed dramatically towards the photographers that had assembled behind the Aberdeen goalkeeper.

Unwilling to buckle in the slipstream of the setback of conceding the equaliser, Aberdeen plugged on. In a game that drifted into extra time, they remained the more likely of the two teams to score, and this they did in the 112th minute, when Weir sent Mark McGhee away down the left, for him to centre majestically for Hewitt's diving header. The Cup Winners' Cup was returning to Scotland after an 11-year gap, with both Ferguson's and Aberdeen's stock rising sharply. Returning home, they would miss out on the league title, but retain the Scottish Cup.

Aberdeen spent the next three seasons as the dominant force in Scottish football. Back-to-back league titles, two more Scottish Cups and a Scottish League Cup were collected. Indeed, when the Dons lost out to FC Porto in the semi-finals of the 1983/84 Cup Winners' Cup it was viewed as quite a shock.

Only returning to the Cup Winners' Cup beyond the departure of Ferguson, Aberdeen never again came close to revisiting the glories of 1983, a success that is as frozen in time as any other the tournament has ever produced. Yet, it is one that is frozen in a gloriously shiny Technicolor due to the way the Gothenburg rain made the 1983 final glisten.

Like him or not, Ferguson's double Cup Winners' Cup success was a work of art.

Chapter Twelve

The Last Stretch, a Speculative Effort and the Final Final

THERE ARE shades of grey when it comes to trying to decipher just when the European Cup Winners' Cup began to unravel.

While the concept of a European Super League stretches back much further than many people would give credit for – inclusive of an intriguing article written by, or ghostwritten for, Des O'Connor in a Millwall matchday programme during the 1972/73 season, in which the entertainer was most dismissive of the idea – a new direction for European club football began to be plotted in earnest in late 1987.

When Real Madrid and Napoli were drawn to face one another in the first round of the 1987/88 European Cup, it was contended by the movers and shakers of football and its commercial partners that what the game needed was this calibre of encounter on a more regular basis.

Indeed, Real Madrid vs Napoli would have made a fitting final, yet ultimately, when the Spanish side emerged triumphantly from the two games, they eventually fell at the semi-finals to PSV Eindhoven. The die was cast, however. Better and bigger was where it was at; the weak were identified and their gradual elimination soon started.

Small congregations in large billowing stadiums at major European finals were frowned upon. While bunfights now take place for 6,000 tickets per team for a UEFA Europa League Final being played out on the opposite side of the continent between two London clubs, there is an entire generation of supporters now who would be stunned to learn they could have bought hundreds, even thousands, of tickets for the 1993 Cup Winners' Cup Final at Wembley between Parma and Royal Antwerp. The tournament became the black sheep of the family quite swiftly.

The demise of European communism played its part. The varying splintering states that used to cluster under the umbrellas of the Soviet Union and Yugoslavia set up their own football leagues, which required extra qualification berths. Czechoslovakia also split in two. In 1990/91, only one preliminary-round game was required while, by the last playing of the tournament, this had increased to 17. It is no coincidence that beyond the 1990/91 campaign, no Welsh or Irish clubs made it beyond the preliminary round. In UEFA's haste for its A-listers to rise collectively, romance died.

As the Champions League came into being, the Cup Winners' Cup started to look tired and dated. Had Margaret

Thatcher been the head of UEFA, she would have called it a managed decline. When extra places per nation began in the Champions League in 1997/98 it was the fatal blow to the Cup Winners' Cup. Barcelona, winners of the tournament in 1997, instead took up a place in the Champions League in 1997/98, despite not winning the 1996/97 La Liga title. More ludicrously, the Netherlands' Cup Winners' Cup representatives in 1998/99 had been beaten semi-finalists in the 1998 KNVB Cup. The two finalists, Ajax and PSV Eindhoven, had already qualified for the Champions League. SC Heerenveen defeated FC Twente in a play-off to clinch Cup Winners' Cup qualification. Meanwhile, of the last six English clubs to qualify for the tournament, only two of them did so as winners of the FA Cup.

None of this is to say the final years of the Cup Winners' Cup were a complete write-off. There was great beauty and immense drama at times. The rise of Nevio Scala's Parma was a wonderful thing, winning the 1993 final and losing as holders in the 1994 final.

Arsenal finally won it 14 years after their penalty shoot-out heartbreak in the 1980 final against Valencia. It was a hard-earned victory against Parma, in Copenhagen, driven by the metronomic efforts of Paul Davis, who won the battle for the centre ground against Massimo Crippa, Gabriele Pin and Tomas Brolin, with only Ian Selley and Steve Morrow for midfield company. Torino and Paris Saint-Germain had been defeated en route, during what was one of the most impressive European runs to success by any British team.

The winning goal scored by the ever supportive Alan Smith, victory was gained without the services of Ian

Wright and against the odds in so many ways. Parma went on to supply five members of the Italy squad that reached the 1994 World Cup Final, four of whom were on duty in Copenhagen.

It is a success that gets swallowed up by George Graham's eventual fall from grace at Highbury, and the way Arsenal lost the 1995 final – yes, as holders – to Real Zaragoza and that speculative winner from Nayim at the Parc des Princes, much to the delight of the supporters of his future employers, Tottenham Hotspur.

Blessed with the availability of Wright and the addition of Stefan Schwarz and John Hartson, it was an infinitely more attacking team that Arsenal took to the 1995 final. Pre-match, Arsenal certainly seemed better equipped to win the 1995 final than the 1994 final.

There was more, however, to Real Zaragoza than simply Nayim's audacious lob. They boasted the services of the inspirational Miguel Pardeza, plus the attacking talents of Juan Esnáider and Gustavo Poyet. They had overcome Feyenoord and Chelsea on their way to reaching Paris, the victory over Chelsea stopping the possibility of an all-English final. It would be a further 24 years before an Arsenal vs Chelsea major European final came into being. The Cup Winners' Cup would forever avoid the dubious honour of two teams from one nation reaching its final, unlike its other two siblings.

Arsenal had dramatically beaten Auxerre and Sampdoria, the latter on penalties in the semi-final, in a stunning end to a difficult season. Caretaker manager, Stewart Houston, had given his players an added degree of freedom and flexibility that looked likely to pay dividends.

In a very even final that could just as easily have fallen Arsenal's way, the club would have been hard pushed not to give Houston the job on a permanent basis had it been Tony Adams reclaiming the trophy. They instead appointed Bruce Rioch, who lasted for a season before Arsène Wenger caught the eye of the Highbury hierarchy.

PSG finally cracked the code in 1996, before becoming the last holders to be defeated in a Cup Winners' Cup Final. Barcelona were their conquerors and what conquerors they were. Led by Bobby Robson and powered by Ronaldo and Luis Figo, they were simply hypnotic. The 1997 final was their fourth success and very last game in a tournament that largely belonged to them at times. It is also nothing but disorientating to see José Mourinho in amongst the Catalan celebrations.

Then came Chelsea again – the pre-Roman Abramovich Chelsea who took over Tottenham Hotspur's position as London's stylists. Producing the type of football, midway through the Britpop era, that appealed to the Cool Britannia generation, despite being littered with expensively assembled players from Italy, France, Spain, the Netherlands, Uruguay, Romania and Norway, to go alongside their ever-diminishing number of British stars.

It was a rebirth for the club of the King's Road, a blast from a mid-1960s and early 1970s past. Style, with cup-winning substance and Gianfranco Zola being impossible to dislike, no matter what your club allegiances. For 1970 and 1971, you could read 1997 and 1998. The dawning of the Austin Powers movies can't have entirely been a coincidence.

A second-leg comeback against Vicenza in the semi-final aside, it was all formulaic for Chelsea, as they reached the 1998 Cup Winners' Cup Final, the penultimate Cup Winners' Cup Final. Even a mildly embarrassing first-leg second-round defeat away to Tromsø was remedied by scoring seven in the return game.

Zola, being nursed back from injury, was named only as a substitute for the final against Joachim Löw's VfB Stuttgart. On the bench he sat until the 71st minute, when he entered the Råsunda Stadium pitch as a replacement for Tore André Flo. He scored the only goal of the game a few seconds later.

Football in England had changed dramatically in a relatively short timespan. Formerly populated predominately by British and Scandinavian players, it was suddenly much more cosmopolitan. The wages increased and the Premier League product was polished until it gleamed greedily. Chelsea were at the forefront of this change, via the initial recruitment of Ruud Gullit as player-manager, utilising his glow to attract players from Serie A and La Liga. It was unheard-of territory; it was uncharted water.

What was strange, however, was that while Chelsea and Lazio, the last team to lift the Cup Winners' Cup, were symptomatic of football's ever-escalating financial power – two previously mid-ranging clubs suddenly demanding seats at the top table – the platform from which they introduced themselves to a watching global audience was by then classed as nothing more than old hat. Two clubs that would be scorned as nouveau riche were the last two winners of an outmoded, handled silver pot.

It was Sven-Göran Eriksson and Héctor Cúper who duelled for the last Cup Winners' Cup at Villa Park, a venue that had never hosted a game in the tournament. Cúper's Real Mallorca, cobbled together and inspired, almost outwitted Eriksson's extortionately assembled Lazio. With the half-time scoreline at 1-1, legend has it that Eriksson was 45 minutes away from losing his job, before they prevailed 2-1; Fabio Capello having supposedly been offered the job as his replacement in the event of the game being lost.

Drama in the Cup Winners' Cup to the very end. Football was never quite the same again after the tournament's demise.

A year earlier, the ground had been prepared when the UEFA Cup Final was changed from a two-legged event to a one-off final. This, when combined with the admittance to the Champions League of multiple teams from individual nations, was a huge redrawing of the borders. The two-legged UEFA Cup Final worked in a perfect symbiosis with the one-off finals of the European Cup and the Cup Winners' Cup. As mentioned at the start of this book, they were three very different siblings to one another. The dying days of the Cup Winners' Cup overlapped with a new but not necessarily pleasing dawning. It was like visiting a much-loved but suddenly ailing family member. The twinkle in the eye was still there, but the spark was largely misfiring.

And then, a tournament definitively frozen in time, it was gone.

Afterword

I SPOKE to a lot of people over the course of writing this book, with the intention of interjecting the views and memories of those who embraced the tournament into the relevant chapters,. Theory and practicalities didn't quite meet in the middle, however, as I'm simply not an interrogator. I am instead a pub conversationalist. I hand somebody a topic they have a passion for and let them pour forth. I then feed off the passion.

What came across as a common thread was the joy everybody had in the Cup Winners' Cup. Joan Gonzalez Martí, a Barcelona fan who has seen his club win all the big prizes contemporary football has to offer, concluded that none of it matched the random joys of facing mysterious opponents in the Cup Winners' Cup. As he spoke of the 1979 final, a game he travelled to with his father, long-forgotten and sometimes mundane memories of the journey to Basel flooded back to him. It was a joy for him to be reminded of time spent with a most precious loved one, at a time when he was without a care in the world.

Friedrich Schacht, a supporter of Fortuna Düsseldorf, beaten finalists in that 1979 final, was no less enthusiastic. He spoke of a city that went wild; the team was welcomed home as vociferously as they would have been had they won the final.

John van der Bruggen tirelessly sifted through his extensive ticket collection, allowing me to see the match ticket of every Cup Winners' Cup Final ever played.

Jørn Brekke, a Norwegian Arsenal fan, spoke reverentially of a tournament that caused him pain in 1980, when Valencia prevailed in the final on penalties. A regular visitor to London for decades, he was even at the Boleyn Ground on the night that West Ham United overcame Eintracht Frankfurt in the 1976 semi-final, there simply as a lover of football and unwilling to pass on the opportunity of being present at such a huge occasion. It remains one of his favourite games of football ever.

Billy Ashcroft, goalscorer extraordinaire for Wrexham during their 1970s Cup Winners' Cup heyday, talked about the spirit of his team, comparing their comradeship to that of a gang of mates turning out for a pub team. They played nothing like a pub team though. A community team that all pulled in the same direction; a spirit that bridged the gap between a good, organised and solid mid-table Second Division team, to Anderlecht's World Cup Final superstars. He also spoke of how far £7 could stretch in Poland in 1975, £7 being the entertainment budget, per player, permitted by the Wrexham management when they went to play Stal Rzeszów.

The feel-good factor extolled by Billy was validated by the enthusiasm of David Evans, who as a Wrexham supporter could corroborate the wonderment of the era, having been present at most of those legendary European nights at the Racecourse Ground and for their very first jaunt across the continent to Zürich, in September 1972. David was of the mind that there were more Wrexham supporters than there were those of FC Zürich. It was something akin to a pilgrimage.

Paul Dempsey, one of the finest Everton fans I have the pleasure to know, spared time to discuss the glory and 'what if' nature of his team, as did the former football journalist Ric George. The years fell away, and schoolboy enthusiasm was impossible to resist for both. Yes, they both believed that Everton would, or at least could, have won the European Cup in 1986, had they not been denied the opportunity to test themselves. Neither of them knew that Everton had theoretically drawn Anderlecht in the 1985/86 first round.

Hamish Tindall, a Rangers supporter, spoke proudly of his club's finest achievement, when they won the Cup Winners' Cup in 1972. He was at the Camp Nou that night, when the SFA refused permission for the game to be broadcast live to the nation.

Christoph Wanger, a Magdeburg supporter born five years after his team's greatest moment, spoke lovingly of their 1974 success, paying a similar type of homage as I do to the Liverpool teams of Bill Shankly, which were just before my time.

Stuart Bateman, a Manchester United supporter who is just a handful of years younger than me, recounted tales of his coach trip to Rotterdam for the 1991 final, and the wider expanse of their run to glory. He spoke of sneaking into school the type of small black and white portable television you could only purchase from the supplements in Sunday newspapers, all in the name of getting a glimpse of those afternoon games in eastern Europe.

Hyder Jawád, author and ex-journalist, offered his memories of travelling to Villa Park for the 1999 Cup Winners' Cup Final, almost as if to pay his respect to the dying tournament, an effort I considered making at the time, only to regret talking myself out of it. Learn from my mistake. When offered the chance to be part of history, don't turn it down.

Many of the stories were repetitive. Similarities were struck. Many of the tales were of the 'you had to be there' nature, which was joyous in itself, as I have a million of those of my own, from my experiences in pursuit of watching 22 men kick an inflated orb around a rectangular patch of grass. But what stood out the most was the passion and affection that people had for the Cup Winners' Cup. It was almost as if they were reaching out for something tangible, only to offer their unconditional joy in the tournament. Writing this book became an out-of-body experience in the end.

In conversational terms, it was all cheese on toast. I was never looking for enlightenment or an epiphany. I set out, in writing this book, to sum up how the European Cup Winners' Cup felt. If the theme tune to *Sportsnight* still stirs your soul, like it does mine, then you'll know exactly where I'm coming from.

Also available at all good book stores

9781785315466

9781785313929

9781785315602

9781785315220

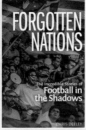

9781785314568

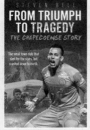

9781785315237

9781785315060

9781785315015

9781785315046

Alex McLeish and his
Aberdeen team-mates
after the 1983 final.